D0206342

Determinism, Blameworthiness, and
Deprivation

Determinism,
Blameworthiness,
and
Deprivation

Martha Klein

CLARENDON PRESS · OXFORD
1990

Oxford University Press, Walton Street, Oxford OX2 6DP

Oxford New York Toronto
Delhi Bombay Calcutta Madras Karachi
Petaling Jaya Singapore Hong Kong Tokyo
Nairobi Dar es Salaam Cape Town
Melbourne Auckland

and associated companies in
Berlin Ibadan

Oxford is a trade mark of Oxford University Press

Published in the United States
by Oxford University Press, New York

© Martha Klein 1990

British Library Cataloguing in Publication Data
Klein, Martha
Determinism, blameworthiness, and deprivation.
1. Man. Actions. Responsibility
I. Title
170
ISBN 0–19–824834–2

Library of Congress Cataloging in Publication Data
Klein, Martha
Determinism, blameworthiness, and deprivation / Martha Klein.
p. cm. — (Oxford philosophical monographs)
Includes bibliographical references.
1. Free will and determinism. 2. Responsibility. 3. Deprivation
(Psychology) I. Title. II. Series.
BJ1468.5.K54 1990   123'.5—dc20   89–28383
ISBN 0–19–824834–2

Set by Eta Services (Typesetters) Ltd, Beccles, Suffolk

Printed in Great Britain by
Courier International Ltd,
Tiptree, Essex

Acknowledgements

I wish to thank Sir Peter Strawson and Paul Snowdon for many years of advice and encouragement. I am very grateful to Derek Parfit for his invaluable comments, and his help in connection with this book's publication by Oxford University Press; and to Paul Snowdon whose comments as an independent adviser for OUP prompted a number of last minute thoughts. Finally, I wish to thank Gabriele Taylor for her comments and encouragement, and Mrs Elsie Hinkes for her excellent typing.

The material in Chapter 5 from Thomas Nagel, *The Possibility of Altruism*, (copyright © 1970) has been reprinted by kind permission of Princeton University Press.

Contents

Introduction

My examination of the debate about determinism and moral responsibility has been prompted by a dissatisfaction with compatibilism and an uneasiness about incompatibilism.

The traditional compatibilist holds that it is sufficient for blameworthiness that when a person acted wrongly his act was the result of what can be called 'a morally reprehensible state of mind'. Roughly, he believes that if an agent has knowingly and willingly done the wrong thing then that agent deserves to be blamed and, possibly, punished.

But this approach to blameworthiness has seemed inadequate to me because it blatantly ignores an anxiety which comes naturally to us when we are asked to reflect on the conditions for moral responsibility and, in particular, when we are asked to reflect on what I call in Chapter 4 'the problem cases' (imaginary cases in which wrongdoers' morally reprehensible states of mind are caused by brain tumours, brain damage, malevolent demons, etc.). This anxiety can be summed up in the question: how can someone be morally responsible for his acts if he is not responsible for the desires and beliefs which motivate him?[1]

But the dissatisfaction with the traditional compatibilist approach is not just prompted by reflection on imaginary cases. It is prompted by reflection on *actual* cases. We are now aware that some wrongdoing is the result of early emotional deprivation, and that many offenders whose motivating states of mind can be regarded as morally reprehensible (in that they are selfish and uncaring states of mind) have become as they are because they have been emotionally deprived.[2] And when we reflect on this, the compatibilist approach seems grossly unjust.[3]

Furthermore, although these worries gain their impetus from reflection on cases like those mentioned above, they can be generalized to include any wrongdoer whose desires, etc. can be traced to causes for which he is not responsible, and hence, possibly, all wrongdoers.

This makes it tempting to turn to incompatibilism. Here, at least, the anxiety ignored by the compatibilist is taken seriously.

But some philosophers have suggested that our intuitions about blameworthiness do not really endorse incompatibilism and that it is, in any event, incoherent.[4]

Such objections make one uneasy about incompatibilism, but they are also, at first glance, rather puzzling. For the anxiety which motivates incompatibilism (let's call this 'the incompatibilist's anxiety') is certainly endorsed by our moral intuitions and there is nothing incoherent about the question which expresses it.

However, the two objections are not directed towards the incompatibilist's anxiety, but to the incompatibilist claim about blameworthiness which is generated *by* that anxiety. As I show in Chapter 3, the anxiety generates incompatibilism because it commits us to the view that it is necessary for blameworthiness that a person's morally reprehensible state of mind should not be caused by factors for which he is not responsible (I call this 'the U-condition') and this in turn commits us to the view that moral responsibility requires the existence of at least some uncaused decisions and choices (see Chapters 3 and 5). And it does seem more plausible to object that our intuitions about blameworthiness do not endorse a U-condition and that belief in such a condition is incoherent. (I argue against the first objection in Chapter 4 and the second in Chapter 5.)

All of this suggests that the debate between the compatibilist and the incompatibilist should be seen as one in which the incompatibilist insists that there is a U-condition for blameworthiness and the compatibilist denies this. And this is in fact how I see the debate and the way I conduct it in Chapters 4–7.

But to present this issue as the focal point of disagreement, I have had first to disentangle it from another issue with which I think it is often confused, namely the claim that it is a condition for moral responsibility that agents could have acted otherwise (the C-condition). Until now the debate has usually gone something like this: both the compatibilist and the incompatibilist have agreed that there is a C-condition for blameworthiness, but have disagreed about what such a condition involves. The incompatibilist has insisted that the C-condition cannot be fulfilled if determinism is true, while the compatibilist has denied this. In insisting that there is such a condition for blameworthiness and that it should be viewed in his own particular way, each protagonist has claimed to be reflecting our commonly shared intuitions.

In Chapters 1–3, I argue that both have been wrong in different ways. The compatibilist has been wrong to think that he is really committed to the belief in a C-condition for blameworthiness (Chapter 1). And the incompatibilist has been wrong to think that he needs to be committed to this belief—wrong because there isn't a C-condition for blameworthiness (in Chapter 2 I examine and defend Frankfurt's powerful arguments for this claim against a recent attack), and wrong also because his commitment to incompatibilism can be entirely and rationally motivated by his commitment to a condition which is separable from the C-condition, namely the U-condition (Chapter 3). I argue that commitment to the U-condition is enough to support the claim that determinism and moral responsibility are incompatible.

This means that if the compatibilist is to maintain that the falsity of determinism is not required for moral responsibility, he must oppose the claim that there is a U-condition. Thus, I make the case for treating the debate as one which is centred on the U-condition.

To return then to the dissatisfaction with compatibilism which motivates incompatibilism and to the uneasiness about incompatibilism which is prompted by the two objections. These suggest that incompatibilism would be vindicated if it could be shown that the U-condition *is* endorsed by our moral intuitions, that belief in it is not logically incoherent, and, perhaps most important, that it can supply what is needed for a just approach to all offenders. By the same token, they suggest that compatibilism would be vindicated if it could be shown that our reflective moral intuitions are all compatibilist ones and that compatibilism can supply what is needed to satisfy our sense of justice in respect of all offenders.

But the arguments in Chapters 4–7 show that while each can claim some victories, neither can be fully vindicated. I argue that the incompatibilist's U-condition is endorsed by our moral intuitions (Chapter 4), that it is logically tenable (Chapter 5), and that it provides the most satisfactory underpinning for a just approach to the problem cases.

But I also argue that it does not appear to provide what is required for a just approach to emotionally deprived wrong-doers. If it really did not this would be ironic since it is partly the inability of traditional compatibilism to cope with the emotionally deprived which motivates (or at least sustains commitment to) incompatibilism. But I go on to argue that there is a good case for concluding that the difficulty the incompatibilist seems to have in coping with such offenders is only apparent. Despite this, I pursue the thought that there is a non-traditional compatibilist principle which would better satisfy our sense of justice in respect of the emotionally deprived.

But there is a more serious problem for anyone whose commitment to incompatibilism (and the U-condition) is motivated by the belief that it alone can provide what is required for a just approach to blame and punishment. And this is that (most probably) the U-condition *cannot* be empirically fulfilled (Chapter 5). So while the U-condition helps to satisfy our belief about what is required for *deserved* condemnation and punishment, the impossibility of its fulfilment means that we cannot have deserved condemnation and punishment.

As will be clear from the above, traditional compatibilism does not fare much better: our reflective moral intuitions do not endorse it because it fails to satisfy our sense of justice. But I argue that there is an intuitively appealing non-traditional, compatibilist principle (mentioned above) which would yield *some* justice for both deprived and problem-case offenders and thus some justice for all offenders (Chapters 4 and 7). This involves what I call 'the payment-in-advance' condition—a condition which has not been argued for before and which must be added to traditional compatibilism. Unlike the U-condition, this condition can be fulfilled. To endorse it as a condition for blameworthiness is (roughly) to endorse the proposal that when an offender has suffered in advance of his wrongdoing, and this suffering is the result of the process which is responsible for his becoming the sort of person who is motivated by morally reprehensible states of mind, then he should be regarded as having already paid a price for his wrongdoing, and this should be taken into account when judgements are being made about the amount of punishment he deserves. Those offenders who have been emotionally deprived have certainly paid a price and I suggest in Chapters 4 and 7 that this can also be said of problem-case offenders.

I end by suggesting that if we want to blame and punish wrongdoers,[5] in the knowledge that we are treating them justly, we ought to adopt the payment-in-advance condition because it offers our only hope of justice. It does not offer *full* justice (the impossible fulfilment of the U-condition would be needed for that) but it is the best we can do. (In Chapter 7 I argue that there is an analogous non-traditional compatibilist approach to praiseworthiness which would (*a*) render us immune from the incompatibilist anxiety about rightdoers and (*b*) satisfy our sense of justice in respect of them.)

Finally, a word about the Appendix: 'Freedom, Moral Responsibility, and Motivation in the *Critique of Practical Reason*'. Here I discuss a very powerful argument of Kant's which, if it worked, would make the debate between compatibilists and incompatibilists superfluous because it would have the consequence that there are no moral requirements. The argument does not work but showing this is not easy and, in the end, the evidence for its not working must be found in my discussion of the debate itself, in particular in my rejection of the C-condition as a requirement for moral responsibility. So, in a sense, I have had to engage in the very debate which is threatened in order to make the case for rejecting the argument which threatens it.

The order of exposition in the book can be summarized by chapter as follows:

1. The compatibilist is not committed to an independent C-condition.
2. Commitment to an independent C-condition is, in any case, mistaken.
3. The incompatibilist is not committed to an independent C-condition but to a U-condition.
4. Our intuitions do endorse a U-condition but this may not be reconcilable with our intuitions in the case of emotionally deprived offenders where a payment-in-advance condition seems closer to what we would endorse.
5. The U-condition is not (empirically) satisfiable.

6. Hence there is a tension between our commitment to the U-condition and our sense of justice.
7. This tension can be *partially* resolved along compatibilist lines.

1

The compatibilist and the could-have-acted-otherwise condition

Introduction

The debate between compatibilist and incompatibilist about determinism and moral responsibility has centred on the could-have-acted-otherwise claim.[1] The incompatibilist has claimed that moral responsibility requires the ability to have acted otherwise and has argued that, since it cannot be true that a person could have acted otherwise if it is also true that there were determining causes for his act, the existence of blameworthiness is inconsistent with the truth of determinism. The compatibilist agrees that moral responsibility requires the ability to have acted otherwise but denies that fulfilment of the could-have-acted-otherwise condition is precluded by the truth of determinism. Thus, while both appear to be agreed that there is a could-have-acted-otherwise condition for moral responsibility, they disagree about the way the claim is to be interpreted.

I believe that both the compatibilist and the incompatibilist have misconceived the nature of their debate. I shall argue that the compatibilist is wrong to think that he is committed to the belief that there is a could-have-acted-otherwise condition for blameworthiness and that the incompatibilist is wrong to think that he needs to be committed to a could-have-acted-otherwise condition. I begin with the compatibilist.

The compatibilist

I hope to show that, despite appearances, the compatibilist is not committed to the belief that there is a could-have-acted-otherwise condition for moral responsibility.

To have a real commitment to the belief that there is a could-have-acted-otherwise condition for moral responsibility is to believe that such a condition is not reducible to any other sort of condition; it is to believe that such a condition has an absolute weight relative to other conditions for moral responsibility. My argument is that most compatibilists can be said not to have such a commitment.

But I shall also argue that any compatibilist who insisted that he was really committed to such a belief would be forced to venture into uncomfortable and dangerous territory—territory which as a compatibilist he need never have entered. It would be uncomfortable because there would be a tension between this belief and his distinctively compatibilist beliefs and it would be dangerous because he would find it necessary to defend interpretations of the could-have-acted-otherwise claim which are both implausible and counter-intuitive.

It might be thought strange that I should be planning to argue for such conclusions for don't both the compatibilist and the incompatibilist advance their accounts of blameworthiness as accounts which accord with our commonly shared intuitions about such matters? And isn't one of our commonly shared intuitions the intuition that there is a could-have-acted-otherwise condition for moral responsibility? After all, we accept that claims such as 'He needn't have done that' and 'He couldn't help it' are relevant to our moral assessments of agents who have offended in some way, and the philosopher's claims 'He could have acted otherwise' and 'He could not have acted otherwise' are simply expedient devices for expressing the essences of such accusations or pleas for exoneration. I shall return to this objection much later in the chapter, but I mention it now because the claim that the compatibilist and the incompatibilist are trying to give accounts which will satisfy commonly held intuitions about blameworthiness leads to a useful starting point for the argument I wish to present about the compatibilist.

So, I begin with the suggestion that it is a commonly shared intuition that underlying our practice of distinguishing between blameworthy and non-blameworthy offenders is the following principle:

> Blame the offender who satisfies both of the following conditions
>
> 1. His offending behaviour was the result of a set of attitudes

(or a combination of attitudes and motives) which are felt to be morally reprehensible; for example, a preparedness to do what the agent knows to be wrong for no reason which would excuse his behaviour. (From now on I shall refer to such attitudes and motives as 'morally reprehensible states of mind', M-states of mind for short.)[2]

2. He could have acted otherwise.

  Excuse the offender who either does not fulfil condition one or does not fulfil condition two.

(I shall call condition one 'The M-condition' and condition two 'the C-condition'.)

Thus, we are to assume (at least provisionally) that we subscribe to a principle in terms of which the blameworthy offender must satisfy both the M- and the C-condition, that is a principle in terms of which each condition has an absolute weight relative to the other.

I shall argue that the compatibilist either is or ought to be committed to the belief that the C-condition does not have an absolute weight relative to the M-condition, but is in fact reducible to it.

My argument will be in three parts. First (part 1), I shall briefly describe the incompatibilist's beliefs about the C-condition. I do this because it is only when the compatibilist is seen as someone who is reacting to the incompatibilist that the essential features of his compatibilism are thrown into sharp relief. Then (part 2), I shall describe what I believe to be the essential features of any response to the incompatibilist which is worthy of the name 'compatibilism'—a position in terms of which the C-condition is held to be reducible to the M-condition. After describing this uncompromisingly compatibilist response I shall (part 3) go on to show that when the compatibilist's response is less uncompromising than this, that is when he attempts to treat the C-condition as one with an independent weight, he runs into serious difficulties.

1. The incompatibilist beliefs about the C-condition

According to the traditional view of him, the incompatibilist believes that both the M-condition and the C-condition must be fulfilled for blameworthiness. The hallmark of the incompatibi-

list's position is his insistence that it cannot be true that agents
could have acted otherwise if it is also true that their behaviour
had determining causes. He insists that the could-have-acted-
otherwise claim is to be understood as a claim to the effect that
it would have been possible for the agent to perform a different
act from the one performed *in-the-circumstances-as-they-were-
when-he-acted*, that is in circumstances which included the
same (kinds of)[3] antecedents as those which led to the original
act, including the same (kinds of) desires and beliefs.[4] To insist
on this is to insist on what has been called an 'absolute' could-
have-acted-otherwise condition for blameworthiness.[5]

2. The compatibilist response to incompatibilism

The hallmark of the traditional compatibilist's position is the
claim that in determining whether or not an offender is blameworthy we rely on a principle which distinguishes between
kinds of causes. Against the incompatibilist, the compatibilist
argues that there is no need to deny the claim that there were
determining causes for an offender's behaviour before we can
appropriately say that he is blameworthy and thus no need to
deny the claim that given the causal antecedents of his act it
would have been empirically impossible for him to have performed a different act. Neither assertion, the compatibilist
argues, is incompatible with the assertion that an offender is
blameworthy, for the cause which explains the occurrence of
the offender's behaviour and (if determinism is true) makes that
behaviour inevitable is at the same time the feature which either
condemns or exonerates him. The compatibilist claims that the
kind of cause for behaviour which condemns the offender is a
morally reprehensible state of mind, while the kind of cause
which exonerates him is either a state of mind which is not morally reprehensible or an event which has produced his behaviour
independently of his psychological motivating states (e.g. his
being pushed). Thus, the compatibilist cheerfully acknowledges
the impossibility, if determinsm is true, of there having been a
different act, an impossibility held against his account by the
incompatibilist, but he turns this to his advantage by claiming
that if the cause which determined the act (thereby making
another act impossible) was the agent's morally reprehensible

state of mind, then the agent is blameworthy. It looks as if the compatibilist, as I have described him, believes not only that the satisfaction of the M-condition is necessary for blameworthiness but also that it is sufficient.[6]

What then of the compatibilist's attitude to the C-condition? If he is to be consistent, he might deny that there is a C-condition for moral responsibility.[7] On the other hand, he might, as many compatibilists do, claim that there is a C-condition for blameworthiness, but treat the could-have-acted-otherwise claim in such a way that it is plausible to maintain that for the traditional compatibilist the claim's moral relevance consists solely in its highlighting of the causal role which was played by the offender's morally reprehensible state of mind. In treating the could-have-acted-otherwise claim in this way, the compatibilist shows himself to be committed to the belief that the role of this claim is not independent of the M-condition, and in revealing his commitment to such a belief, the compatibilist reveals that he does not have a real commitment to the claim that there is a could-have-acted-otherwise condition for moral responsibility, or, better, he shows that he does not believe that such a condition has an absolute weight relative to the M-condition. I shall now show why this is so.

If the compatibilist is to maintain that there is a morally relevant could-have-acted-otherwise claim whose truth is compatible with the truth of determinsm, then he must allow that it could be true that 'X could have acted otherwise' and also true that 'It was not possible in the causal circumstances as they were for there to have been a different act from the one X performed.' Thus he must interpret the could-have-acted-otherwise claim in a way which does not imply that an agent could have performed a different act in the existing circumstances. As we have seen, the compatibilist is not worried by the fact that (if determinism is true) X's act was causally determined, for he maintains that it is the *kind* of cause which determines whether or not X is blameworthy. Also, like the incompatibilist, he believes that the fulfilment of the M-condition is necessary if X is to be appropriately judged as blameworthy.

So when the compatibilist claims that he believes there is a C-condition for blameworthiness, he must, if he is to be faithful to his compatibilist beliefs, endorse an interpretation of 'X

could have acted otherwise' which accommodates two requirements:

  (*a*) it must not be inconsistent with the claim that X's acts
        were causally determined; and
  (*b*) it must be consistent with the belief that X has satisfied
        the M-condition.

I would suggest that it is his desire to accommodate both
demands which leads the compatibilist to interpret the 'X could
have acted otherwise' claim in the following ways:

  (i)   When X acted certain causal constraints (whose presence
        would have exonerated X from moral responsibility)
        were absent; and
  (ii) X had the ability and opportunity to act otherwise such
        that if he had willed (chosen, wanted) to act otherwise, he
        would have acted otherwise.

These claims can be said to accommodate successfully
demands (*a*) and (*b*) by suggesting that the cause which
accounts for X's act is his morally reprehensible state of mind.
For (i) can be seen as a way of saying that it was not because X
was prevented from acting otherwise by anything which would
have excused him that he acted as he did. And (ii) can be seen as
a way of saying that X did not act as he did because he lacked
the ability or opportunity to act otherwise, but because he
wanted to act that way.

Interpreted in either of these ways, the claim serves to remind
us of the role played by X's morally reprehensible state of mind;
it obliquely underscores the fact that X's morally reprehensible
state of mind was responsible for his acting as he did. On
neither interpretation can the claim be seen as representing a
condition which must be satisfied over and above the
M-condition.

Any compatibilist whose attitude to the C-claim is as I have
described it above is someone of whom it is appropriate to say
that he has no more than the appearance of someone who is
committed to the belief that there is an independent C-condition
for moral responsibility.

But it might be objected: why should anyone accept that the
compatibilist interpretations of the could-have-acted-otherwise
claim which have been described above are such that the claim

ought to be seen as reducible to the claim embodied in the description of the M-condition? The C-claim interpreted in either way has a different meaning from the M-claim and interpreted in both ways it seems to be a claim which can stand on its own, playing an independent role in our moral assessment procedures.

My answer to this is that if the compatibilist treats the C-claim as one whose role is something other than the highlighting of the fulfilment of the M-condition, serious difficulties arise for him. I shall now attempt to show this.

3. The compatibilist who treats the C-claim as if it represented an independent condition

Let us assume that the compatibilist's position is that he believes an offender is blameworthy if he fulfils two conditions:

M   his act was caused by a morally reprehensible state of mind and

C   he could have acted otherwise.

As we have seen, the compatibilist interprets the C-claim in the following ways:

(i)   When X acted certain causal constraints (whose presence would have exonerated X from moral responsibility) were absent; or

(ii) X had the ability and opportunity to act otherwise such that if he had willed (chosen, wanted) to act otherwise, he would have acted otherwise.

It must be remembered that we are testing the belief that these claims refer to something which is independent of the M-condition. But it seems impossible to view the first interpretation as anything other than an underscoring of the M-condition, while the second interpretation, viewed as referring to an independent condition, provokes uneasiness. It provokes the thought: could X have willed (chosen) otherwise and oughtn't we to know this before we can decide whether or not he is blameworthy?

If this question were asked of the compatibilist described earlier, for whom the C-claim is not independent of the M-claim, he could reply without compromising his position at all that the question, 'Could X have willed (or chosen) otherwise?'

simply doesn't arise because the fact that X has fulfilled the M-condition is sufficient for blameworthiness. But this answer is not available to the compatibilist who claims that the C-condition has an independent weight. He must either try to show that the question does not arise for different reasons, or he must attempt to give a compatibilist analysis of the claim 'X could have willed (chosen, decided, wanted) otherwise'—an analysis which will satisfy our intuitions about blameworthiness.

One reason interpretation (ii) might be thought *not* to give rise to the question 'Could X have willed (chosen, etc.) otherwise?' is that it could be taken to imply (*a*) that the agent's ability to act otherwise is separable from his ability to will (etc.) otherwise; and (*b*) that *as so separable* this ability is fully constitutive of what we refer to when we say that the agent could have acted otherwise and we mean this claim to be understood as a claim whose truth is a condition of the agent's blameworthiness. But both (*a*) and (*b*) are counter-intuitive. For both imply that an agent could have acted otherwise in a morally relevant sense (that is a sense which would have had a bearing on his moral responsibility) even if he could not have willed (etc.) otherwise.

But I shall argue that if the moral relevance of the C-claim is not held to reside in its underscoring of the existence of the M-condition then the only plausible way of interpreting the claim which would render it relevant to an agent's moral responsibility is one in terms of which it entails a claim to the effect that he could have willed (or chosen, or decided, etc.) otherwise. And this means that the kind of compatibilist who insists that the C-claim is independent of the M-claim is thereby committed to providing an account of the *could-have-willed* (etc.) otherwise claim which is compatible with determinsm, relevant to our moral assessment of offenders, and independent of the M-claim.

Difficulties for the compatibilist who believes the C-condition is independent

My argument will be in two parts:

(*a*) First, I shall argue for the entailment claim and will show that it cannot be true that X could have performed an act for which he would have deserved a different moral assessment if it is false that he could have willed (chosen, decided) to perform a different act.

(*b*) Then I shall argue that the sort of compatibilist we are considering (that is one who is committed to an independent C-condition) cannot provide a satisfactory account of the could-have-willed (etc.) otherwise claim.

Before I begin the argument for (*a*) there are two obviously irrelevant interpretations of the X could-have-acted-otherwise claim (the C-claim) which are worth mentioning because their irrelevance helps to bring into focus those features which any morally relevant C-claim has to involve. The first is an interpretation of the claim as one about the logically possible, that is as an assertion to the effect that the claim that X did not act otherwise could be denied without contradiction. The second is an interpretation of the claim as one about what one might call the 'metaphysically possible'—that kind of possibility which followers of Kripke would attribute to any individual and situation so long as essential properties were not called into question. If the C-claim were one about the metaphysically possible it would at best be a claim about X conceived of in the most minimal way, simply as the living continuation of a particular zygote (if Kripke is right).[8]

Since, according to this doctrine,[9] metaphysically the only thing which could not have been different about X was the fact that he had the biological parents he did, the metaphysical possibilities for him are endless. Not only could X have *acted* otherwise, he could have been a different sort of person with different motivations and different abilities; and he could have been in a different sort of situation from the one he was in when he acted wrongly. It should be clear that all these thoughts are totally irrelevant to the question of X's blameworthiness. When we are passing moral judgement on X, we are judging X-as-he-was in the situation as-it-was, not X as he conceivably might have been in a situation which might conceivably have obtained. This one can say is a minimal requirement for any judgement which is to be relevant to the question of someone's moral responsibility.

This has a bearing on the next point. We are testing whether fulfilment of the C-condition is something we have to know about *in addition* to knowledge of fulfilment of the

M-condition. This means that the sort of agent with whom we are concerned is someone who is known to have fulfilled the M-condition. Thus the judgement of this agent (X) as he was will be a judgement of him as someone who is known to have acted as the result of a willingness to do the wrong thing. I turn now to the argument.

(a) *The C-claim entails an X could-have-willed (or chosen, decided) otherwise claim.*   We are imagining that the role of the ability–opportunity formulation of the C-claim is not to highlight the fact that the M-condition has been fulfilled, but that it is relevant for different reasons to our moral assessment of X. Clearly, we are supposed to assume that its relevance depends on the fact that it is referring to abilities and opportunities whose possession by X, in conjunction with the moral requirement, made it reasonable to have expected him to act differently.

But what kind of morally relevant abilities is X being credited with? To know this we must consider what the notion of 'acting otherwise' involves. In the contexts with which we are concerned—contexts in which X is being blamed for having performed a morally unacceptable act—there is an understanding that not just *any* act different from the one performed would be a morally acceptable substitute. Rather, the notion of 'acting otherwise' in these contexts is one which refers to specific kinds of acts. When X is being criticized for what he has done it is understood that had he not acted in that way, he would not be vulnerable to that criticism. When he is being criticized for not acting it is understood that had he acted and thus fulfilled the moral requirement he would not be vulnerable to criticism. Now, as has already been said, we are judging X as he was, and this means that involved in our judgement of him must be the knowledge that when he acted in the morally unacceptable way, he did so because (in some sense) he wanted, or was inclined, to act in that way, as well as the knowledge that he was aware that what he was planning to do was wrong. Therefore, I would suggest that the sort of act we feel X ought to have performed when he acted wrongly was an act of self-restraint. We feel X ought to have resisted the inclination to do something which he knew to be wrong. In those cases where X is blamed for not acting we feel that he ought to have made himself do the right thing, that is he ought to have overcome his disinclination to act. In both sorts of cases X is seen as someone who could have deliberately done something other than he was inclined to do. He is seen as someone who could have deliberately acted against (some of) his inclinations. It is the ability to have done this with which he is being credited when it is claimed that he had the ability to do otherwise.

But for X to have deliberately stopped himself from acting as he was inclined to do his state of mind would have had to be different from that state of mind which preceded and caused the act for which we blame him. It would have had to involve either a different decision or choice or the willing of a different act and a different motivating desire (since it is plausible to assume that decisions, choices, and willings are often based on desires). This seems so obvious that it is embarrassing to be offering arguments for it. But the hypothetical compatibilist against whom we are arguing is envisaged as someone who thinks it plausible to maintain that there is a sense in which X could have acted otherwise even if he could not have willed (chosen or decided) otherwise and that it is (partly) in virtue of this non-dependent ability to act otherwise that X is blameworthy. But what reason could anyone possibly have for thinking this?

There is a sense, other than that of bare logical or metaphysical possibility, in terms of which it is true that X could have acted otherwise even if he could not have been in a different state of mind and perhaps the compatibilist we are addressing has mistakenly assumed that because it is true in this sense it is true in all senses. The sense in which it is true is that X could have performed an act with different consequences even if he could not have willed (chosen, etc.) otherwise. And since it is legitimate to describe actions in terms of their consequences (as well as their intentions), it would be legitimate to say that had X's act had different consequences it would have been a different act.

But *this* sense in which X could have performed a different act is *not* one which is relevant to his blameworthiness. Imagine that X's offending act was an act of harming Y and that X intended to harm Y when he acted. Now imagine that X's act might not have harmed Y even though X peformed it intending to harm him. Y might have been someone who (unknown to X) could not have been harmed by this sort of act. It should be clear that to say on this account that X could have acted otherwise is misleading if this claim is supposed to be relevant to our judgement of X's blameworthiness. For the claim that X's act might have had different consequences from the ones it had is hardly a claim about X at all, or *a fortiori* about what X could have deliberately done to avoid those consequences (that is to avoid harming Y). It is rather a claim about the possibility that the world in respect of Y's physical or psychological sensitivities might have been different from the way it was when X acted. This claim is therefore not relevant to the question of X's moral responsibility.

Of course, if X's act had not harmed Y there would have been no obvious motive for regarding him as a prima-facie candidate for blame. Nevertheless, had we known what he was attempting to do we would (all things being equal) have regarded him as blameworthy. X's moral unacceptability does not follow from what he actually brings about but from what he attempts to do.[10] This last point must be stressed for someone might want to claim that in a situation in which X's act has not had harmful consequences, we cannot speak of blaming X for his act, but only for what he intended to do. But acts can be characterized as attempts to do something or other. X can therefore be blamed for having made the attempt to do something which he thought would hurt Y. In respect of the act's characterizability as one which does or does not reflect badly on X, X could only have performed a different act if he could have made a different attempt. But X could only have made a different attempt if he had willed (or chosen or decided) to do something other than he in fact did. For the sort of attempt X can be said to make depends on what he thinks of himself as trying to do, and these thoughts will be embodied in his willings, or decisions, or choices. Therefore, the claim that X could have acted otherwise as a claim about what X could have attempted to do entails the claim that X could have willed (or chosen, or decided) to act otherwise.

So the compatibilist who treats the could-have-acted-otherwise claim as one which is independent of the M-condition cannot deny that there is a could-have-willed (etc.) otherwise condition for moral responsibility. Unlike the compatibilist who insists that the fulfilment of the M-condition is sufficient for blameworthiness, this compatibilist has no basis for claiming that the question 'Could X have willed (or chosen etc.) other- wise?' does not arise. Such a compatibilist is, therefore, bound to show that there is an interpretation of the claim that X could have willed (etc.) otherwise which (1) is not reducible to the M-claim, (2) is consistent with the truth of determinism, and (3) satisfies our intuitions about blameworthiness.

(*b*) *Two compatibilist accounts*   I shall discuss an account of the could-have-willed-otherwise claim and an account of the claim that an agent could have altered his intention. Both have been offered as accounts which are compatible with determin- ism. The account of the could-have-willed-otherwise claim has been advanced by Richard Foley.[11] Although Foley has not sug- gested that his account is relevant to judgements of blame- worthiness, I think it is legitimate to enquire whether it can accommodate the beliefs involved in such judgements. The account of the could-have-altered-his-intention claim has been advanced by Johnathan Glover in *Responsibility*[12] and it has been offered by him as an account which is both compatible with determinism and our beliefs about blameworthiness. I shall argue that when viewed as accounts of a C-condition which is independent of the M-condition, neither can satisfy our intuitions about blameworthiness.

The essential ingredients of Foley's compatibilist analysis of the 'ability to will otherwise' are contained in the following pas- sage from 'Compatibilism':

A person is in our paradigmatic sense able to will z only if there might exist a situation in which the person would will z because he would recognise that of all the practical alternatives available to him in the situation, y is the one which would yield the most of what he values. Thus, although he may in fact never find himself in a situation where y is his best option and hence may never find himself in a situation where he is induced to will z, it may nevertheless be true that he was able to will z, since it may be true that situations could arise in which he would be so induced. (pp. 424–5)

By the 'ability to will in the paradigmatic sense', Foley means the ability to will an act z knowing that the act z will produce certain consequences y. It is clear that we are to read into this account the assumption that doing z as the result of willing z will bring about y.

Foley is at pains to explain that he is offering an analysis of the ability of a person *as he is* to will—an analysis, therefore, of the ability which is attributable to him in virtue of certain characteristics which are intrinsic to him. If the analysis is to succeed in this respect it cannot bracket off any intrinsic characteristics on which the existence of the ability might depend. And if it is to succeed as a compatibilist analysis it must bracket off some causal conditions. The causal condition which is bracketed off, therefore, must be one whose presence is irrelevant to the existence of the ability. Foley claims that what can be bracketed off as irrelevant is the situation in which the person (called by Foley 'S') finds himself at the moment. He says:

The compatibilist can claim that the fact that there happens to obtain a set of conditions which make it advantageous or attractive for the person to will in a certain way is not relevant for deciding whether he is able to will something else z. Instead, we should ask if there might obtain a set of conditions in which it would be advantageous or attractive for the person to will and, hence, a set of conditions in which he would will z. If there is such a set of conditions, then the person can be said to be able to will z. (p. 423.)

Foley specifically mentions as relevant intrinsic characteristics of S, his basic desires and physical capacities. Thus, he claims that S can be said to be able to will otherwise if it is the case that there are physically possible situations in which S would recognize that a different act would produce consequences which, all things considered, would yield most of what he basically wants.

Can Foley's analysis of what it is to be able to will otherwise be seen as one which would be relevant to our moral responsibility judgements if, as we are supposing for the time being, we are *not* interested in the existence of that ability because it indicates fulfilment of the M-condition, but because we think that its existence is independently important?

I think that the answer is 'no'. For Foley's analysis makes the situation which S was in (when he didn't will otherwise) irrelevant to the question 'Could he have willed otherwise?' He claims that what S would have done in other situations constitutes what he is capable of. But if we *had* judged S to be blame-worthy in virtue of his ability to will otherwise, we would not have been interested in what he would have willed in other situations. What would have concerned us is whether in *that* situation, the situation in which he had acted wrongly, S could have willed differently. When we say of an offender that he ought to have acted differently, we mean that he ought to have acted differently in the situation as it then was and if, as many believe, ought implies can, then this would seem to commit us to the view that he could have acted differently (and therefore willed differently) in the situation as it then was. We would consider it neither necessary nor sufficient for his blameworthiness that in another situation he could have been induced to will otherwise.[13]

The compatibilist account of the conditions for blameworthiness which is offered by Johnathan Glover in *Responsibility* is briefly summarized by him as follows: 'To sum up crudely: for purposes of blame, a person is his intentions, except where his intentions are unalterable.'[14] Thus, Glover can be said to endorse the view that an offender must satisfy *two* conditions for blameworthiness—an M-condition *and* an alterable intention condition.

In keeping with his compatibilist position, Glover insists that the truth or falsity of the claim that an agent could have altered his intention is independent of the truth or falsity of determinism. It can be true, he claims, that the agent could have altered his intention even if it is also true that, given the causal antecedents of his intention, he could not have had a different one. For the test of alterability of intention is 'whether or not reasons providing a fairly strong motive for doing so would have persuaded the person to change his course of action.'[15] But it can be objected that (i) there are people who would fail Glover's test but who would not *on that account* fail the test for responsibility and (ii) there are people whose intentions would pass the test for alterability but whom we would be reluctant *on that account* to call morally responsible for their acts. One sort of person who would fail Glover's test is the sort who is so committed to an ideal that he is prepared to die in order to fulfil it. Nothing would induce such a person to alter his intention and yet we would feel it wrong to say that because his intention to pursue his ideal is unalterable, he is not responsible for acting in pursuit of it.[16]

The sorts of people who would pass Glover's test for alterability of intention but who would not on that account be considered blameworthy are people like drug addicts who might, on pain of death, resist the next dose of drugs, or kleptomaniacs who might, if threatened with having their arms cut off, resist the temptation to steal. These would be people who might pass the test in the sense that they might be persuaded to change their courses of action because they have been provided with very strong reasons for doing so. But the fact that in such extreme situations the addict and the kleptomaniac might be able to alter their intentions is no evidence for the claim that in circumstances where such dangers were not present they would have been able to alter them. Glover concedes this and suggests that the proper test for alterability is whether offenders would be persuadable in normal circumstances (p. 99). Presumably, such circumstances would be those in which the agent is not in a life-threatening situation but in which there are reasons present which normal people would accept as sufficient to induce anyone to act in a certain way. Glover must be assuming that such reasons would be reasons of self-interest for *ex hypothesi* in those morally problematic situations in which agents have failed to act morally, there were *moral* reasons which should have outweighed the motivating reasons for acting, but which failed to sway the agent. Glover's idea seems to be that if the agent could not be persuaded to alter his course of action when it is in his interest to do so (p. 100), then his intention must be one which he is incapable of altering. But this is precisely the case with the person whose act follows from an unshakeable commitment to an ideal and we do not say on that account that he is not responsible for acting as he does. Furthermore, it is not clear how a test designed to show what someone would be capable of doing if he knew his interests were threatened can indicate whether he is capable of disregarding his interests as the man in a morally problematic situation is sometimes required to do. Candidates for blameworthiness are those who have not been swayed by moral reasons all the way to action. They have failed to respond sufficiently to the thought that what they were about to do was wrong or harmful. And, it might be argued, in blaming them because these moral reasons did not weigh enough with them, we are implying that they could have responded to such reasons. Of what relevance then is a test which is designed to show that they would have responded to other reasons? As we saw when discussing Foley's account, what concerns us when we are apportioning blame is the fact that the agent failed to do the right thing in the circumstances as they were. It seems prima-facie implausible to suggest that the test for whether or not it is excusable for a man to perform an act in one set of circumstances is whether in a different set of circumstances he could have been persuaded to change his mind.

Doesn't it seem overwhelmingly likely that the true relevance of information about what someone would have done in different circumstances is that such information indicates what his motivation in *these* circumstances is? Indeed, in his recent British Academy Lecture, Glover says: 'normally when reacting to the behaviour of others, our interest in their abilities is primarily as a source of evidence about their motivation'.[17] This suggests that, as I have argued, the role of such information is to emphasize fulfilment or lack of fulfilment of the M-condition.

It would be tempting to assume at this point that a strong enough case has been made for the claim that any compatibilist who holds that there is a C-condition which must be satisfied in addition to the M-condition is committed to a position with counter-intuitive consequences which can only be avoided if he treats the C-claims as nothing more than ways of highlighting the fulfilment of the M-condition.

But it might be objected that we cannot draw general conclusions about all compatibilist accounts from the failure of two such accounts. After all, both accounts failed for the same reason: they were accounts of an agent's ability to have willed otherwise in a different situation from the one in which he acted, whereas what can plausibly be said to be required of a blameworthy agent is the ability to have willed otherwise in the situation he was in at the time—the situation in which he failed to will the act which was morally required of him. But this doesn't mean that all compatibilist accounts are bound to make this mistake. We cannot rule out the possibility that another account might succeed in satisfying our moral intuitions.

I find myself unable to give an *a priori* argument for the claim that any compatibilist account which treats the could-have-willed-otherwise claim as one with an independent role to play in our moral assessment procedures is bound to fail. But I can show that on some very plausible interpretations of what such an attempt would have to involve, it does fail.

A general discussion of the compatibilist attempt to offer an account of an independent could-have-willed-otherwise claim

It would be helpful if we reminded ourselves of the sort of account which the compatibilist we are considering is trying to give. He is trying to provide an interpretation of the claim which fulfils three requirements:

1. It must be an interpretation which shows the claim to be something other than an oblique way of underscoring the fact that the M-condition has been fulfilled.
2. It must be compatible with determinism.
3. It must be morally relevant.

Since the compatibilist we are considering is asking us to treat the could-have-willed-otherwise claim as something other than an oblique way of underscoring what did happen, it seems plausible to say that he believes its role is to refer to what 'could-have-happened', that is he believes the C-claim is to be taken at its face value. The most obvious way of taking the claim at its face value is to interpret it in a way which does justice to its appearance of referring to (unrealized) possibilities. The other way of interpreting the C-claim is the one we have just been discussing—the one which treats it as a claim about the agent's ability and opportunity. These seem to be the only interpretations of the claim which are both plausible and able to suggest that its role might be independent from that of the M-claim.

I shall consider the 'possibility' interpretation first. The compatibilist who interprets the C-claim as one about possibility must take it to be implying that even if in the causal circumstances as they were the agent could not have willed otherwise, nevertheless in those causal circumstances there was the possibility of alternative willing. But in what sense was alternative willing possible if, as the compatibilist acknowledges, it was (or might have been) causally impossible? What kind of possibility is being invoked?

It cannot be *logical* possibility for, as we saw earlier, no morally relevant claim can be referring to the merely-logically-possible. If the compatibilist is to show that the C-claim is morally relevant, he must show it to be referring to a more than logical possibility of alternative willing, and if he is to show that it is compatible with determinism, he must show that this more-than-logical possibility of alternative willing is consistent with the causal impossibility of such willing. But what kind of possibility is left once we have ruled out mere-logical-possibility and causal possibility?

There is a kind of natural possibility which might be invoked: this is the possibility which could be said to exist in virtue of the existence of a natural law. Thus, a particular event which did not occur can be said to have been naturally possible in this sense if a natural law exists such that if different circumstances had obtained, that event would have occurred. So if the X could-have-willed-otherwise claim referred to this sort of possibility then it would be interpretable as follows: when X willed as he did, it was possible for him to have willed otherwise in that if an event which did not occur had occurred, X would have willed otherwise.

But such an interpretation does not fulfil the third requirement of moral relevance. It seems counter-intuitive to suggest that X might be blameworthy because he would have willed otherwise if a particular event which did not occur had occurred.

Now someone might object that it is not counter-intuitive to suggest this if the event which would have been needed to bring about his willing otherwise was the occurrence of the right kind of desire. The objection would be that it *is* relevant to the question of X's blameworthiness that *had he wanted* something else, he would have willed differently.

However, I cannot see how such a claim could be relevant *unless* its role is to emphasize X's fulfilment of the M-condition. And if this is right, then the interpretation does not meet the first requirement.

As the compatibilist is committed to invoking a non-causal possibility if he is to invoke possibility at all, and since neither the merely-logically-possible nor this very remote sense of natural possibility will do, it seems safe to conclude that there is no hope of providing an account of the could-have-willed-otherwise claim which will fulfil all three requirements so long as the claim is thought to be a claim about possibility.

But suppose we take the C-claim to be one which is referring to X's ability (and opportunity) to will otherwise.[18] We have already seen that two compatibilist analyses of the ability to will (or to intend) otherwise have failed to fulfil the third requirement because they were not analyses of an agent's ability to have willed otherwise in the circumstances as they were. But isn't any compatibilist analysis bound to fail on this account? Whatever analysis is offered must be one which is consistent with the claim that it was causally impossible for there to have been a different event of willing. How then can an agent be said to have been 'able' to will otherwise in the circumstances as they were?

The compatibilist might reply that to say this is to confuse the existence of an ability with the conditions for its exercise. His argument would be this: granted that in the causal circumstances as they were the agent could not have *exercized* his ability, but this does not mean that he did not *have* the ability.

But this reply rather than answering the overall objection to the compatibilist analysis only serves to reinforce it. For unless one accepts that the role of the ability–opportunity interpretation of the C-claim is to underscore the satisfaction of the M-condition, it remains completely inexplicable why it should be thought relevant to the question of an agent's blameworthiness that he had an ability which he could not have exercised (and an opportunity he could not have taken advantage of).

Surely, the most plausible explanation for the relevance of claims like 'He had the ability and the opportunity to . . . otherwise, such that if he had wanted (willed, chosen, decided) to . . . otherwise, he would have . . . otherwise' is that they highlight the fulfilment of the M-condition.

At the beginning of this chapter, I suggested that everyday pleas for exoneration like 'He couldn't help it' and 'She couldn't do anything else' might be taken as evidence of widespread commitment to a could-have-acted-otherwise condition for moral responsibility.

But perhaps we are now in a position to accept the suggestion that such pleas do not represent this kind of commitment but are instead oblique ways of indicating that when the offender acted as he did, he did not fulfil the M-condition.

A way of testing this is to reflect on the apparent absurdity of a statement like 'He couldn't help doing that, he wanted to do it.' I think the statement is absurd because it contains an implicit contradiction. The first clause, 'He couldn't help doing that' implies that it was not because he wanted to that he acted as he did, while the second clause contradicts this. This persuades me that when statements like 'He couldn't help it' are made in conjunction with judgements of moral responsibility, they are being used to refer to the offender's non-fulfilment of the M-condition. It seems reasonable, therefore, to conclude that claims like 'He needn't have done that' are used to refer to the offender's fulfilment of the M-condition.

Conclusion

I have argued that the compatibilist is not committed to an independent C-condition and that to the extent that he thinks he is he makes himself vulnerable to objections which he cannot satisfactorily meet.

Addendum: Some remarks on the M-condition

There are some elements of my description of the M-condition which I would like to explain further and some criticisms of it which I should like to examine. These specifically concern what I have called 'the morally reprehensible state of mind'. It will be remembered that as an illustration of such a state of mind I suggested 'a preparedness to do what the agent knows to be wrong for no reason which would excuse his behaviour'.

But it can be argued that while some aspects of this illustration would have to be satisfied by any state of mind which deserved the label 'morally reprehensible', not all aspects would have to be. In particular, the M-state of mind need not include the agent's *knowledge* that his intended act was wrong. For example, an agent might mistakenly think that his act was morally right and yet still have a state of mind which qualified as reprehensible, if his thought was based on a conviction which is morally abhorrent, for example the conviction that those who belong to a particular racial group can be treated with less consideration than those who belong to a different racial group.[19]

Furthermore, it can be argued that an agent's motivating state of mind could qualify as morally reprehensible even if it contained no beliefs about the morality of his act; for instance, the state of mind of someone who is motivated by the sadistic desire to hurt another and who has no thoughts one way or another about the rightness of his act.

These examples are convincing, but it is difficult to see how one could give a general description of the M-state which took account of them without that description becoming far too unwieldy. What would be needed would be some claim to the effect that the agent's state of mind must either (a) contain knowledge that his act is wrong or (b) contain a belief about the nature of his act which is such that were any normal and morally knowledgeable person to hold it, he or she would immediately be aware that such an act is wrong.[20] This is obviously too cumbersome and I can think of no shorter substitute for the addition which would not provoke the objection that it hadn't covered other possible reprehensible states. For the time being, therefore, I propose to retain the original description with the proviso that it should be seen as an abbreviated version of the more adequate description just given.[21]

I must now explain what I mean when I say that the M-state of mind would be one which did not include excusing reasons. The term 'reason' here refers to motives. I think that excusing motives can be divided into three sorts. One sort would involve the agent's mistaken belief that the good nature of his act morally outweighs its bad nature. But there are two ways in which someone could be mistaken about the moral nature of his act, only one of which can be called 'excusing': (a) he could have the true belief that his act satisfied a certain morally neutral description[22] and falsely believe that under this description it was morally justifiable; or (b) he could falsely believe that his act satisfied a certain morally neutral description and have the true belief that acts which satisfied this description were morally justifiable.

An agent who had the true belief that his act was disadvantageous to Catholics and advantageous to Protestants and who also believed that differences in religious belief justified such differential treatment would satisfy description (a). Someone who attacked another because he mistakenly believed that he was about to be attacked and who also believed that he was morally entitled to defend himself would be an example of (b). But only the agent who satisfied description (b) could

be said to have an excusing motive. The agent who satisfied description (*a*) could not because his 'moral' convictions are morally unacceptable.

A second sort of excusing motive would be an agent's morally neutral and false belief about the nature of his act. It would be 'morally
neutral' in the sense that it contained no thoughts about the act's
moral nature. And it would be 'excusing' because if it had been true,
the agent would have been justified in acting as he did. Someone who
falsely believes that his neighbour is about to attack him and who
therefore strikes out in what he imagines to be an act of self-protection
can be said to be acting from this kind of excusing motive. Many paranoid delusions would come under this heading of 'excusing motive'
and could also satisfy description (*b*) above.

The third kind of excusing motive involves a true belief whose
ignoring, or a desire whose overcoming, would require a saint or
someone of exceptional courage or fortitude. An example of such a
motive would be the justified belief that one's life was in danger in circumstances where one had to choose between one's own life and the
lives of others. Imagine a possible incident from World War II. A Ger-
man soldier is ordered to open fire on a group of women and children
who have been picked at random in reprisal for the villagers' alleged
harbouring of resistance fighters. He refuses to do so and is told that
unless he does, he himself will be shot. A gun is then pointed at his
head. He opens fire on the women and children. His action cannot be
justified since his life does not morally outweigh the lives of the
women and children, but we might agree that his motive for acting (to
save his own life) is a morally excusable one.

2

Frankfurt, van Inwagen, and the could-have-acted-otherwise condition

I shall begin by examining some arguments of Frankfurt's which, I believe, constitute a powerful case for the claim that there is not an independent C-condition for moral responsibility. And I shall end by examining van Inwagen's claim that even if Frankfurt's arguments succeed, it is still true that moral responsibility requires the ability to have acted otherwise.[1] I shall argue that van Inwagen fails to establish this.

Frankfurt's arguments

In 'Alternate Possibilities and Moral Responsibility', Frankfurt argues that the following principle, called by him the 'Principle of Alternate Possibilities' (P.A.P.)[2] is false:

'A person is morally responsible for what he has done only if he could have done otherwise.'[3]

At the end of his paper, he suggests that the P.A.P. should be replaced by the following principle:

'A person is not morally responsible for what he has done if he did it only because he could not have done otherwise.'[4]

And, in a more recent paper,[5] he gives specific examples of the sorts of cases to which this replacement principle would apply.

In the counter-example which Frankfurt offers as the strongest one to the P.A.P., he imagines a world containing an agent, Jones, and a creature with unusual power, Black. In this world, Jones has always decided on his own initiative to (say) ϕ. It is also the case, however, that if Jones had ever been inclined to decide to not-ϕ, Black would have brought it about that he (Jones) did decide to ϕ. But Black has never had to intervene for Jones has always decided to ϕ. Frankfurt concludes that this is a world in which Jones could not have done otherwise, but that we would agree with the judgement that Jones is morally responsible for what he has done (p. 835). He says:

It would be quite unreasonable to excuse Jones ... for his action ... on the basis of the fact that he could not have done otherwise. This fact played no role at all in leading him to act as he did. He would have acted the same even if it had not been a fact ... In this example, there are sufficient conditions for Jones performing the action in question. What action he performs is not up to him. Of course it is in a way up to him whether he acts on his own or as a result of Black's intervention. That depends on what action he himself is inclined to perform. But whether he finally acts on his own or as a result of Black's intervention he performs the same action. He has no alternative but to do what Black wants him to do. If he does it on his own, however, his moral responsibility for doing it is not affected by the fact that Black was lurking in the background with sinister intent; since his intent never comes into play. (p. 836.)

It it clear from this passage and from other things which Frankfurt says in this paper that he believes we would attribute moral responsibility to Jones in virtue of his having acted (as he did) *because he wanted to.*

But someone might object to this as follows: we do not consider it sufficient for moral responsibility that a man's behaviour is determined by his desires. We would, for instance, excuse a person who acted as the result of a desire which was irresistible. And this surely suggests that we are committed to a C-condition for blameworthiness. For we would excuse such an agent for not having been able to resist the desire. Thus the reason we find Jones blameworthy, even though he could not have performed an act with different consequences, is that we take it that the desire he acted on was not irresistible and that he, therefore, could have acted otherwise in the sense that he could have resisted the desire to act as he did by deliberately refraining from acting on it. His deliberate refraining would have been an act of self-control. The objection would continue: it looks as if Frankfurt has seen that Jones could not have acted on his desire for he says 'Of course it is in a way up to him whether he acts on his own or as a result of Black's intervention.' But he has not seen that it is precisely this ability to have not acted on his desire which makes Jones morally culpable. Thus, it is only partly true to say as Frankfurt does that whether Jones 'acts on his own or as the result of Black's intervention he performs the same action'. What is correct about the statement is that the consequences of Jones's behaviour would have been of the same type whether they were brought about by his intervention-free act or the Black-induced one. Of course, because the Black-induced act would have had different causal antecedents from the intervention-free act, it would have been a different act-token. But the *important* difference between the two is that each represents a different act-type. Jones's act instantiates the act type: act-performed-as-the-result-of-a-resistible-desire. While his Black-induced act would have instantiated the type: act-performed - as - the - result - of - a - desire - whose - outcome - is - determined-by-someone-other-than-Jones. And in virtue of this difference Jones's intervention-free act instantiates a different moral type. It is an act for which he is morally responsible, while his Black-induced act would not have been one for which he was morally responsible.

But one can object that it is wrong to say that in the counter-example to the P.A.P., provided by Frankfurt, Jones could have deliberately refrained from acting as the result of his desire and thus to imply that he could have decided not to act on it. For, in fact, as Frankfurt describes the situation, if Jones had begun to manifest an inclination which threatened to lead to a non-Black approved decision, Black would have stepped in. Black is ready to intervene as soon as it becomes clear that Jones is about to decide not to act on his desire. Since he is unable to decide not to act in accordance with the desire of which Black approves, it is not true that Jones could have acted otherwise by refraining from acting as he did.

A possible reply to this objection is that it overlooks the morally crucial fact that Jones *has* the ability not to act in an intervention-free way; that is, he has the ability to force Black to take over (and thus an ability not to be morally responsible for the act he performs).[6]

But it is not clear why this should be thought to be morally crucial unless the objector thinks that Jones's ability not to act in an intervention-free way is an ability to *refrain* from acting and thus an ability to act otherwise. But this would be wrong. For remember that Jones is not given the opportunity by Black to decide in any way other than the way of which Black approves or to 'do' anything which could be construed as an alternative act. This means that Jones's ability to force Black to intervene cannot consist in an ability deliberately to refrain. The most it could consist of is the presence in Jones of stronger desires not to do what Black wants him to do than the desire of which Black approves. But without the ability to decide in favour of these stronger desires, Jones cannot be said to have an ability to act otherwise.

There is one more argument which might be thought to suggest that, *pace* Frankfurt, the ability to act otherwise *is* crucial for moral responsibility. Consider the sort of psychological state Jones has to be in for Black to see no reason to intervene. There seem to be two such states of mind:

A. One which consists in a compulsive desire to do what Black approves of and
B. one which consists in a stronger desire to do what Black approves of than any countervailing desire Jones might have.

Yet, surely, there is a morally relevant distinction between A and B for one feels that when Jones is in state A he should not be blamed for acting, but when in state B he should. Why is this? Is it not because we believe that when in state B Jones possesses an ingredient, for the ability to act otherwise, which he lacks in state A? Perhaps, then, if we think Jones *is* morally responsible, in the world which contains Black, it is because we assume that the desire on which he acted in that world was one which, *if he had lived in a world without Black*, he would have been able to refrain from acting on.

We can test this by imagining a world inhabited by Jones, Black, and another creature with unusual powers, White. In this world Jones has an irresistible compulsion to ϕ, White has the power to turn Jones's compulsion into a resistible desire, but Black has the power to implant another compulsion to ϕ in Jones should White tamper with the original compulsion. White never intervenes and therefore Jones always acts as a result of his self-originating compulsion to ϕ. In such a world the alternatives open to Jones are either to act as the result of his self-originating compulsion or to act as the result of the Black-induced compulsion.

Although Jones can be said always to act as the result of his desire, we would not say that he is morally responsible for his act. But why should the compulsiveness of Jones's desire make us feel that he is not morally responsible unless it is because compulsiveness rules out the possibility of acting otherwise?

The answer to this is that, despite appearances, if the compulsiveness of Jones's desire does excuse him it is not because it makes it impossible for him to do otherwise. To see why this is so we must turn again to Frankfurt and a distinction he makes between acting as the result of a desire which happens to be irresistible and acting as the result of a desire *because* it is irresistible. In 'Three Concepts of Free Action' Frankfurt argues that the inability to have resisted a desire and thus the inability to have acted otherwise can only serve as an excuse if the inability explains *why* the agent acted as he did.

To test Frankfurt's suggestion, let us imagine the following situation. There is an agent, A, who has been moved to flout a moral requirement by a desire which was both morally reprehensible and irresistible; morally reprehensible in that it was (say) an unprovoked desire to harm an innocent man and irresistible in that had A tried not to act on it his attempt would have failed. A was unaware that his desire was irresistible; so far as he was concerned if he hadn't wanted to harm the man he would have been able to refrain from doing so. According to Frankfurt, our moral intuitions would lead us to condemn A despite the fact that he could not have resisted his desire. We would condemn him because the irresistibility of his desire played no role in producing his act.

The intuition to which Frankfurt is appealing is this: what matters for blameworthiness is why the agent did what he did. It is irrelevant that other options were closed to him unless their non-availability *explains* his action. I find Frankfurt's argument completely convincing. I feel that it shows conclusively that there is not an independent C-condition for blameworthiness.

Before I take up van Inwagen's challenge, I wish to discuss Frankfurt's suggestion that a person who acts because of the irresistibility of his desires is not blameworthy. What does it mean to say that someone has acted *because* of the irresistibility of his desires?

In the course of his paper, Frankfurt refers, not always, I

think, with a clear idea of the differences between them, to three ways in which a man might be said to do this:

1. He could be 'defeated' by a desire which he does not want to be effective after an unsuccessful struggle to resist it (p. 114);

2. This is a case described by Frankfurt as one in which the agent is not defeated by a desire because he has not attempted to resist it, and yet as one in which he 'acts because of the irresistibility of his desire'. Such an agent, says Frankfurt, is not autonomous 'since his action does not result from an effective choice on his part concerning what to do' (p. 116). It is not clear from these remarks what sort of case Frankfurt is envisaging. The only situation I can think of which could be characterized as one in which the agent acts because of the irresistibility of his desire, in such a way that he is not to be seen as either having been defeated or as autonomous, is one about which it would be misleading to say that his act has not resulted from an *effective* choice for it is a situation about which it would be more accurate to say that his act has not resulted from *any choice at all*. Such a situation would be one in which the desire could be said to take a person by storm, in that it so quickly results in behaviour that there is no room (time) for even the *attempt* to resist on his part. Here there would be no question of the agent's choosing to act or not choosing to act as he desires: the desire would occur and before the agent could do anything about it, the 'act' would occur as well. One might be tempted to say about such a situation that the agent has not acted, because his behaviour cannot be called intentional. (The claim that the act has not resulted from an effective choice is more appropriate to situation 1—if this is understood to mean that in that situation the agent's choosing to do otherwise was ineffective.)

3. The agent acts as he does because he *believes* that he can't resist the desire which prompts him (p. 116). Case 3 is suggested by the following remarks of Frankfurt:

the fact that someone acts because of the irresistibility of a desire does not mean that he acts in a panic or with a great rush of feeling. A person may believe of himself that he cannot resist a certain desire, and therefore proceed in calm resignation to satisfy it, without experiencing the uncontrollable compulsive thrust that he might indeed encounter if he should attempt to refuse it satisfaction (p. 116).

Of course, acting because one *believes* that a desire is irresistible is not correctly characterized as 'acting because of the irresistibility of a desire' which is what Frankfurt seems to do. Even so, such a case is relevant to our discussion of blameworthiness, for it is plausible to suggest that the person who acts because he believes his desire is irresistible, whether or not it in fact is, is in a morally superior position to the person who acts believing that the desire which prompts him is not irresistible, although it in fact is, or the person who acts to satisfy a desire about whose resistibility he has no beliefs at all.

But is it true that an agent who acts *because* of the irresistibility of his desires in any of the above senses is *ipso facto not* blameworthy? The most useful way to approach this question is, I think, to consider whether the agents in these cases would fail to fulfil the M-condition. I shall deal first with cases 2 and 3 because the conclusions reached in respect of them will affect our assessment of case 1.

Concerning case 2, when a desire takes a person by storm so that it issues in behaviour before he has had time to think about what he is doing it seems right to say that his behaviour is not intentional. And it also seems right to say that an agent who does not have time to think before his desire issues in behaviour does not fulfil the M-condition, for the description of that condition strongly suggests, although it does not state, that the agent who fulfils it has made a choice between a morally required (or morally permissible) course of action and the morally prohibited course perhaps made attractive to him by one of his desires. The suggestion is implicit in the words 'preparedness to do what the agent knows to be wrong' (see Chapter 1). The agent who is aware that what he is about to do is wrong and who, despite this awareness, acts wrongly is, in virtue of that awareness, someone of whom it is appropriate to say that he chose (or decided) to do one thing rather than another. The distinction between choices and decisions will be discussed in Chapter 5, but both presuppose an awareness on the part of the agent that there is an alternative course of action to the one he proposes to take. The agent in case 2 cannot be said to have either chosen or decided to act because he is envisaged as someone who has had no time to consider alternative courses of action. If it is right to say that for this reason he cannot be said to have fulfilled the M-condition, then this suggests that we should amend the description of the M-condition to make explicit what was implicit. It suggests that we should say in future that an agent fulfils the M-condition if his offending behaviour was the result of a decision or choice to do what he knew to be wrong for no reason which would excuse his behaviour.[7]

But there is an objection which has to be dealt with before we can accept this suggestion. It will be remembered that when I discussed the M-condition, at the end of Chapter 1, I acknowledged that an agent could fulfil it even if he didn't *know* that his proposed act was wrong; he could fulfil it if (*a*) he mistakenly thought that his act was morally right, so long as this thought was the result of a morally obnoxious belief, and he could fulfil it if (*b*) he had no opinions one way or the other about the rightness of his act, so long as most normal, morally knowledgeable agents could be expected to know that such an act was wrong. Thus the objection would be that—since in these examples from Chapter 1 there is no awareness on the part of the agent that what he is doing is wrong and yet he can be said to fulfil the M-condition—it is not true that any agent who fulfils the M-condition must have made a decision or choice.

I think that this objection can be met. When the agent wrongly thinks that what he is about to do is right and then does it, he can be said to have chosen or decided. This is because the belief that one's action is right implies an awareness of alternative courses of action which in turn suggests that a decision or choice was made.

Now example (*b*) above does not strongly suggest a decision or choice because it is one in which the element of moral belief, which would have implied an awareness of alternatives, is missing. And yet I wish to say that it is an example of a morally reprehensible state of mind. So doesn't this mean that I am committed to saying that M-states of mind do not need to include decisions or choices?

No, I think that although example (*b*) does not *strongly* suggest a decision or choice, reference to a decision or choice is not ruled out. There is nothing to prevent us from supposing that the agent in example (*b*) made a decision or choice to do what any morally knowledgeable person would have known to be wrong.

I also think that reflection on case 2 should persuade us that unless the agent's state of mind does involve something like a decision or choice, it cannot qualify as morally reprehensible, for the M-condition is supposed to represent the kind of psychological cause for action which we take to be essential to blameworthiness. But it seems wrong to say that a desire (however unattractive) which takes a person by storm so that it bypasses any process of deliberation (however minute) that he might have gone through *is* such a cause. There needs to be at least *some* measure of deliberateness about the agent's behaviour (not necessarily full-blown deliberation) for it to qualify as having been caused by a blame-conferring psychological state.[8] And this measure of deliberateness would be appropriately represented by including in the description of the M-state reference to a choice or decision. On balance, therefore, I think the description of the M-condition should be amended to include such a reference.

The agent in case 3 is envisaged as someone whose act is motivated by the belief that even if he tried, he would not be able to resist his desires. But are people ever motivated by such beliefs? And if so, does this mean that they don't fulfil the M-condition? I can think of *some* people who might be motivated by such a belief; namely those who suffer from compulsive urges which they have unsuccessfully tried to resist in the past. It has been found that when people who suffer from such compulsions attempt to resist them, they are subject to intense anxiety.[9] Perhaps someone who knew he would suffer from intense anxiety if he did not give in to his desire would be motivated to do so by the thought that there was no point in his trying to resist it now since he would eventually give in to it anyway in order to allay his anxiety.

But I do not think that if an agent were motivated by such a thought he would automatically escape fulfilment of the M-condition. If his compulsive desire was one whose fulfilment would cause great harm and he knew this, then it seems right to say that he ought to try to resist it however dubious he is about his powers of resistance. On the other hand, if the fulfilment of his desire involved only a minor wrong and the alternative to non-fulfilment was believed by the agent to be something which would cause him *great* anxiety (ending in his giving in anyway), then it is possible that acting on this belief would not count as fulfilling the M-condition.

Turning now to case 1, we must first distinguish between two ways in which an agent could be defeated by a desire after an unsuccessful struggle to resist it:

(*a*) the desire might breach the agent's consciously erected defences, spilling over into 'action' (offending behaviour); or

(*b*) the agent might decide to give in to the desire, that is he might perform an act of surrender.

If the agent in case 1 were defeated by his desire in an (*a*)-type manner, then he would not fulfil the M-condition (as amended), for his behaviour, in occurring despite him, would not have resulted from a decision or choice. But if he satisfied description (*b*) then he *might* fulfil the M-condition. Whether he did would depend both on the nature of the desire and how much harm giving in to it would cause. If the desire were a compulsion and he believed that acting on it was likely to cause great harm then—in giving in to it—he would fulfil the M-condition. On the other hand if he believed that no *great* harm would be done and he knew that not giving in to it would cause him great suffering, then in giving in to it, he would not fulfil the M-condition.

Thus, it looks as if there are *some* cases of acting *because* of the irresistibility of a desire for which an agent could be morally responsible. But, in respect of those cases for which an agent would *not* be morally responsible, I think Frankfurt has argued convincingly that the reason for exoneration would *not* be that the agent could not have acted otherwise.

But now we must examine van Inwagen's challenge to this claim.

Van Inwagen's challenge

In his book, *An Essay on Free Will*, van Inwagen argues that although Frankfurt has shown that the Principle of Alternate Possibilities is 'possibly false' (p. 164), there are three principles very close in spirit to the P.A.P. which are true and therefore immune to Frankfurt-type counter-examples. He concludes that the truth of these principles constitutes proof that there is a could-have-acted-otherwise condition for moral responsibility.[10]

These three principles are:

1. The Principle of Possible Action (PPA): 'A person is morally responsible for failing to perform a given act only if he could have performed that act'.[11]
2. The Principle of Possible Prevention 1 (PPP1): 'A person is morally responsible for a certain event (particular) only if he could have prevented it'.[12]
3. The Principle of Possible Prevention 2 (PPP2): 'A person is morally responsible for a certain state of affairs only if (that state of affairs obtains and) he could have prevented it from obtaining' [13]

I shall examine van Inwagen's arguments for each of these principles in turn.

The Principle of Possible Action (PPA)

To illustrate the invulnerability of his first principle (PPA) to a Frankfurt-type of counter-example van Inwagen imagines that an agent, having noticed that a man is in danger of being harmed by several other men, first considers whether to telephone the police and then decides not to. Unknown to him, however, the telephone exchange is out of order so that even if he had decided to telephone the police he would not have been able to get through to them. Van Inwagen argues:

Am I reponsible for failing to call the police? Of course not. I couldn't have called them. I may be responsible for failing to try to call the police—that much I *could* have done—or for refraining from calling the police ... But I am simply not responsible for failing to call the police. This 'counter-example' therefore is not a counter-example at all: PPA is unscathed. (p. 166)

The phrase 'failing to perform a given act' is ambiguous. It could mean:

(*a*) not succeeding in the attempt to perform a given act; or
(*b*) simply not performing a given act.

Since in van Inwagen's example no attempt has been made to

inform the police, interpretation (*a*) cannot be relevant to his argument against Frankfurt.[14] This leaves us with (*b*) as the relevant interpretation. But what act has van Inwagen's agent (let us call him 'X') not performed (and hence in van Inwagen's terms 'failed to perform')? It must be the act of bringing-it-about-that-the-police-were-informed, for, unlike trying to inform them, it is that that X could not have done. Although it seems strained to describe an act in this way, since we do describe acts in terms of their consequences, one can say that it is as acceptable to claim that there are acts of bringing-it-about-that-the-police-were-informed as it is to claim that there are acts of harming (bringing it about that someone is harmed).

So van Inwagen's case amounts to this: X is not morally responsible for not performing the act of bringing-it-about-that-the-police-were-informed because he could not have brought this about.

But this wrongly implies that the question of X's blameworthiness for not bringing it about that the police were informed can only be settled when we know whether he could have brought it about. But the question of X's blameworthiness doesn't even *arise* in such a situation. The question of blameworthiness only arises when someone has failed to fulfil a moral requirement, and X has not failed to fulfil a moral requirement in not bringing it about that the police were informed because there is no moral requirement to *bring things about*. Moral requirements are not of the form 'Succeed in ϕ-ing', but rather 'Do what you can to bring about ϕ', so the reason X is not morally responsible for not bringing it about, etc. is not, as van Inwagen thinks, that he couldn't, but that he was not required to perform *that* act; he was not required to bring it about. What he was required to do was to initiate that part of the process which *so far as he was aware* would have culminated in the police being informed. He ought to have gone to the telephone and dialled the number.

In the situation as described by van Inwagen, the agent has decided not to make a telephone call to the police despite his awareness that he ought to. He is thus guilty (as van Inwagen himself suggests) of deliberately refraining from trying to reach them and this is the only fact which is relevant to his moral responsibility. But van Inwagen's arguments do not show that if we blame X for refraining from trying it is because he could have not refrained.

Frankfurt's challenge to the thesis that there is a C-condition for blameworthiness is therefore not touched by anything which is said by van Inwagen in support of PPA.

I turn now to the second principle proposed by van Inwagen.

The Principle of Possible Prevention 1 (PPP1)

("A person is morally responsible for a certain event (particular) only if he could have prevented it.") Van Inwagen argues for this as follows: events as *particulars* must be individuated (at least) in terms of their causal antecedents. Since this is so, it would be inconsistent to claim that an event-token which would have occurred had the agent not taken a certain course of action would have been the same event-token as the one which did occur as the result of the agent's course of action. But a Frankfurt-type counter-example would rely on such an inconsistency, for it would represent an attempt to show that an agent was morally responsible for an event-particular even though he could not have prevented it from occurring, by positing a world in which the *same* event-token would occur whether or not the agent caused it. Van Inwagen rests his case for PPP1 on the claim that since a Frankfurt-type counter-example would be inconsistent it cannot threaten the principle.

It is worth bearing in mind that the actual Frankfurt counter-example to the P.A.P. does not rely on such an inconsistency. This is, of course, irrelevant to the claim that the Frankfurt *type* of counter-example to PPP1 (described above) *would* do so, but the fact that it would is not a good enough reason for claiming that the principle is true.

In fact, the principle should be rejected because, as I shall show, it has counter-intuitive implications: PPP1 has been purposely formulated (I take it) so that it doesn't state that a person is morally responsible for causing a certain event only if he could have prevented himself from causing it, because such a formulation would simply beg the question against Frankfurt by asserting what he has denied. Formulated like that, it would simply be a statement of the P.A.P. against which Frankfurt's arguments are decisive. Instead we are supposed to assume that the event (particular) which the person, referred to in the principle, might or might not be morally responsible for, is the *consequence* of an act which that person has performed.[15] And understood in this way, the principle is open to serious criticisms: suppose that X presses a button knowing that once he does so a dam will burst its banks and hundreds of people will drown. Suppose also that he rightly believes that once he presses the button he will not be able to do anything to prevent the drownings and that he falsely believes that if he had wanted to he could have not pressed the button. According to the principle, X is not morally responsible for the drownings because he could not have prevented them. But this is counter-intuitive.

And because PPP1 is formulated as it is, it has an even more counter-intuitive implication. Since it carefully avoids stating that the person to whom it refers is morally responsible for *bringing about* the event to which it refers, it is possible to read the principle as suggesting that that person could be any person who was able to prevent the consequences of the act which was performed, whether or not he was causally responsible for bringing about those consequences. So, imagine that X is exactly as described above when he presses the button, that is he rightly believes that he cannot prevent the drownings once the button is pressed and he wrongly believes that if he wishes he will be able to not press the button. But imagine also that this time X is being watched by Y who can prevent the drownings and does not. According to PPP1, Y would be morally responsible for the drownings and X would not. But it is counter-intuitive to claim that X would not also be morally responsible. PPP1 is thus not acceptable as a principle of moral appraisal. I turn now to the third principle.

The Principle of Possible Prevention 2 (PPP2)

("A person is morally responsible for a certain state of affairs only if (that state of affairs obtains and) he could have prevented it from obtaining.") Van Inwagen claims that the state of affairs to which the principle refers is a universal. By "a universal state of affairs" he means one which can be consistently described in the same way, although it is capable of being brought about by different people in different ways. For example, the universal state of affairs describable as 'Caesar is killed' remains describable as 'Caesar is killed' whether it is brought about by one assassin rather than many, or by the use of poison rather than knives. There are, van Inwagen says, 'different causal roads' to the same state of affairs *qua* universal. To test PPP2 against a Frankfurt-type of counter-example van Inwagen imagines the following story:

Gunnar shoots Ridley (intentionally), an act sufficient for the obtaining of Ridley's being dead, a certain state of affairs; but there is some factor, F, which (i) played no causal role in Ridley's death and (ii) would have caused Ridley's death if Gunnar had not shot him (or had decided not to shoot him) and (iii) is such that Gunnar could not have prevented it from causing Ridley's death except by killing (or by deciding to kill) Ridley himself. (p. 172.)

Van Inwagen then says that although the example *seems* to show that PPP2 is false and that Gunnar is responsible for Ridley's being dead; in fact PPP2 is true and Gunnar is not responsible for Ridley's being dead.

It seems strange for van Inwagen to claim that the counter-example does not *actually* show PPP2 to be false since it appears in all respects to incorporate the intuition to which Frankfurt appeals, namely that if the reason for a man's acting as he does is of a certain sort, than it is irrelevant that he could not have acted otherwise. Indeed, the van Inwagen posited world is just like the sort of world Frankfurt has conjured up in order to show that the agent would be morally responsible for the choice of a causal route to the bound-to-obtain-state-of-affairs if that choice followed naturally from his desires. Frankfurt's counter-example to the P.A.P. is one in which, although whatever the agent decides, the same universal state of affairs obtains, the agent is morally responsible for his intervention-free realization of that state of affairs.

Van Inwagen produces two explicit arguments for his claim that PPP2 is not false and it is possible that there is a third implicit argument which is linked with his insistence that the principle is quantifying over universals. At the risk of tedium, I shall examine all three of these arguments, because I feel it is important to *demonstrate* that *none* of them succeeds.

The first argument goes like this: if the story is to be a counter-example to PPP2, and not some other principle which involves *particulars*, then the words 'Ridley's being dead' must denote a universal—the universal C(Ridley dies), which according to van Inwagen we are to interpret as 'its being the case that Ridley dies' (see pp. 171–2). And, van Inwagen claims, Gunnar is not responsible for C(Ridley dies). He continues:

Why should anyone think he is? Well, Gunnar did something—shooting Ridley—that was sufficient for C(Ridley dies). What is more he performed this act intentionally, knowing that it was sufficient for that state of affairs. This argument however is invalid. For consider the state of affairs C(Ridley is mortal). When Gunnar shot Ridley he performed an act sufficient for the obtaining of this state of affairs. But it would be absurd to say that Gunnar is responsible for C(Ridley is mortal). God, or Adam and Eve jointly or perhaps no one at all, might be held accountable for Ridley's mortality; certainly not his murderer. (pp. 172–3.)

Van Inwagen goes on to suggest that the state of affairs C(Ridley dies) is the same state of affairs as C(Ridley is mortal) because the two sentences in brackets express the same proposition—a proposition which is also expressed by 'Ridley does not live for ever' and 'Ridley dies at some time or another'.

I take it that the essence of this argument is as follows: although by shooting Ridley, Gunnar performed an act which was sufficient for C(Ridley dies) he is not morally responsible for C(Ridley dies) because, given the equivalence between 'Ridley dies' and 'Ridley is mortal', this would mean that he was responsible for C(Ridley is mortal) and this is absurd.

But I find it very hard to follow this argument. It seems, at one point, to rely on an equivocation between claims about logical sufficiency and claim about causal sufficiency, and, at another point, on the dubious assumption that a person's mortality can be equated with his being killed. But even if I am wrong about its particular failings, I am confident that the argument should be rejected, since it would have the consequence that no one is responsible for anyone's death.

Van Inwagen's second argument is simply that there are two highly plausible principles which suggest that Gunnar is not

morally responsible for its being the case that Ridley is dead.
These are:

1. 'If a certain state of affairs would have obtained no matter
   what X had done, then X is not morally responsible for it.'
2. 'If a certain state of affairs would have obtained no matter
   what choices or decisions X had made, then X is not morally responsible for it.'

But both principles seem vulnerable to Frankfurt's argument
that if a man's particular realization of a bound-to-obtain state
of affairs is of a certain sort (that is if it includes his fulfilment of
the M-condition) then the fact that the state of affairs would
have obtained anyway does not absolve him from moral responsibility.

However, as I have suggested, it is possible that there is a
third argument which van Inwagen is tacitly relying on which is
linked to his insistence that PPP2 is a principle about universals
and not particulars. That there might be such an argument is
suggested by some things which van Inwagen says in the course
of his first two arguments. It would go like this: Frankfurt's insight relates to a person's moral responsibility for his particular
bringing about of a state of affairs, but because PPP2 is not concerned with a person's responsibility for particulars Frankfurt's
argument is not relevant. And as a principle which is concerned
with moral responsibility for a *universal* state of affairs (pp. 178–
9), PPP2 is invulnerable to a Frankfurt-type of counter-example.

But it is not clear what content a principle which is concerned
with a universal state of affairs could have which would make it
invulnerable to a Frankfurt-type of counter-example.[16]

For instance, suppose that the PPP2 principle is this: 'A person is morally responsible for a state of affairs which is such that
it can be realized in many different ways, only if he could have
prevented it from being realized in any way.' Surely, such a principle *would* be vulnerable to Frankfurt's counter-example.

Van Inwagen might say that we think this because we are
assuming that the person concerned has brought about the state
of affairs referred to in the principle and in thinking this we have
not taken seriously the claim that the principle is quantifying
over *universal* states of affairs. That this might be something he
would say is suggested by a passage in which he claims that the

agents he has been considering in his Frankfurt-type counter-examples (Gunnar and Ryder) cannot be said to have brought about the universal states of affairs mentioned (pp. 177–8). He continues:

The states of affairs we have been considering are universals. There are many ways the concrete particulars that make up our surroundings could be arranged that would be sufficient for their obtaining. What Gunnar and Ryder can bring about is *which* of these possible arrangements of particulars—which murderer, which road—the universals will be 'realized in'; that some arrangement or other of the particulars will realize these universals is something totally outside their control; it is not something they bring about. (p. 178.)

But these remarks cannot be used in defence of the claim that PPP2 is true, for PPP2 is supposed to be claiming that a person who *is* causally responsible for a certain state of affairs is not morally responsible for it unless he could have prevented it. It is supposed to refer to the consequences of what *that person has done* (or left undone) (see pp. 164–5). Therefore, we must take it that the person referred to in the principle has done something which is sufficient for the obtaining of the state of affairs mentioned.

Bearing this in mind, and taking into account that fact that van Inwagen seems to think that the *inevitability* of the obtaining of these states of affairs is relevant, this suggests that the person mentioned in the principle is superhuman, for only such an agent could be responsible for it being the case that whatever happens a certain state of affairs will be realized in one way or another. Van Inwagen would not be happy with this interpretation because he wants his principles to apply to ordinary human beings, but this seems the only way of interpreting the principle given all the conditions which it apparently has to fulfil.

Let us assume then that the principle refers to a superhuman agent. Then it might be formulated like this: 'A person is morally responsible for bringing about a world in which a certain state of affairs will be realized in one way or another, only if he could have prevented himself from bringing about such a world.' But this is simply the P.A.P. in disguise and as such it is vulnerable to Frankfurt's arguments.

I can think of no way in which PPP2 can be formulated to

take account of van Inwagen's claim that it is about universals which does not either render it vulnerable to a Frankfurt-type of attack or reveal it to be counter-intuitive.

We can conclude that none of van Inwagen's three principles is true and that he has accordingly failed to show that there is an independent could-have-acted-otherwise condition for moral responsibility.

3

The incompatibilist, the could-have-acted-otherwise condition, and the U-condition

Introduction

The arguments in Chapter 2 have established that there is not an independent C-condition for blameworthiness (that is a C-condition which must be fulfilled in addition to the M-condition). Where does this leave the incompatibilist? He has been described as someone who assumes that there is an independent C-condition and whose commitment to such a condition is what motivates his incompatibilism. For he has traditionally reasoned as follows:

Premiss 1. It is an independent condition of blameworthiness that offending agents could have acted otherwise.

Premiss 2. It cannot be true that agents could have acted otherwise if their acts were causally determined.

Conclusion: Unless determinism is false, agents cannot be morally responsible for their offending acts.

But since the arguments we have just considered show that the first premiss is false, doesn't this mean that the incompatibilist should abandon his belief that moral responsibility requires the falsity of determinism?

In fact, it does not. For, as I shall argue, his incompatibilism has not just been motivated by the belief in a C-condition; it has also been fuelled by the belief in what I shall call 'a U-condition for blameworthiness'—the condition that an agent's morally reprehensible decision or choice should not be caused by factors for which he is not responsible.

My main concern is to show that the commitment to a U-condition for blameworthiness is enough to motivate the belief that determinism and moral responsibility are incompatible. But I shall also suggest that the incompatibilist might have mistaken his commitment to a U-condition for a commitment to an independent C-condition for blameworthiness.

The traditional picture of the incompatibilist, which presents him as someone whose anxiety about determinism is based on the belief that its truth would rule out the possibility of an agent's acting otherwise, often includes the suggestion of another anxiety—the worry that if determinism is true, then agents' acts are caused by factors for which they are not responsible. The worry can be put like this: if agents' acts are caused by factors for which they are not responsible, then how can they be morally responsible for acting as the result of those factors? This is obviously different from the thought: if agents' acts are causally determined, then how can they act otherwise than they do? But although these worries can be distinguished they are often spoken of as if they were inseparable. An example of this can be found in Nozick's question: '. . . how can we punish someone or hold him responsible for an action if his doing it was causally determined eventually by factors originating before his birth and hence outside his control?'[1] Another example can be found in Thorp's book, *Free Will*, when, as a prelude to providing a defence of libertarianism, he describes the threat thought to be posed by determinism as follows: 'Any given decision of an agent was made necessary by a law of nature together with some initial conditions which were beyond that agent's control or even his knowledge.'[2] In both passages two distinguishable aspects of the causal antecedents of action (or decision) are assumed to provide one indivisible source of anxiety:

(a) their allegedly determining (causally necessitating) aspects, and
(b) their being outside the agent's control.

At least three things might be meant by the claim that the antecedents of action were outside the agent's control:

(i) The agent was powerless to prevent their occurrence.
(ii) The agent was powerless to prevent their effects.
(iii) The agent played no part in their occurrence.

I believe that when incompatibilists make this claim about the antecedents of action, they are often prompted to do so by all three of these thoughts. But it is (iii) which can be said to constitute a source of anxiety which is independent from the worry about the agent's powerlessnes to do otherwise.

It is this separate anxiety which commits the incompatibilist to the belief in a U-condition for blameworthiness. For his conviction, that one of the things which disqualifies an agent from blameworthiness is his not having been responsible for the causes of his decisions or choices, commits him to the belief that it is a condition of agent accountability that agents should be ultimately responsible for their morally relevant decisions or choices—'ultimately' in the sense that nothing for which they are not responsible should be the source of their decisions or choices. This is what I have called 'the U-condition'.

Either some reference to this other anxiety or an endorsement of something very much like the U-condition can be found in many incompatibilist discussions of determinism. Rarely, however, does one sense an awareness in these discussions that this anxiety is separable from the anxiety about acting otherwise, or that each anxiety can be seen as separately reflected in commitments to two distinct conditions for blameworthiness (the U-condition and the C-condition). To show this, I shall briefly discuss some passages from the works of three incompatibilist philosophers—Kant, Edwards, and van Inwagen. The passages of Kant and Edwards contain explicit endorsements of something very much like a U-condition for blameworthiness, but only Edwards seems to be aware that the commitment to this condition is distinct from the commitment to a C-condition. And, as we shall see, it is not clear whether he really is aware that there is a distinction. The passage of van Inwagen's suggests that his incompatibilism has been prompted by an anxiety which is distinct from the anxiety about the impossibility of acting otherwise and yet he seems unaware that these anxieties are distinct.

I turn first to Kant. In *Religion Within the Limits of Reason Alone*, Kant states his opposition to compatibilism in a way which suggests that he believes determinism threatens moral responsibility solely because it rules out the possibility of acting otherwise:

what we wish to understand and never shall understand is how pre-determinism according to which voluntary actions as events, have their determining grounds in antecedent time (which, with what happened in it, is no longer within our power) can be consistent with freedom according to which the act as well as its opposite must be within the power of the subject at the moment of its taking place. (p. 45.)

But the solution Kant proposes to the problem of reconciling determinism in the phenomenal world with the existence of moral responsibility and human freedom, suggests that it is not just the impossibility of acting otherwise which he sees as a threat to moral responsibility, but the fact that men might not be responsible for being the sort of moral agents they are, for he says:

Man himself must make or have made himself into whatever in a moral sense, whether good or evil, he is or is to become. Either condition must be an effect of his free choice for otherwise he could not be held responsible for it and could therefore be morally neither good nor evil. (p. 40.)

To claim that men can only be morally responsible if they freely choose their moral natures is to be committed to the claim that there is a condition for moral responsibility which is different from the could-have-acted-otherwise condition. It suggests commitment to a U-condition—since freely choosing one's moral nature would count as being responsible for the causes of one's actions and being responsible in this sense would constitute fulfilment of the U-condition. Such a commitment is a response to the anxiety about determinism which, as I have argued, is distinguishable from the anxiety about the possibility of acting otherwise.

A much more recent example of the incompatibilist concern that men's actions might be caused by factors for which they are not responsible can be found in Paul Edwards's paper, 'Hard and Soft Determinism'. In this paper, Edwards describes and endorses C. A. Campbell's claim that those who are reflective about their judgements of moral responsibility will conclude that it is incompatible with determinism. Edwards describes Campbell as claiming that before holding anyone morally responsible a reflective person will:

. . . require not only that the agent was not coerced or constrained but also—and this is taken to be an additional condition—that he 'could have chosen otherwise than he actually did.' ... I should prefer to put this somewhat differently, but it will not affect the main conclusion drawn by Campbell with which I agree. The reflective person, I should prefer to express it, requires not only that the agent was not coerced, he also requires that the agent originally chose his own character—the character that now displays itself in his choices and desires and efforts. (pp. 122–3.)

Here is a clear commitment to something very much like the U-condition, since to choose one's character would count as being responsible for the causes of one's actions. But it is not clear whether, when Edwards says 'I should prefer to put this somewhat differently', he is acknowledging that the could-have-acted-otherwise condition and the U-like condition are different or whether he sees his statement as a more precise way of expressing what Campbell was trying to say. If the latter, then he is wrongly equating the two conditions. Whichever is the case, Edwards's statement too points to the existence of an anxiety which is separable from the anxiety about agents' abilities to have acted otherwise, namely an anxiety that if determinism is true, agents are motivated by psychological states for which they are not responsible.

Finally, I turn to van Inwagen who is one of the most recent defenders of incompatibilism. He devotes a large part of his book, *An Essay on Free Will*, to establishing that there is a C-condition for moral responsibility. (I discussed this in Chapter 2.) But he sometimes describes the incompatibilist's anxiety about determinism in a way which suggests that it is not really determinism's threat to the possibility of acting otherwise which exercises him:

If determinism is true then our acts are the consequences of the laws of nature and events in the remote past. But it is not up to us what went on before we were born and neither is it up to us what the laws of nature are. Therefore, the consequences of these things (including our present acts) are not up to us. (p. 16, p. 222.)

From this passage one might conclude that determinism is seen by van Inwagen as a threat to moral responsibility not because, given causes, agents cannot act otherwise, but because the causes which determine our acts are 'not up to us'.

Since the anxiety about the causes of our actions not being

'up to us' is often not distinguished from the anxiety about the impossibility of acting otherwise, it is possible that the philosopher who is motivated to endorse incompatibilism has mistaken one anxiety for the other. Perhaps the incompatibilist, like the compatibilist, is not really committed to an independent C-condition for blameworthiness, but only thinks he is; perhaps despite appearances his incompatibilism has not really been motivated by a belief in a C-condition at all, but only by a belief in a U-condition.

Such a thing would be impossible to prove. So far as I know all incompatibilists have used the claim that there is a C-condition for blameworthiness as a basis for their incompatibilist arguments. Nevertheless, it would be worthwhile to be able to show that it is possible that they are not really committed to a C-condition, not least because, as we have seen from the discussions in Chapter 2, they ought not to be committed to one.

One way ot trying to demonstrate this is to ask the incompatibilist to imagine that determinism is true and then to consider, in turn, two different stages in the process which is normally thought to lead from an agent's motivating psychological states to his performance of an act. First, we can ask him to consider the link between an agent's decisions and his actions, and then to answer the following question: if all you knew of an agent was that his decision had causally determined his act and you had no reason to think that the decision had itself been causally determined, would you conclude *on this* account that he could not be blameworthy? That is, would you conclude that because, given his decision, he could not have acted otherwise, he was therefore not blameworthy? I am sure that the incompatibilist's response would be that the agent could be blameworthy even though his act had to follow his decision.

Secondly, we can ask the incompatibilist to consider the link between an agent's desires (and beliefs) and his decisions, and then to answer this question: could an agent be morally responsible for his actions if the decisions which caused them were themselves causally determined by his desires and beliefs? I am certain that the incompatibilist would reply that the agent could not be morally responsible in these circumstances. But why should there be this difference in reaction to the thought that an act had been causally determined by a decision and the thought that the decision had been causally determined by a desire and belief?

I would suggest that the difference can be accounted for by the view that desires and beliefs are states which occur to us; while deciding is something we can be said to do. We *make* decisions, we don't make desires (or beliefs); these (for the most part) come to us unbidden.

Now if the difference in reaction can be explained in this way, doesn't this suggest that what worries the incompatibilist about causal determination is not that it rules out the possibility of acting otherwise, but that, given the fact that we do not choose the desires and beliefs which motivate us, if determinism is true our decisions are caused by states for which we are not responsible?

However, the incompatibilist might reject this explanation and say that so far as he is concerned all that has been shown is that strictly speaking he is not so much worried by the thought that, if determinism is true, no agent could have *acted* otherwise as he is by the thought that, if determinism is true, no agent could have *decided* otherwise.[3]

We might try to convince him that it is not this which really worries him about determinism by asking him to imagine the following possibility: there is a world in which each agent is able to determine for the entire course of his life the sorts of desires he will have and the sorts of desires which will determine his decisions in morally problematic situations. Each agent makes his choice of desires in the knowledge that, once he has them, his decision to act will be causally determined by them. It is reasonable to assume that, in contemplating such a world, the incompatibilist would feel that the agents in it could be morally responsible despite the fact that they cannot decide otherwise than they do. And it might be argued that if this is what he would feel then what he sees as a threat to accountability is not that each decision might be caused in such a way that no other decision is possible, but that each decision might be caused by events and states for which the agent is not responsible.

But the incompatibilist could object that his putative reaction to the world he has been asked to envisage does not necessarily indicate a lack of concern about the fulfilment of the could-have-decided-otherwise condition, for as the world is described, it is possible to assume that the original choice of desires which each agent makes was not determined. And if this is so, then at the moment of original choice each agent was able to decide otherwise. Thus, the incompatibilist might say, if he does not feel that the agents in the envisaged world lack moral responsibility it is because at the moment of original choice they could have decided otherwise.[4]

Now it might be thought that if we could construct a logically possible example in which there was never a time at which the agent could decide otherwise, but in which he was nevertheless responsible for the causes of his decisions, then we would be able to convince the incompatibilist that he is not really committed to a C-condition. But the only example I can think of is one which, while not perhaps logically impossible, is too incomprehensible to be taken seriously. This example is suggested by John Wisdom who advances what he takes to be a compatibilist version of what I am calling the U-condition. He says: 'It appears . . . that if (i) the Law of Causation is true and (ii) we are to blame for our acts, then each decision is due to an either infinite or world long series of determinations of the will by the will.'[5] Now, a series that is world long would be incompatible with the Law of Causation and, because it would imply a non-causally determined first cause, it is not the kind of example which would persuade a C-condition advocate to give up his advocacy. Rather, it is the infinitely long series of determinations of the will, by the will, which might plausibly be thought to constitute the kind of convincing example we need. For the infinity of the chain of causes means that there is no uncaused cause and this, plus the fact that the causes are determining, means that there was never a time at which the agent could have willed or decided otherwise. And finally, the fact that the causal chain consists of nothing but willings (or perhaps decidings or choosings) seems guaranteed to assuage any fears the incompatibilist might have had about psychological states such as desires which, being the kind of states which occur to an agent, are not ones for which he can be responsible. Willing and deciding are, after all, things we do; we are active in respect of willing and deciding.

But we are not given any idea of what kind of willings the causal chain is supposed to consist of. If this example is to work at all as an illustration of how an agent could be responsible for the causes of his decisions it must be because the agent is deemed to be responsible for each link in the chain of willings and this suggests that each willing is deemed to be caused by his having willed that willing and so on *ad infinitum*. But what, apart from willing to will, is the agent supposed to will? There is no explanation of how these willings acquire a content which could contribute to a morally relevant decision and there seems no room for such an explanation.

In fact, it is not clear how a *decision* could emerge from this series since, as I shall argue in Chapter 5, decisions are necessarily made between competing considerations and there is no room for competing considerations in the picture of uninterrupted willings which is conjured up by Wisdom's suggestion. So, in the absence of any explanation of these mysteries, the incompatibilist we are addressing is entitled to conclude that the infinite chain example does not provide any reason for him to abandon his conviction that he is committed to a C-condition.

It seems, then, that the strongest case we can make for the claim that the incompatibilist has mistaken a commitment to a U-condition for a commitment to a C-condition is the fact that his attitude to desires differs from his attitude to decisions. But as we have seen it is open to the incompatibilist to deny that the reason for this difference is one which precludes commitment to a C-condition.

However, this does not matter very much. For on the basis of the arguments in the preceding chapter, we can say that even if the incompatibilist does believe in a C-condition he ought not to.

Furthermore, as I shall now argue, the incompatibilist's belief in the U-condition is enough to motivate his claim that the falsity of determinism is required for moral responsibility. The U-condition is satisfied when an agent's (morally reprehensible) decision or choice has not been caused by anything for which he is not responsible. This suggests that it would be satisfied in any one of the following ways:

(*a*) if the agent's decision (or choice) was caused by a preceding decision (choice, or volition) which had a causal history consisting in a never-ending chain of causally linked decisions (choices, or volitions) (despite my reservations about this, I am including it, provisionally, as a *logical* possibility); or

(b) if all the agent's morally relevant decisions or choices had a causal history which began with one ultimate decision or choice (of his) which was uncaused by preceding events or states[6]—a decision or choice which determined for all time the motives on which the agent would act in morally problematic situations; or

(c) if at some point in his history the agent made a decision or choice uncaused by preceding events or states which determined what his choice or decision would be in this particular case; or

(d) if the agent's decision or choice in this particular case was uncaused by preceding events or states.

Something which needs to be added to these descriptions is that the motivation-determining choice must be one which is taken in the knowledge that the choice will affect how the agent acts in morally problematic situations. The agent does not have to know that he will be in morally problematic situations, but merely that if he is in such situations, then the motivational states he is choosing will motivate his choices in them.

In saying this I am following Kant who argues, in *Religion Within the Limits of Reason Alone*,[7] that if the original choice is to confer moral responsibility on the agent for his subsequent choices, then it must be one for which the agent can also be said to be morally responsible, and hence it must be one which is made with the moral law in mind so that it is itself praise- or blame-conferring. I think that Kant is right with respect to blameworthy choices (although I do not think that the content of the choice needs to involve explicit reference to the moral law). If the original choice is to be one which results in subsequent blame-conferring choices, then it must itself be blame-conferring. This means that the original choice must be one which qualifies as morally reprehensible (see Chapter 1). I do not believe though that the choice which determines praise-conferring choices must itself be praise-conferring. This last point will come up again in Chapter 7.

It is important, in the context of this discussion, to bear in mind the difference between making an effective decision about what one's motivations will be in the future and making a decision or choice which effectively determines what one's motivations will be. Someone could make a choice which effectively determined what his motivations would be and yet not fulfil the U-condition for blameworthiness if in making the choice he did not realize:

1. that the choice would determine what his motivations would be; or
2. that these motivations would lead him to behave in morally repugnant ways.

To return to the descriptions of how the U-condition could be fulfilled, the kind of choice made by the agent in (b) could be something like this: 'Whenever I have to decide how to act, I shall always decide in the way which gives me the most pleasure, even if acting in this way is not moral' (or, 'even if acting in this way I end up hurting someone').

The agent in (c) could make a choice like the one in (b), prefaced by the words 'In the future', or he could be more specific, for example, 'The next time I have to decide between paying my debts and investing in the stock market, I'll decide to invest in the stock market.'

As for the infinite chain of decisions in (a), since, as I have argued, such decisions seem to have hardly any content and, *a fortiori*, no moral content, it looks very much as if (a)-type decisions could not logically fulfil the U-condition. But even if the U-condition could logically be fulfilled by (a), it could not be empirically fulfilled: human agents do not have infinite histories. Nor are they in a position at the beginning of their lives to make decisions about the kind of desires which will motivate them in morally problematic situations. We have motivating desires and develop habitual patterns of behaviour to respond to them long before we are in a position to understand the concepts of moral rightness and wrongness. So this rules out (b) as a way in which the U-condition could be fulfilled empirically and leaves us with (c) and (d).

There are two objections which might be raised against (c). The first is that it is not clear how the decision or choice which is supposed to determine future choices could have any content. However, we can add to the description of (c) to overcome this problem. The decision which determines future decisions is one about the kind of *motivation* on which such future decisions will be based. An illustration of the kind of thing I have in mind is this: an agent surveys his desires and thinks about the kind of considerations which normally move him all the way to action. He decides that he will undergo aversion therapy so that some of his desires are weakened (for example the desire not to be thought badly of by others) and some strengthened (for example the desire to 'get ahead in life'). His aim is to ensure that in the future he will be swayed by the desire to get ahead, whatever the considerations against it seem to be. This example seems to be both logically and empirically possible.

The second objection to (c) is that even if the agent's subsequent M-state decisions (and choices) were caused by his original M-state decision (or choice) this would not be enough to generate blameworthiness for those subsequent decisions or choices. For it seems that for blame-conferring responsibility to spread from his original choice to his present choice, there must be a certain sort of psychological connectedness between the original chooser and the present chooser.[8] Logical identity would not be sufficient (and might not even be necessary).[9] But what sort of psychological connectedness? The following example suggests that the connectedness needs to consist in memory of the original choice: suppose that X makes an M-state choice to have a brain operation (which will not involve a change *of* brain but a change *to* his brain), knowing that this operation will transform him into someone who is always motivated in a morally reprehensible way and knowing also that the operation will leave him with no memories of his former self including no memories of his original choice. Would X, after the brain operation, retain blame-conferring responsibility for his original choice? Would he now be blame-conferringly responsible for his present M-state choices? I feel that the answer to both questions is 'no'. X was blame-conferringly responsible for the original uncaused M-state choice but is no longer blame-conferringly responsible either for that choice, or the present choices caused by it.[10]

So the example suggests that memory of the original choice is necessary if responsibility is to spread from that choice to subsequent ones. But why should this be so? Perhaps because memory of the original choice plus the continuation of M-state motivation implies continued endorsement of that original choice.[11]

But *is* memory necessary? Suppose that X just forgets that he made this original choice. We would not think that someone would be exonerated by just forgetting that he had committed a crime.[12] So, doesn't this suggest, contrary to the first intuition, that memory of the original choice is not necessary for moral responsibility?

I do not yet know how to resolve this conflict between intuitions about memory. And this means that I cannot describe what would be necessary *in addition* to the causal chain between the original M-choice and subsequent ones to make those subsequent ones blame-conferring. (It should be noted that this difficulty only applies to c-type and not to d-type decisions and choices.) But perhaps I can say what would be sufficient for the inheriting by a 'later self' of blame-conferring responsibility, namely that in addition to the causal chain between the original and subsequent M-choices, the later self also remembers his original choice.[13]

I said earlier that the example I gave of an agent's making a c-type original decision to undergo aversion therapy seemed to be both logically and empirically possible. But is it empirically possible that such a decision would not itself have been caused by desires for which the agent is not responsible, for example the desire to be a more forceful (ambitious, or successful) person? At this stage of the discussion we have no conclusive reason for saying that it is not empirically possible, however unlikely it might seem to us that such a decision would not be caused by this sort of desire. In Chapter 5, arguments will be provided which support the view that neither (c) nor (d) is empirically possible and that both require modification to make them logically possible. But until we examine these arguments, we can proceed on the assumption that they are logically and empirically possible.

Since both (c) and (d) require the falsity of determinism because both require (some) uncaused decisions and choices, it is clear that the incompatibilist who is committed to the belief that there is a U-condition for blameworthiness is, by virtue of this commitment, committed to the belief that blameworthiness requires the falsity of determinism.

But it is not enough to say that the incompatibilist is committed to a belief in the need for the falsity of determinism by his commitment to the belief in a U-condition, for it would be possible for a decision or choice which was not determined to fail to fulfil the U-condition. Such a decision or choice would be one which had been caused by a state for which the agent was not responsible but which had not been determined by that state. Those who believe that causes must necessitate will say that this is not possible. There is a long philosophic tradition in favour of the view that causes must necessitate.[14] But this tradition has, I think, rightly been challenged by some philosophers who argue that the concept of causation is such that we are not required to conclude that because an event was caused it *had* to occur.[15] They suggest instead that what is essential to the concept of causation is the idea of 'productiveness' (if one is considering events as causes) or 'derivativeness' (if one is considering events as effects). Anscombe argues that the derivativeness of an effect from its cause is 'the core, the common feature, of causality in its various kinds'.[16] And, inspired by Anscombe's arguments, van Inwagen suggests that so long as we are satisfied that one event has produced another event, we will conclude that it has caused that other event, even if we are told that determinism is false.[17] I am convinced by their arguments that, while our concept of causation involves the idea of production, it does not necessarily involve the idea of necessitation.[18] I conclude, therefore, that there could be a decision or choice which was caused but not determined.

The incompatibilist who believes that an agent cannot be morally responsible for his decisions (and the acts which follow them) if those decisions were the results of states for which he is not responsible, would not be relieved by the thought that a decision, although caused by these states, was not determined by them. Why should he be? The possibility that the decision might not have occurred as the result of his desires and beliefs does not negate the fact that it *did* occur as the result of his desires and beliefs. It is no more up to the agent that the decision did occur because it might not have, than its occurrence would have been up to him had it been determined.

This shows that the advocate of the U-condition cannot be committed to requiring, as a condition of responsibility, that kind of indeterminism which consists of non-determining causes. The kind of indeterminism he must be committed to requiring is the uncausedness of some decisions or choices by preceding events or states.

Conclusion

I have suggested that the incompatibilist might not really be committed to a C-condition for blameworthiness and I have argued that he is committed to a U-condition for blameworthiness—a commitment which on its own is sufficient to motivate his belief that the falsity of determinism is required if agents are to be morally responsible for their actions.

If the arguments in this and the two earlier chapters are correct, then we must reject the traditional picture of the debate between compatibilist and incompatibilist and replace it with a new one. The picture we must reject is one in which both are seen as committed to the claim that there is a C-condition for blameworthiness but disagree about what is required to fulfil it. In the new picture, what motivates the opposition beween compatibilist and incompatibilist is the incompatibilist's commitment to a U-condition. For it is (now) in virtue of his commitment to this that he must argue, against the compatibilist, that the falsity of determinism is required for moral responsibility. In the next chapter, I shall consider arguments for and against the claim that our reflective judgements about moral responsibility involve a commitment to the U-condition for blameworthiness.

The reader might have been struck by what appears to be the vulnerability of the U-condition to certain criticisms and might wonder why I am not discussing them immediately. Here are two criticisms he might have thought of:

(i) the idea of a blameworthy decision or choice which is uncaused by preceding events or states is logically incoherent; and

(ii) the U-condition cannot be fulfilled because there cannot be a decision or choice which is not due (at least in part) to some aspects of the agent and the world for which he (the agent) is not responsible.

I would ask the reader who believes that the U-condition is vulnerable to these (or other) criticisms to bear with me until after the discussion in the next chapter. That discussion would seem to have a greater priority, since if it emerged from it that our reflective beliefs about moral responsibility did not involve a commitment to the U-condition, then an examination of any other criticisms would be somewhat superfluous. In fact, as we shall see, the case against the claim that our intuitions endorse a U-condition is less persuasive than the case which can be presented in favour of the claim.

Before leaving this chapter, I shall consider an objection which might be made to the claim that the incompatibilist should no longer be seen as committed to a C-condition for blameworthiness. The objection is simple: in being committed to a U-condition for blameworthiness, the incompatibilist is thereby committed to a C-condition, for satisfaction of the U-condition implies satisfaction of the C-condition. This holds in whichever of the two ways the satisfaction of the U-condition is provisionally allowed to be empirically possible (see (*c*) and (*d*) above).

For suppose (*c*): the agent makes an uncaused choice of future motivations, in full awareness of the moral character which acts emerging from these motivations will have. Then, since the choice of motivations is uncaused, it is possible that he should have chosen differently. But if he had chosen differently, his subsequent (differently motivated) choices, decisions, and acts would have been different. So it is possible that he would have chosen, decided, acted differently on those subsequent occasions. In summary he could have chosen his motivations differently; if he had chosen them differently, he would have acted differently; therefore he could have acted differently.

Or suppose (*d*): the decision or choice which immediately issues in the act is itself uncaused. Then it follows immediately that it is possible that a different choice should have occurred and hence that the agent should have acted differently.

The argument in case (*c*) is, however, unsound. The most that follows from the premises is that it is possible that the total circumstances prevailing at the time of the act might have been such that the agent chose and acted differently (because the total circumstances might have included a different original choice).

But it does not follow that in the total circumstances actually prevailing at the time of the act it is possible that the agent should have chosen and acted differently. And it is the latter, not the former, that is required for the satisfaction of the C-condition. (The total circumstances actually prevailing include the motivations actually chosen.) The position of the modal operator ('it is possible that') is crucial.

The argument for case (*d*) is in better shape. But three comments are in order. First, the case itself requires further discussion, which will be forthcoming in Chapter 5, as to its genuine possibility and significance. Secondly, even if it is admitted that in case (*d*) satisfaction of the U-condition implies satisfaction of the C-condition, the implication, thus limited, is not, as the objection suggested, a *general* implication. And finally, even if that limited implication holds, it is only as a consequence of his more fundamental commitment to the U-condition that the incompatibilist is shown as committed, in certain cases, to the C-condition for blameworthiness. It is, at most, a commitment to a non-independent C-condition.[19]

4

Are we committed to a U-condition for blameworthiness?

Introduction

As I indicated at the end of Chapter 3, there are two ways in which a compatibilist might oppose the claim that there is a U-condition for blameworthiness. He might object that our moral intuitions do not endorse such a condition. Or he might claim that if we do endorse such a condition, we ought not to, for the belief in it is incoherent or unsatisfactory in some other respect. It is with the first of these objections that this chapter will be concerned.

Since, as I argued in the last chapter, some philosophers have explicitly endorsed conditions like the U-condition, it might seem that one has simply to point to these endorsements as evidence that there is commitment to a belief in it. But this clearly won't do, for most people who think about these issues (philosophers and non-philosophers) have not explicitly committed themselves to a U-condition for blameworthiness.

However, one does not have to endorse a belief explicitly in order to be committed to it. There could be other beliefs we hold which commit us to the belief in a U-condition and I shall argue that this is, in fact, the case. I shall argue that some of our reflective moral intuitions are 'U-condition generating beliefs', that is beliefs which commit those who hold them (whether they realize it or not) to the belief in a U-condition. (This will be argued for in Section 2.) These intuitions are all beliefs to the effect that agents are not morally responsible if their actions are caused by certain specific factors; what these factors have in common is that they are states or events for which the agents are not responsible. Among such beliefs is the one that an agent whose M-state of mind is attributable to brainwashing is not morally responsible. Another is the belief that an agent whose M-state of mind is the result of brain damage is not morally responsible. (Cases involving stories of brain damage, brainwashing, etc., I shall call 'the problem cases'.) I shall argue that it is the fact that agents are not responsible for the causes mentioned, rather than any other fact which these causes might have in common, which best explains the belief that agents who act as the result of these causes are not morally responsible. By 'best explains' I mean 'is the only defensible reason (or adequate justification) for holding' such beliefs.

Obviously, the compatibilist is committed to opposing this and I shall present the sort of arguments I think he would use—arguments in which non-U-condition justifications for these intuitions are offered (Section 2). I hope to show that although the U-condition opponent has some powerful arguments at his disposal (Section 5), the arguments in favour of the claim that we are committed to a U-condition are, on balance, more persuasive (Section 5).

However, I also argue (in Section 3) that there is a distinction we make (or are prepared to make) between wrongdoers which seems hard to account for by reference to the belief in a U-condition—a distinction between offenders who are emotionally deprived and those who are not. And although the U-condition advocate has a strong case for saying that his inability to account for the distinction is only apparent, I suggest that it could be accounted for and justified by a compatibilist principle which is quite different from traditional compatibilist principles governing blameworthiness.

In Section 4, I consider and reject the suggestion that the proposed compatibilist justification for reactions to deprived offenders can be reconciled with the U-condition justifications for reactions to the problem cases.

In Section 5, I consider and reject attempts by the compatibilist to extend his new justification to cover the problem cases, but I leave open the question of whether the U-condition solution to the problem cases offers a better account of our reaction to emotionally deprived offenders than that offered by the compatibilist justification.

I end by provisionally suggesting that our moral reactions might commit us to both compatibilist and incompatibilist principles for blameworthiness. But since some of these reactions *are* U-condition generating, the compatibilist is forced to con-

tinue his argument by claiming that we ought not to be committed to the U-condition.

Section 1: Do our everyday moral appraisals indicate commitment to a U-condition?

One of the first moves a compatibilist might make in support of
his claim that we do not endorse a U-condition is to argue that
U-condition generating beliefs play no part in our everyday
practices of moral appraisal.

I say this because some compatibilist philosophers have
thought it relevant to argue that the distinctions we actually
make between offenders do not depend on any beliefs about the
truth or falsity of determinism.[1]

I take it that this is thought by them to be relevant because
they assume it establishes that the incompatibilist is suffering
from some kind of delusion in imagining that our beliefs about
accountability involve worries about determinism.

But of course what we *actually* do is not sufficient evidence
for what we think we ought to do, and, also, even if our practices and our feelings about these practices coincide, it is possible that after further thought or philosophic argument, we
could be persuaded that we ought not to be satisfied with our
actual practices of moral appraisal. Indeed, the argument in Section 2 is intended to convince us that whatever the truth about
our actual practices of moral appraisal they ought to depend on
commitment to a U-condition.

What kind of beliefs about blameworthiness do our actual
practices of moral appraisal reveal?

I think it can be plausibly claimed that many of the distinctions we make between wrongdoers can be accounted for by
supposing that we are committed to the traditional compatibilist belief that fulfilment of the M-condition is both necessary
and sufficient for blameworthiness. For instance, when we condemn the agent who has acted wrongly from pure selfishness
and excuse the agent who has acted wrongly because he suffered
from a psychotic delusion, both condemnation and exoneration
can be fully explained by appeal to the traditional compatibilist
belief. The psychotic who attacks because he believes he is

under attack is morally excused because he does not fulfil the M-condition; the selfish agent who pursues a goal which he knows will harm others and for which he has neither excuse nor justification is blamed because he fulfils the M-condition.

And it might be argued by the compatibilist that there is no hint in our reaction to the selfish wrongdoer, which is typical of many of our moral reactions to wrongdoers, of any belief which could be called 'U-condition generating'. We do not ask ourselves before we pass judgement on him, 'Is he responsible for his selfish nature?'

But it could be objected that this is not true in the case of emotionally deprived offenders. Our attitude to these offenders suggests that we do ask such questions before we pass judgement on them. It is held that many offenders who lack concern for others and whose behaviour can be described as selfish and uncaring have become as they are because they have been deprived of affection and care in childhood.[2] And information like this about the childhoods and upbringings of young delinquents is increasingly taken into account by magistrates, police, social workers, before recommendations and orders are made in respect of them. Often offenders who have been deprived of affection are thought to be not so much candidates for condemnation and punishment as candidates for an environment which will help to make up for what they have lacked—an environment which will provide them with affection and an interest in their well-being.[3]

And the U-condition advocate might argue that such a response can plausibly be said to reveal a commitment (no doubt unrecognized) to a U-condition for blameworthiness, for it can be said to be a response which is prompted by the belief that the deprived offender is not responsible for having the kind of inclinations he has. Indeed, such a belief seems to be the natural accompaniment of the beliefs which are to be found in many of those who are concerned with 'disadvantaged' young offenders, for example social workers, child guidance therapists, and some psychologists. Such people often have thoughts like this: the young person's offending (or offensive) behaviour can be explained by his history of emotional deprivation; because he has had no experience of being cared about, he has become someone who does not care about others. Through no

fault of his own, he has become the sort of emotionally impo-
verished individual who is likely to behave with scant regard
for others.

There will be further discussion of our attitudes to emotionally deprived offenders in Section 3, but I want next to consider
a different incompatibilist argument for the existence of
U-condition generating beliefs.

Section 2: An argument for the existence of U-condition generating beliefs

The argument is this: our reactions to imaginary problem cases,
which are used by philosophers to test our intuitions about
moral responsibility, are such that the only satisfactory explanation for them is that we are implicitly committed to a
U-condition. Such imaginary cases are those in which an
agent's fulfilment of the M-condition can be attributed to his
having a brain tumour or to his having had certain states of
mind produced in him by brainwashing, hypnosis, or malevolent supernatural agents. We would be inclined to say that
the victims of such implantations, brain tumours, etc. are not
blameworthy and the incompatibilist would say that this
response is strong evidence of our being committed to the
belief that, when an agent's decisions can be traced to causes
for which he is not responsible, he ought not to be blamed for
what he does as the result of those decisions. It is only such a
belief, he would argue, which can be said to underly and justify
these responses.

But it might be felt that the incompatibilist is being too hasty
in assuming that our response to these cases amounts to a commitment to the U-condition. There are other possibilities, one of
which is that there is no belief which underlies and justifies these
responses—they are basic. In other words, we simply do feel
that people in these groups ought to be excused and this is not
based on any further reason or deeper justification. At some
point justification must stop and perhaps it stops here, with the
natural fact that we have such reactions in these cases.

But this seems unsatisfactory. The thought that there is a
unifying principle which links these cases for us and justifies

our responses is more persuasive than the suggestion that there isn't, particularly since there is a candidate for such a principle, namely the U-condition.

The opponent of the U-condition might suggest that our need for a deeper basis could be satisfied by a unifying *explanation* of these responses—an explanation which does not consist in an appeal to a belief which is thought to justify these responses. One suggestion for such an explanation is that we are so constituted that our moral indignation (or approval) is aroused by knowledge of an agent's motivational states so long as we do not concentrate closely on the fact that these states have been caused. But when we know the causal history of these motivational states, the motive explanation becomes absorbed into the longer causal explanation of the offending act, and in doing so it loses its power to arouse our moral feelings.

This seems to amount to the suggestion that our moral reactions will dissolve simply because we see the agent's motives as part of a longer causal chain—as if the sort of causal chain these motives are a part of does not matter for us. But the U-condition advocate would protest at the suggestion that the sort of causal chain doesn't matter by invoking his intuition that if we thought the agent himself was responsible for his motives, then the fact that these motives were later links in an extended causal chain would not affect our feeling of moral indignation. Our moral reactions would not dissolve if we believed that the longer causal chain was one whose initial links consisted in the agent's own choices.

At this point the compatibilist opponent of the U-condition claim could say that he accepts that we are concerned about the sort of causal chain which leads to a man's act and that in fact it is he, the compatibilist, who has always insisted that the *sort* of cause, rather than the mere fact of causation, is what distinguishes the blameworthy from the non-blameworthy offender. But, he might say, there are justifying explanations which can be given of our reactions to the problem cases (in which the agent's fulfilment of the M-condition is attributable to a brain tumour, or a malevolent demon, etc.) which differ from that given by the U-condition advocate.

For instance, he might say, our propensity to believe that an agent, X, is excusable if the states of mind which motivate his behaviour have been produced in him by a malevolent demon could be explained and justified by the belief that they are the demon's desires and not X's desires, since he is merely the receptacle for them.

But it is not clear that we are bound to say that the desires are not X's. Certainly, if we were imagining a situation in which the demon has bypassed X's motivational system and directly connected his own brain to the muscles controlling X's arms and legs, then we would say that X's behaviour was the result of the demon's desires. But in the situation we are actually imagining the desires are assumed to have been introduced into X's motivational system. Thus the reasons someone might have for assuming that they are not X's could either be:

1. that they have been implanted in X by someone else; or
2. that they have not been produced in X in the way desires are normally produced in X; or (possibly)
3. that the desires produced in X in this abnormal way are not the sort of desires which X characteristically has.

None of these reasons seems to me either necessary or sufficient for the claim that the desires are not X's. After all, X *has* the desires.

It would be more plausible, I think, for the compatibilist to argue that X is not responsible for acting on the desires which have been implanted in him for one or more of the reasons stated above. But, although more plausible, such an argument would fail. I shall postpone discussing why arguing on the basis of 2 or 3 would fail until later in the section, but I turn to the first argument the compatibilist might use, namely that X is not morally responsible for acting on the desires which have been placed in him *because* they have been placed in him by someone else. Suppose that X had asked the other agent to place these desires in him. Would we not then say that X was morally responsible for acting as the result of them? I think we would. And this suggests that the mere fact that X's desires were placed in him by someone else is not a sufficient justification for excusing him. To make this an excusing claim we should have to add to it the claim that X did not agree to these desires being implanted in him. But with this addition, the claim that X is excusable because his desires have been implanted in him comes down to the claim that he is excusable because he is not responsible for those desires *and this is what the U-condition advocate would say.*

In reply to this, the compatibilist might resort to the rather desperate strategy of claiming that our belief that X is excusable if his states have been chosen for him by someone else is basic and cannot be explained by any further belief. Now if we accepted that this belief was *sui generis*, we should have to accept that it had no connection with the sort of reactions we have to cases in which M-states of mind are caused by brain tumours or brain damage. For obviously, in these cases the motivations have not been *chosen* by someone else. But the U-condition advocate's suggestion seems superior to his opponent's, precisely because it provides a unifying justification for both sorts of cases.

Can the compatibilist provide a unifying non-U-condition justification for our reactions to all of the problem cases? There are several candidates for such unifying justifications which are available to him, but I find none of them satisfactory alternatives to the U-condition.

First, the compatibilist might say that in all of the problem cases we see the causes of X's motivational states as intrusive and it is their being seen as intrusive which makes us say that the agents who act as the result of these motivational states are not morally responsible. Or he might say that we react as we do to the problem cases because we see the causes of X's motivational states as abnormal, or that we react as we do to the problem cases because we assume that desires which are produced by abnormal causes are likely to be uncharacteristic desires for X to have.

The first suggestion, that it is the intrusiveness of the causes of X's motivational states which excuses him, can be easily turned against the compatibilist. This is why: to say that a cause is intrusive is to say that it, or its effects, are either uninvited or unwelcome. If we feel that X is not responsible because he did not invite the deliberate tampering with his psyche or the motivational changes wrought by his tumour, then this supports the U-condition advocate's claim that our reaction is based on the intuition that X ought not to be blamed because he did not choose (to have) these states of mind.

Suppose, though, it is claimed that we feel X is not respons-ible because he finds these 'external' influences unwelcome. Why should this fact make us feel that he is not responsible for the acts which issue from his motivational states? Perhaps it is thought that, if X is unhappy that external forces are respons-ible for his states of mind, he will find the states of mind them-selves unwelcome and, if he finds the states of mind he acts on unwelcome, he will have endeavoured to prevent them from issuing in action, therefore he ought not to be held responsible for his failure to prevent something he tried to prevent.

But it can be objected that:

(a) it need not be the case that an agent who is unhappy about the causes of his states of mind is unhappy about the states of mind themselves; and

(b) it need not be the case than an agent who finds his states of mind unwelcome tries to prevent them from issuing in action; and

(c) an agent can find unwelcome those states of mind which arise from natural or normal causes so that the fact of unwelcomeness cannot serve to distinguish these particu-lar cases in the way in which they ought to be dis-tinguished if it is true, as the compatibilist wants to claim, that an offender who acts from states of mind which have arisen naturally or normally can be morally responsible.

I turn now to the compatibilist's suggestion that we react as we do to the problem cases because we see the causes of X's states of mind as abnormal.

This can be objected to on the grounds that if these abnormal means for changing himself had been deliberately sought by X, the fact of abnormality would not produce the reaction in us for which we are seeking an explanation. Once again, it seems that the U-condition advocate has the only satisfactory explanation for this reaction.

The final compatibilist suggestion that we excuse X because we assume the desires produced in him by abnormal causes are uncharacteristic can be objected to on two grounds. First, the uncharacteristicness of the desire is not in itself a reason for excusing the agent who acts on it. Secondly, even if the abnor-mal causes for which X was not responsible produced desires which were characteristic of X (and this is certainly a logical possibility), we would feel that X is excusable and the U-condition advocate's explanation for this feeling seems more plausible than the explanations which have been offered by his compatibilist opponent.

The compatibilist does not seem able to suggest a rationale for our reactions in these cases which is as good as the rationale suggested by the U-condition advocate. It seems that the more adequate explanation of and justification for our holding the agents in these cases to be not morally responsible for their actions is that we believe they are not responsible for their motivations.

The U-condition advocate will go on to argue that if we think it wrong for the offenders in these cases to be blamed because they are not responsible for their motivations we ought, in all consistency, to think it wrong to blame any offender who is not responsible for his motivations. Using the strong intuitions which are aroused in us by the thought that brainwashing or brain tumours are responsible for an agent's motivations, he seeks to persuade us that we ought to have similar reactions to cases in which the agent's motivations are said to be attributable to the relatively pedestrian and non-threating-sounding causes of genetic endowment and environment. For, he reasons, the agent is no more responsible for his genetic endowment and upbringing than he is for the designs of a malevolent demon or a brainwasher. He is no more responsible for a personality which (perhaps) depends on his brain in a normal state, than he is for the personality change attributable to his brain tumour. The argument is a familiar one which seems almost crude in its simplicity, but I find it persuasive.

A strong case has been made for the claim that we are committed to the view that blameworthiness requires fulfilment of the U-condition. In the next few sections, I shall present arguments about our attitudes to emotionally deprived offenders which seem to point to a view about blameworthiness which cannot be reconciled with this.

Section 3: Blameworthiness and emotional deprivation

In Section 1, the traditional compatibilist belief that fulfilment of the M-condition is sufficient for blameworthiness was challenged by the claim that this would not accommodate our moral reactions to emotionally deprived offenders who fulfil the M-condition. These reactions were then used by the U-condition advocate to suggest that they indicated commitment to a U-condition. But further reflection might tempt us to challenge this.

Let us imagine that there are two offenders, only one of whom has had a history of emotional deprivation. The other offender has not been emotionally deprived but has had both affection and material comforts lavished on him. However, because he has never been taught to consider other people he has become selfish and insensitive. The emotionally deprived offender is also selfish and uncaring but his selfishness and lack of concern for others is attributable to his not having been cared about.[4]

The U-condition advocate is committed to claiming that since the behaviour of both offenders is causally due to states and events for which they are not responsible, neither is blameworthy. But there is something unacceptable about lumping both offenders together. One feels that the emotionally deprived offender merits some sort of special consideration, that he should be judged differently from the non-deprived offender. I shall call this feeling the 'sense of difference'.

The U-condition advocate could argue that the 'sense of difference' can be explained by our finding it easier to imagine initially that the U-condition is not fulfilled in the case of the deprived offender than it is to see that it is not fulfilled in the case of the non-deprived offender.[5] If so, then far from being incompatible with the U-condition, the sense of difference can actually be explained by it. And once we realize that the non-deprived offender also does not fulfil the U-condition, the sense of difference should disappear.

Or, if it does not disappear, it can be explained as a feeling that the deprived offender deserves more sympathy than the non-deprived offender. This would be perfectly compatible with the idea that both are equally non-deserving of blame because neither has fulfilled the U-condition. To accept this, would be to accept than an offender's history of deprivation has no more bearing on his blameworthiness than any other kind of history which might have been responsible for his fulfilment of the M-condition. It would be to accept that if deprivation is morally significant, it is so only because it is a cause for which the offender is not responsible. And in this respect, of course, the history of the offender who was not deprived would be of equal moral significance.

But there is a compatibilist non-U-condition justification for the sense of difference which is worth exploring. This alternative is based on the suggestion that there is something about the fact of deprivation itself which makes it an excusing condition. There are two forms such a suggestion might take:

1. it might be held that deprived offenders should be judged to be not blameworthy simply because they have been deprived; or
2. it might be held that deprived offenders should be judged to be less blameworthy because they have been deprived. Here the fact of deprivation would act as a mitigating condition influencing the amount of blame (condemnation or punishment) which is held to be deserved.

It is the second suggestion which I shall argue for, but its plausibility will emerge in the course of a discussion of the first suggestion, in particular as the result of our showing that the various justifications a compatibilist might offer for the first suggestion are not satisfactory.

What is it about the fact of emotional deprivation which could be thought to justify the belief that the deprived offender does not deserve to be blamed? The first thing a compatibilist might say is that, contrary to the assumption in Section 1, deprived offenders do not really fulfil the M-condition. The argument could take several forms:

1. it might be argued that, despite appearances, the deprived offender's behaviour is not the deliberate flouting of a moral requirement but is instead 'a cry for help', or an attempt to fill the emotional gaps left by his deprivation. In other words, such

agents are motivated by the desire to be helped or loved and this is not morally reprehensible; or

2. it might be argued that while not consciously motivated by the desire for affection, such offenders are unconsciously motivated by it, with their conscious desires taking a variety of different forms, for example a craving for possessions.[6] But, the argument would run, whatever form their desires take, they will have an intensity and persistence which is due to their being prompted by the unsatisfied need for affection. This need is such a pressing one that any desire which is prompted by it will be hard to resist. And (see Chapter 2) if someone acts because of the irresistibility of his desire he might not fulfil the M-condition; or

3. it might be argued that where the desire for affection which motivates the offender is unconscious, the offender, because ignorant of the desire which motivates him, cannot be said to know what he is doing and is excusable for this reason.

To this last point, one can reply that ignorance of one's motivating desire does not necessarily entail the kind of ignorance of what one is doing which would be excusing. For example, even if it is true that what appears to the offender to be a desire to steal things is really a disguised desire for affection, the fact that he does not realize this does not preclude his knowing that he is stealing or that stealing is wrong.

But there is a general objection to all three arguments, namely that it cannot be legitimately assumed that *whenever* a deprived person does something wrong, he is motivated (either consciously or unconsciously) by the desire for affection. It is likely that by the time many of the more grossly deprived offenders have grown up, any hope of affection from others has long since died in them. But many of them continue to offend and when they do their motivating states of mind are often selfish and uncaring.

The compatibilist needs to explain why deprivation might excuse offenders who *do* fulfil the M-condition.

One explanation he might give is that put forward by Milo in 'Amorality' that deprived offenders are likely to suffer from emotional impairments rendering them incapable of caring about others:

... it is not necessary to hold that the psychopath fails to understand the difference between right and wrong in order to explain why ... we consider his responsibility for his behaviour to be diminished. The reason for this is simply that he suffers from a genuine emotional impairment—he is unable to feel any genuine love or affection for others. Perhaps he has been so deprived of love and affection in childhood, so emotionally undernourished that he has been rendered completely cold and unsympathetic, no longer capable of being moved by the prospects of pain or harm to others ... if so, then it is these things—emotional impairment and lack of self-control—that justify us in excusing or withholding blame from the psychopath. (pp. 486–7.)

Obviously, this passage is not ideal for my purposes since the author seems to believe on the one hand that emotional impairment justifies a verdict of diminished responsibility and, on the other, that it could justify a verdict of non-responsibility, if it is coupled with lack of self-control.[7] But it is not a misrepresentation to say that he regards emotional incapacity as *an* excusing condition, and I have decided to include the passage because it expresses the thought that emotional deprivation is a reason for excusing because it results in emotional incapacity. We must remember, though, that we are trying to judge whether emotional incapacity would provide a *sufficient* reason for excusing.

Let us assume for the sake of argument that only those who have been emotionally deprived are incapable of caring. Then, why should their emotional incapacity be considered sufficient to excuse them? Perhaps because it is thought that it renders them incapable of acting otherwise. But this answer is not acceptable because it implies that we are committed to an independent could-have-acted-otherwise condition for blameworthiness and, as we have seen, this is false.

What other reason could there be for assuming that the difference in capacity for caring would justify a judgement of blameworthiness in the case of the non-deprived offender and a judgement of non-blameworthiness in the case of the deprived? It is possible that those who believe that the facts of capacity and incapacity are morally relevant have been prompted to do so by the vague thought that the offender who has the capacity to care is at fault for not exercising that capacity. Perhaps they have a vague picture of such an offender as someone who has deliberately not allowed himself to be moved enough by consideration for another's welfare, and an accompanying and equally vague picture of the emotionally incapacitated agent as someone who would have cared if he could have, perhaps, as someone who tried to care and failed. But these thoughts when reflected on, will be seen to be untenable.

It is absurd to suggest that an agent is capable of exercising his capacity for caring for others at will, as if he could determine when he would be moved more by the thought of others than he is by the thought of himself. And the image of the uncaring offender who, at the time of action, tries and fails to feel any-thing for his intended victim is equally far-fetched. What would move an agent who is incapable of being moved by another's plight to try to be moved by it? Even if one could construct imaginary situations in which such an attempt would be made, they would be unlikely to mirror the everyday situations in which uncaring agents act.

And, in any event, even if uncaring agents could sometimes be motivated in this way, it would not be relevant to our present discussion, since that discussion is concerned with discovering whether the fact of deprivation is an excusing condition for agents who have fulfilled the M-condition, and an offender who acted because he had failed in his attempt to be moved to per-form a different act might not fulfil the M-condition (see Chapter 2).

Another compatibilist justification which might be offered for the claim that the deprived offender is not blameworthy is that such offenders have had abnormal childhoods. The term 'ab-normal childhood' suggests one which has been both out of the ordinary and unnatural. Since there is obviously nothing in the fact of non-ordinariness which could justify the claim that an out of the ordinary childhood is excusing, anyone who thinks that abnormality is excusing is probably prompted by some thought about unnaturalness. But what is it to say that some-thing is unnatural? The phrase which springs to mind is 'against nature'. Now it could hardly be claimed that emotional depriva-tion is 'against nature' in the sense that it is not covered by natural laws. It is neither miraculous nor supernatural. How-ever, the term 'unnatural' could be used to mean something like 'not right' as in 'It's unnatural for a mother to deprive her child', where what is being conveyed is the belief that it's not normal, plus something like a feeling of disapproval for the depriver, and sympathy for the deprived. But, of course, such feelings would not constitute justifications for the claim that offenders do not deserve to be blamed.

Another suggestion is that we feel the deprived and non-deprived offenders should be judged differently because we believe the deprived offender has been denied what is due to him. The suggestion would go like this: it is the birthright of every child to be given an upbringing which will ensure his emotional and physical well-being. The emotionally deprived child has not been given such an upbringing and has therefore been deprived of his birthright and, in this respect, of what is due to him. On the other hand, the non-deprived offender who has been indulged has been given more than his due. Therefore, some compensation is deserved by the deprived offender which is not deserved by the non-deprived offender. For this reason, the deprived offender should be judged to be undeserving of blame.

But there are two objections to this: first, it can be objected that the indulged child (as we have described him) has not been given more than his due. He is similar to the under-indulged child in being selfish and insensitive to others and these qualities are attributable to his upbringing. And his selfishness and insensitivity could prevent him from finding fulfilment in relationships with other people who might prudently shy away from involvement with him. He has not, therefore, been given an upbringing which ensures his emotional well-being any more than the deprived child has and, in this respect, cannot be said to have been given what is due to him either.

Nevertheless, unlike the deprived child he has been given warmth and affection and as a result he has been able to enjoy feelings of security and self-esteem denied to the first child. He has at least, then, been given more of his due in the way of the ingredients for emotional well-being than the first child, and we might feel that in consequence the first child deserves more in the way of compensation and therefore less in the way of punishment for his offence than does the second child.

This brings me to the second objection which is that the claim does not take into account the fact that we are concerned with what an offender deserves *for his offence*. It does not follow that because an offender has had an undeservedly hard life, he deserves a softer response for his offence than he would if his life had been easier. This can be seen if we imagine an offender who fulfils the M-condition and has suffered a series of misfortunes but whose fulfilment of the M-condition is not attributable to those misfortunes. In the absence of an explanatory causal link between his misfortunes and his offences we would not be tempted to say that he deserved less harsh treatment. The principle of desert we seem to be looking for is a principle which stipulates that if an offender's misfortunes are causally responsible for his having an M-state of mind, he deserves to be judged less harshly than an offender whose M-state of mind is causally attributable to experiences which have not been unfortunate. Only such a principle will justify the intuition that an offender deserves less harsh treatment for what he has done *because* what he has done is attributable to a history of emotional deprivation.

Perhaps the principle we are looking for could be called a 'principle of retributory balance'. I shall explain: when a man does something wrong one common response to this is the thought that he must 'pay' for what he has done. But suppose we believed that he had already paid something for his behaviour compared to another offender who had not. We would then conclude that he ought to pay less than the other offender. Perhaps we could say that the offender whose behaviour can be attributed to deprivation has paid something in advance for that behaviour. He has paid something in advance in the sense that the causal process which has culminated in his becoming someone who lacks feelings for others is one which has involved suffering for him. In the process of becoming someone who is a prima-facie candidate for blame, he has suffered undeservedly.

On the other hand, the offender who has been indulged has not suffered in the process of becoming someone who is a prima-facie candidate for blame. It has cost him nothing in advance. He deserves, therefore, to pay a higher price for a similar offence.

Commitment to such a principle would help to explain our feeling that the sort of causal sequence which leads to an agent's offence is important for determining his blameworthiness or excusability, but it should be noted that in discussing the principle and how we would apply it, it has been assumed that the principle is not one which determines whether an agent deserves blame, but how much blame he deserves.

Until now we have concentrated exclusively on conditions for blameworthiness, that is conditions which determine that an offender deserves to be condemned or punished *tout court*. But there are certain facts whose obtaining we take to be relevant to how much criticism or punishment an offender deserves for a particular offence. We believe, for instance, that physical harm merits more punishment than theft; we believe that severe physical harm merits more punishment than slight physical harm. And we also believe that the severity of condemnation or punishment ought to depend on how morally reprehensible an offender's state of mind is. Thus, we might say that an offender who is motivated by greed is more morally reprehensible than an offender who is motivated by sexual jealousy and that the greater reprehensibility of his motive merits greater condemnation although the offences of both offenders are similar.

So the suggestion is that if two offenders, deprived and non-deprived, commit the same offence, then the deprived offender should be held to deserve less blame than the non-deprived offender.

To sum up, we have considered various justifications which might be offered for the claim that the fact of emotional deprivation is sufficient to excuse an offender who has fulfilled the M-condition and we have found that none of these justifications is acceptable. But we have found a justification which seems intuitively acceptable for the claim that the fact of emotional deprivation should be taken into account when we are deciding how much blame a particular offender deserves. It has been suggested that in so far as the offender's history of emotional deprivation can be said to be causally responsible for his fulfilment of the M-condition, the suffering which he experienced as the result of his deprivation can be regarded as a payment in advance for the offence he committed.

Now it might be thought that in terms of the notion that one ought to pay for one's offences, the distinction between being blameworthy at all and being more or less blameworthy is in danger of collapsing, for one could envisage circumstances in which the price (in suffering) paid in advance was so great that it would be felt that the offender had discharged his debt for all but the most serious of wrongs. Suppose for instance he had suffered greatly as a child from neglect and lack of affection and as a result had become someone who was cold and selfish. Suppose further that he was motivated to perform an act of petty theft. Then it might seem that he deserves to pay nothing for his offence. But if he deserves to pay nothing for his offence, doesn't this mean that he is not blameworthy? I would suggest that the claim that he deserves to pay nothing for his offence is misleading. It is not that he is deemed to deserve to pay nothing; it is rather that he is deemed to deserve to pay nothing more for he has already paid (with interest) what he deserved to pay.

I can think of no further objection to the claim that if deprivation is to count against blame, then it should mitigate rather than abolish it. However, since it has been shown to be the assumption that the deprived offender paid a price in suffering which justifies the belief that he should be judged less harshly, we should perhaps rename the condition, calling it instead 'the payment-in-advance-condition'.

Section 4: Why reconciliation is not possible

At first glance, it might look as if commitment to a payment-in-advance-condition could be reconciled with commitment to a U-condition. For since the role of the payment-in-advance-condition is to mitigate the amount of blame, it is clear that it is supposed to be appealed to only after the offender has been judged to be blameworthy. And since this is so, the offender must be deemed to have already fulfilled the conditions for blameworthiness. Why then could not one of these conditions be the U-condition?

The answer is that this is impossible because fulfilment of the payment-in-advance-condition would preclude fulfilment of the U-condition. This is why: it has been shown in Chapter 3 that an offender could only fulfil the U-condition if his morally relevant decision was uncaused by anything for which he is not responsible. But if his decision were uncaused by anything for which he was not responsible, then he could not fulfil the payment-in-advance-condition which is that the depriving (or other unfortunate) circumstances should be causally responsible for his fulfilling of the M-condition.[8]

Commitment to the belief that there is a payment-in-advance-condition involves commitment to the belief that we live in a world in which at least some decisions are caused by states and events for which we are not responsible and it also involves a commitment to the belief that offenders whose decisions are caused by states and events for which they are not responsible can be blameworthy. It is, thus, incompatible with a commitment to the belief in a U-condition for blameworthiness.

However, there is a further argument which might be advanced for the claim that commitment to the U-condition is compatible with commitment to the belief in a deprivation condition. Suppose that an offender's history has only been partly responsible for his fulfilment of the M-condition, that is suppose it has not been the complete cause of his fulfilment of the M-condition, but that it has played an essential role, that it has been necessary but not sufficient for his fulfilment of the M-condition. If we think of moral responsibility as something which requires fulfilment of the U-condition, that is as something which requires that nothing for which the offender is not responsible should be the source of his motivation, then we might be willing to concede that moral responsibility is diminished if something for which the offender is not responsible is *partly* responsible for his motivation. If we were willing to concede this, then we would judge the offender who had a history of deprivation to be less blameworthy because he had a history which was partly responsible for his decision. In this way, the belief that deprivation diminished responsibility could be compatible with the belief in a U-condition for blameworthiness.

As it stands, this suggestion does not meet the demand for something which will justify and explain our sense that deprived and non-deprived offenders should be judged differently. For the offender who is not deprived could also be someone whose history is partly responsible for his fulfilment of the M-condition and as such, according to the suggestion, he too would qualify as someone whose moral responsibility was diminished.

But the suggestion could be modified to meet the demand: we could add to the claim that moral responsibility is diminished if something for which the offender is not responsible is partly responsible for his fulfilment of the M-condition and further claim that a history of deprivation would diminish even more that responsibility which is already diminished by the fact that his chosen mental states are partly responsible for his decision. In other words, the U-condition advocate could hold that while, given the thesis of partial causation, both deprived and non-deprived offenders bear less than full responsibility for their decisions, the deprived offender deserves to pay even less than the non-deprived. This would seem to allow the U-condition advocate to retain his belief that total uncausedness is necessary for full responsibility and to believe (without inconsistency) in a deprivation degree-of-blameworthiness condition.

But the extent to which these two beliefs really are compatible depends:

1. on what sense can be made of the idea of partial causation; and

2. on whether we can interpret the thought that the agent might be partly causally responsible in such a way that it is made clear why he is only *partly* morally responsible.

The need to consider 2 follows from this thought: if the fact that partial causation of (say) an M-condition decision by an agent's unchosen mental states is supposed to *diminish* but not *obliterate* the agent's moral responsibility, then this must be because the agent is deemed to be also partly (causally) responsible for fulfilment of the M-condition. So in what sense are we to take it that the agent is partly but not fully causally responsible and how does his being partly causally responsible in this sense make him only partly morally responsible?

Here is one unacceptable suggestion which relies on the thought that partial responsibility for S can be construed as full responsibility for a part of S. Let us imagine that we can make sense of the thought that the agent has contributed part of the cause of his decision and that his unchosen mental states have contributed the remaining part. Let us suppose further that the agent is fully causally responsible for contributing part of the cause. Then would it not make sense to say that because the agent has only contributed *part* of the cause he doesn't deserve the condemnation which would be deserved by someone who contributed the whole of it, but because he is fully causally responsible for contributing part of it, he deserves some condemnation?

Such a suggestion is unacceptable for two reasons:

1. it implies an absurd claim about the relationship of a decision maker to his desires; and
2. its model of partial causal responsibility, far from justifying belief in partial moral responsibility, as suggested, actually justifies belief in full moral responsibility.

To explain both of these points further: the claim that an agent is fully morally responsible for a part of the decision implies that his contributions have not been caused (even if the contributions of his desires have been). This would follow from the U-condition demand that full moral responsibility requires total uncausedness. But if his contribution to the decision is uncaused then of course it cannot be even partly caused by his desires. And this would imply that he and his caused desires have made separate contributions as if they were totally independent factors which happened to combine to produce the decision. Now this would suggest that our attitude to the agent should be similar to the attitude we might have to someone who intends to push open a door and not having the strength to do it on his own is helped by a wind to push it open. Surely, our attitude to such a person would be that he should bear full moral responsibility (if something morally problematic were at stake) for opening the door. The wind can't take moral responsibility any more than his desires can. Furthermore, even if the agent had combined with another agent to perform an act which neither of them could perform on his own we would feel that each should be held fully morally responsible for the act.

Obviously then, it can't be this kind of partial causation which partly exonerates the agent. But we should also reject this way of interpreting the claim about partial causation because it implies, absurdly, that the agent and his desires are only coincidentally joined when surely the correct thought is that if desires and mental states are partly responsible for the agent's decision, it is because his decision, in some way which falls short of full causation by them, is partly the result of their existence. But can we understand how this might be? That is, can we understand how his decision might be partly but not fully caused by these states?

One thought might be that we are to understand this as meaning that his decision is partly caused and partly uncaused. But this is surely incomprehensible. It seems therefore that we must again resort to the thought that the agent and his states constitute the full cause of his decision, but not in the form suggested and rejected above (that is both independently combining to cause the decision). Rather, it seems plausible to say that the full cause is to be seen as one which involves the agent's basing his decision on these states. And we might construe the idea of each (that is, the agent and his states) being a partial cause as meaning that the decision to do such and such must be caused by:

  (i) an agent who decides and
  (ii) the states which give rise to considerations which he decides between.

Both, it could be said, are necessarily involved in his basing his decision on his mental states.

Unfortunately, this construal of partial causation does not take us very far, for it is compatible with there being a complete causal explanation of the agent's deciding as he does which resides in his antecedent mental states. This is because the construal is simply a conceptual point about basing one's decisions on considerations.

So, we are still left with the problem of finding an acceptable construal of partial causation *and* showing how this kind of partial causation justifies partial moral responsibility. I can see no way of doing this. The only model of decision making I can think of which comes close to expressing the idea that a man's mental states are partly responsible for his decision is one which is supposed to support the thought that the agent is fully morally responsible for his decisions.

The idea is this: the agent's decision is to some extent constrained by the materials provided by the past. He is not responsible for the fact that the desires which form the ingredients for the decision making process (or choosing process) are those desires; that these are the ingredients for the decision making process is caused by factors for which he is not responsible.

Thus, that this decision will have to be based on these ingredients is not something he is responsible for. But which decision he actually makes, which of the courses of action open to him he opts for is something he is responsible for.

This model of the agent's decisions is one which would be invoked by a libertarian as a way of making sense of the idea that desires are relevant to but not causally responsible for decisions. The agent as decision maker is presented as someone who is influenced but not caused by his desires to come to the decision he makes. I later argue that this model should be rejected (in Chapter 5), but even if it were acceptable it would not provide what is needed to make sense of the idea of partial causation, except in a form which is supposed to underwrite the claim that the agent is fully morally responsible for his decisions, and in this form it can hardly be called a notion of partial causation, for the idea is supposed to be that there is *no* causal relationship between the agent's desires and his decisions.

I conclude that there is no way of reconciling the requirements of the U-condition with those which would have to be fulfilled if the deprivation payment-in-advance-condition were to be considered relevant to our assessment of blameworthy offenders.

Section 5: A compatibilist attempt to accommodate the problem cases

The irreconcilability of these principles only presents a problem if we are committed to both of them. But are we? The compatibilist might opt for a colonizing move by suggesting that the intuitions which are linked with the belief in a payment-in-advance-condition could provide as good an explanation for our reactions to the problem cases (brain tumours, brainwashing, etc.) as belief in a U-condition.

The suggestion would be that our reactions to the problem cases could be justified by the belief that the agents in all of these cases have paid a price in advance. This is a very persuasive claim because we would no doubt agree that in each of these cases the cause of the agent's morally reprehensible state of mind is such that he can be said to have suffered as a result of it. The agent with a brain tumour has suffered from the deterioration of his faculties and the inescapable change in his personality. The agent who is at the mercy of the demon has suffered from the loss of his independence. The agent who has been brainwashed has suffered from being changed without his agreement.

But I have two reservations about this suggestion, one less serious than the other. The less serious reservation is about the use of the term 'suffering' in connection with *all* these cases. It cannot be said that the agent who has been changed is necessarily unhappy because of this. If he doesn't know that he is at the mercy of a demon, if he doesn't know that he has been subjected to brainwashing techniques, he might not feel any uneasiness as a result. Indeed, he might know that he is being subjected to such techniques and not feel unhappy about this. And if he cannot be said to have experienced suffering, we might feel that he cannot be said to have paid a price in advance. Against this, it might be said that feeling unhappy or in pain is only one way of paying a price. There are other ways which needn't involve actual suffering. Many would feel that lack of independence, being unwittingly manipulated, a change in personality for the worse, a loss of intellectual ability, physical deterioration, are all evils whose character as such is distinct from any feeling which the victim might have about them.

Those who do feel this would say that the offenders in our imaginary problem cases have all paid a price, whether they would be willing to acknowledge this or not, a price which, since it is a causal concomitant of their becoming the sort of people who fulfil the M-condition, can be said to have been paid in advance for their offences.

Nevertheless, the stubborn thought persists that if the offender himself has not felt his circumstances to be unhappy ones then he has not paid the sort of price which would be plausibly construed as an advance on the discomfort (or shame) he can be said to deserve as the result of his wrong.

The second more serious reservation is this: the payment-in-advance-condition is a degree-of-blameworthiness condition and our reaction when we hear of the problem cases described above is that the agents in them are not blameworthy at all. We would not accept, I think, that the agent whose desires are implanted in him by a malevolent demon, or whose new personality is the result of brainwashing or a brain tumour is less blameworthy than an agent who has not been subjected to such interference. We would feel that the first agent was not blameworthy at all.

Thus, I conclude that belief in the payment-in-advance-condition cannot be used to explain our reactions to the problem cases, and that the claim that we are committed to a U-condition for blameworthiness via our reactions to these cases must be allowed to stand.

Furthermore, there is a fairly powerful case for saying that we are not really committed via the sense of difference to a payment-in-advance-condition, a case which consists in the U-condition advocate's earlier suggestion that our reactions to emotional deprivation can be fully explained as a consequence of our commitment to the U-condition, or construed as a feeling of sympathy which is compatible with the U-condition commitment (or perhaps both).

Nevertheless, I do not think we should simply dismiss the payment-in-advance-condition, partly because it has an intuitive appeal and partly because, as I shall argue in Chapter 7, there is a compatibilist condition for praiseworthiness which is analogous to the payment-in-advance-condition and which I think we would be willing to endorse at the expense of the U-condition.

So I end with the provisional suggestion that we might be committed to both compatibilist and incompatibilist principles for moral responsibility. I shall discuss this further in the concluding chapter (7).

In the meantime, the fact remains that the compatibilist cannot dismiss belief in the U-condition out-of-hand as something which is not endorsed by our intuitions. If he is to continue to oppose it he must do so on different grounds. So, in Chapter 5, I shall discuss some claims about the U-condition belief which, if true, might constitute a case for saying that we ought not to be committed to it.

5

Can the U-condition for blameworthiness be fulfilled?

Introduction

In this Chapter, I discuss the arguments for two claims:

1. that belief in the U-condition for blameworthiness is logically incoherent; and
2. that the U-condition cannot be fulfilled.

The success of arguments for the first claim would constitute a conclusive case for saying that we ought not to be committed to the U-condition. The success of arguments for the second claim would make it reasonable to ask whether we ought to be so committed.

I conclude that there is no incoherence in the belief that fulfilment of the U-condition is necessary for blameworthiness, but I also conclude that the U-condition for blameworthiness cannot be fulfilled. So the U-condition advocate who is simply concerned to establish the logical coherence of his particular brand of incompatibilism against the charge that he is committed to a condition which is 'ultimately unintelligible'[1] can take comfort from some of the arguments in this chapter (Part I and Part III).

But the U-condition advocate who is a libertarian can take no comfort from the conclusions which emerge. For libertarians believe that we have the non-causal freedom required for moral responsibility and the arguments in this chapter show that blameworthiness as the U-condition advocate conceives of it is probably not an empirical possibility (Part IV), but is at best a logical possibility which is restricted to reasonless choices, and decisions or choices which have themselves been caused by reasonless choices. (Why the choices must be reasonless and why the distinction between decisions and choices is important will become clear as the argument progresses.)

In the discussions which follow, a number of different but

connected issues wil be explored. The structure of the argument as it moves from one issue to another can be summarized as follows. Part I involves a discussion and rejection of the claim that we cannot (logically) be morally responsible for uncaused events. In Part I(*a*) I discuss the doctrine of agent-causation and imply that because a convincing case has not (yet) been made for it, it should be avoided by the U-condition advocate. In Part I(*b*) I argue that we can be morally responsible for uncaused decisions and choices. In Part I(*c*) a challenge to Part I(*b*) is discussed and rejected; and this leads to Part I(*d*), a discussion of the distinction between decisions and choices. This distinction is important for the subsequent discussion in Part II—can there be uncaused decisions and choices?

The argument in this section is in three stages. In Part II(*a*) it is argued that decisions must (logically) be based on reasons, but that choices can be reasonless. In Part II(*b*) the thesis that reasons are causes is defended, and in Part II(*c*) Thorp's suggestion that motives are influences but not causes is rejected. The conclusion which emerges from these arguments is that the U-condition can only be fulfilled by a reasonless choice, or a choice or decision which is caused by a reasonless choice. This is challenged in Part III, by an argument to the effect that *blameworthy* reasonless choices are not logically possible. I reject this argument. By the end of Part III, I have reached the conclusion that it is logically possible for the U-condition to be fulfilled by reasonless choices. But in Part IV, it is argued that such choices are (probably) not empirically possible. This conclusion depends mainly on a defence of the claim that desires are necessary as motivators for action against some recent challenges to it by Nagel and McDowell.

Part I: Can we be morally responsible for uncaused events?

As we saw in Chapter 3, the U-condition advocate holds that, given certain facts about the way the world is, blameworthiness is only possible if the decisions or choices which lead to action are either uncaused by preceding events or states, or caused by choices and decisions which are themselves uncaused by preceding events or states.

But it has been objected that if an event is uncaused then it will be 'accidental', 'random', 'chance' or 'fortuitous' in a way which militates against its being the sort of event for which an agent can be morally responsible.[2] This amounts, I think, to the charge that it is incoherent to suggest that we could be morally responsible for an uncaused event.

This criticism is often levelled at the libertarian who insists that we have the freedom required for moral responsibility and that this freedom requires the falsity of determinism. The libertarian is then challenged to show how an event which is not causally determined can be one for which the agent is morally responsible, for it is assumed that if the event is not causally determined, then it is not caused and if not caused then accidental, or random.

In Chapter 3, I suggested that an event could be caused without being causally determined, and it might be thought that one way of answering the objection would be to say that the falsity of determinism does not necessarily entail uncausedness. But this is not a way which is open to the U-condition advocate who, for reasons which have been discussed in Chapter 3, believes that moral responsibility requires the uncausedness of (some) decisions or choices. He must, therefore, answer the challenge about uncaused events.

Some libertarians have invoked the doctrine of agent-causation as a way of meeting this challenge. They have suggested that whereas moral responsibility is incompatible with an agent's acts being caused by preceding events, it will not be threatened if the agent himself causes his actions. If actions are caused by agents, they reason, then they are not the uncaused events for which it is assumed that agents cannot be morally responsible and since *ex hypothesi* such actions are not caused by events, they have the kind of freedom required for moral responsibility.[3]

One can imagine that the U-condition advocate would find it tempting to apply the doctrine of agent-causation to a person's decisions, saying that when a person decides to do something it is not his desires which cause his decisions, but he, the person, who causes them; and to suggest that there is some relationship other than a causal one between a person's desires and his caus-ing himself to decide (as Thorp does: see Part II(*c*)).

I(*a*): The doctrine of agent-causation

But is the doctrine of agent-causation a tenable one? It has attracted a great deal of criticism. The objections against it range from the claim that it is 'mysterious' to the claim that it is incoherent. I shall examine some of the objections which have been made, some objections which can be made, and the answers to them—answers which have either actually been given by agent-causationists or which might be given by agent-causationists.

One objection concerns the nature of actions. It goes like this: either agent-causation of actions is nothing more than desire and belief causation of actions or there can be no such thing as agent-causation. For the concept of an act just is the concept of desire-and-belief-caused behaviour (via a non-deviant causal chain). Goldman can be seen as mounting such an argument when he suggests in *A Theory of Human Action* that:

1. the claim that an agent has caused his act is explicable in terms of the claim that his behaviour has been caused (in the right way) by his desires and beliefs; and
2. that 'it is part of the concept of an act that an act is caused by a want'.[4]

There are two replies which can be made to this. One is to deny that the concept of action is necessarily that of desire-and-belief-caused behaviour. This reply works, I think. The second is to claim that the concept of action *cannot* be that of desire-and-belief-caused behaviour. This reply does not work.

In support of the first point, I would say this: it is intuitively more acceptable to think of the term 'action' as standing for 'in-tentional behaviour' than it is to think of it as standing for 'be-haviour which is caused by desires and beliefs'. And the concept of 'intentional behaviour' is not one which must in turn be understood as standing for desire-and-belief-caused behaviour. This runs counter to the suggestions of Davidson and Goldman who see the concept of 'intentional behaviour' as analysable into 'behaviour which is caused in the right way by desires and beliefs'.[5] But I do not find these suggestions compelling. It might be true that *as a matter of fact* all intentional behaviour is caused by desires and beliefs but the concept of intentional behaviour does not imply this. There is no incoherence in the idea that a person's behaviour has been intentional although it has not been caused by a desire; and if not caused (in part) by a desire, then not caused (in part) by any belief about the means of satisfying this desire. (It might be claimed that the mere fact of intentional behaviour entails an implicit belief that what is intended is possible; but, if so, such a belief, when not desire related, is irrelevant to the argument.)

The second reply to the claim that action should be viewed as desire-and-belief-caused behaviour is that such a definition fails to capture two essential constituents of the thought that someone has acted:

1. that it is a person, an integrated being, who acts, and not some part of him; and
2. that to act is to do something, as opposed to having something happen to you.

Richard Taylor seems to be arguing for the first point in *Action and Purpose* when he says:

in acting, I make something happen, I cause it or bring it about. Now it does seem odd that philosophers should construe this natural way of expressing the matter as really meaning, not that I, but rather some event, process or state not identical with myself should be the cause of that which is represented as my act. It is plain that, whatever I am, I am never identical with any such event, process or state as is usually proposed as the 'real cause' of my act ... Hence, if it is really and unmetaphorically true, as I believe it to be, that I sometimes cause something to happen, this would seem to entail that it is false that any event, process or state not identical with my self should be the real cause of it. (p. 111.)

Perhaps Taylor feels that it is odd to construe a claim about my doing something as a claim to the effect that my desires and beliefs cause my behaviour because he assumes that what is being claimed by those who construe action in this way is that the desires and beliefs have acted and not me. But need someone who defines actions as Goldman does be seen as claiming this? It is surely open to him to say that when he construes action as desire-and-belief-caused behaviour he is not claiming that the states within the agent have acted, but rather than it is in virtue of the fact that his behaviour has been caused by his desires and beliefs that he, the agent, can be said to have acted.

This leaves us with the claim that to construe the relationship between an agent and his act as a causal relationship between his desires and his behaviour is to fail to do justice to the second constituent of the thought that a person acts, namely the belief that to act is to do something, as opposed to having something happen to you.

Nagel seems to suggest that to construe action as *an event of any kind* is to fail to do justice to the second constituent when he says that 'something in the idea of agency is incompatible with actions being events'.[6] And he apparently bases this claim on the belief that since all events are happenings there cannot be events which are the *doings* of agents:

Something in the ordinary idea of what someone does must explain how it can seem necessary to subtract from it anything that merely happens, even though the ultimate consequence of such subtraction is that nothing remains. (p. 36.)

In a later passage he speaks of the 'gradual erosion of what we do by the subtraction of what happens.'[7]

I think that Nagel has failed to distinguish between the claim that all events are happenings and the claim that all events are hapenings *to* the substances which are involved in them. While the first claim is undoubtedly true, the second claim is not. For example, the event of an agent's trying to do such and such is something which happens, but it is not something which happens to him. The event of an agent's deciding or choosing to do such and such is something which happens, but we do not think of deciding and choosing as things which happen *to* him. Only if every event which involved agents consisted entirely of things which happened *to* them would events *per se* be incompatible with agency.

But it might now be argued that even if events *per se* are not incompatible with agency, events resulting from desires and beliefs are. The objection would be that if an agent's behaviour or his deciding or choosing are the causal consequences of desires and beliefs, then these cannot be things he *does*, but events which *befall* him. I see the imaginary objector as someone who thinks that an event in respect of which an agent is active cannot be the result of an event in respect of which he is passive. I see him as reasoning that since a person's desires and beliefs are states in respect of which he is passive (in the sense that these are states which occur to him), if these do cause his behaviour then that behaviour is not action. Or, to put his objection another way, if an agent has acted, then this cannot have been caused by desires and beliefs.

Now, we think of trying as necessarily something we do; we tend to think of deciding and choosing as necessarily things we do. All seem to be of their nature active doings.[8] This view of them precludes a view of them as events which occur to agents. If we combine this claim with the claim that activity cannot emerge from passivity, and if both claims are correct, then deciding, choosing, and trying cannot be caused by desires and beliefs.

Such a conclusion might please the U-condition advocate even if it did not have a bearing on agent-causation, for if decisions and choices cannot be caused by desires and beliefs then given two further assumptions, it is plausible to conclude that they cannot be caused at all. These two assumptions are:

1. that our decisions and choices are not caused directly by previous decisions and choices; and
2. that any other state which might be a candidate for the cause of a decision or choice will be a state in respect of which the agent is passive.

And if decisions and choices *could not be caused*, then the U-condition advocate would be entitled to claim that far from suggesting something logically absurd when he speaks of uncaused decisions and choices, he is describing how things logically must be.

But ought we to accept that activity cannot emerge from passivity? Is such a claim self-evident, or should we think of it as based on some other claim (or claims)? Someone who believes that activity cannot emerge from passivity might be tacitly committed to a belief in what I shall call 'the causal transference of passivity principle' (the c.t.p.).[9] The belief can be expressed schematically as follows: if X is passive in respect of ψ-ing and ψ-ing causes X's ϕ-ing, then X is passive in respect of his ϕ-ing.

Ought we to accept the c.t.p.? Is it self-evident or is there some more general principle underlying it which can be examined? The only candidate for such a principle which I can think of is one about the causal transference of all properties, namely that the properties of events are transferred to the events they cause.[10]

Leaving aside for the moment whether this new principle is acceptable, it can be argued that it does not apply to the question we are interested in because being passive in respect of an event is not a property of that event, but a property of the agent.

Perhaps though we could get over this problem by saying that an event's being one which *occurs to* an agent (rather than being one which is brought about by him) is a property of that event. We could then express the c.t.p. as follows: if the onset of X's ψ-ing is an event which occurs to X and X's ψ-ing causes X's ϕ-ing, then his ϕ-ing is an event which occurs to X; or, roughly, if an event which occurs to X causes an event to occur which involves X's mind or body, then that succeeding event can be said to have occurred to X.

But even if it is acceptable to claim that the property of 'occurring to' is attributable to events, there are obvious counter instances to the general principle of the causal transference of properties. Here is one: the event consisting of an orchestral concert has a number of properties. Among these properties are that it lasts for three hours and it involves an orchestra of 80 musicians. The music making event causes various events to occur in the audience, for example their hearing the music, their enjoying it or being bored by it, their having certain thoughts. But there is no reason to think that the fact the music lasts for three hours means that all of these effect-events last three hours. Some members of the audience might enjoy the music for fifteen minutes, be bored by it for half an hour and indifferent to it for the rest of the time. The thoughts which are prompted by it are likely to be discontinuous and when continuous are unlikely to last for three hours. The property of being given by an orchestra of 80 musicians will not be transferred to any of the events which the concert causes.

So if the c.t.p. does depend on this general principle about the transference of all properties, then it should be rejected. But it might be argued that it does not depend on any more general principle, that it is *sui generis*. Or, it might be said that there is a less general principle than that of the transference of *all* properties which could account for the transmission of the 'occurring to' property and perhaps some others, but which could not be invoked to underwrite other claims about alleged transferences. I cannot think of what such a principle might be.

Suppose we assume that the c.t.p. is *sui generis*. Viewed in this way, is it acceptable? While I find the thought that the 'occurring-to' property is causally transferred persuasive in the abstract, I do not find it persuasive when it is applied to concrete cases. It seems indisputable to me that, for instance, trying to do something is not an event which can occur to an agent. But I am not convinced that trying to do something cannot be caused by events which do occur to the agent, such as the onset of desires and beliefs. To accept that tryings can be caused by desires and beliefs is to accept that activity can emerge from passivity, but this seems to be no harder to accept (and perhaps easier) than the belief that at some time in the distant past animate matter emerged from inanimate matter, and yet many of us do accept this, although we find it astonishing.[11]

Since I can think of no compelling arguments for the c.t.p., I conclude that there is no logical barrier to an event's counting as an act even if it is caused by states and events in respect of which the agent is passive, for example his desires and beliefs.

To sum up: so far we have considered an argument against agent-causation to the effect that acts must be caused by desires and we have rejected it. We have also considered three arguments on behalf of the agent-causationist, the first to the effect that action cannot consist in a relationship between an agent's internal states and his behaviour; the second to the effect that acts cannot be events,[12] and the third to the effect that acts cannot be caused by desires and beliefs. All of these arguments have been rejected. So there appears to be a stalemate between the agent-causationist and his opponent.

But there are other arguments against agent-causation which need to be considered. One relies on the claim that the concept of causation is such that we do not count anything as a cause unless (*a*) it is an event and unless (*b*) it is related in a law governed way to the events it causes.[13] The objection based on these claims is that since the doctrine of agent-causation implies that things can bring about events and that the relationship between the thing-cause and the effect-event need not be law governed, the doctrine is logically untenable. I do not find this objection convincing. It does not seem to me to be logically incoherent to claim either that things could cause events or that causal sequences might not instantiate laws. I have already argued for the logical possibility of non-law-governed causal sequences in Chapter 3 and I will not repeat those arguments here.

Those who argue that causation must involve a relationship between events are not daunted by the reply that we often speak in a way which suggests that we think things do cause events. They will acknowledge that in ordinary speech reference is made to the bringing about of effects by substances, for example we say that stones smash windows, trees flatten houses and people cause harm to one another. But the opponents of agent-causation insist that such talk is always translatable into talk of event-causation. In support of this they say things like this: 'When we say that the stone smashed the window what we mean is that the throwing of the stone (or its motion or impact) caused the breaking of the window.[14] When we say that the tree flattened the house, we mean that the falling of the tree caused the flattening of the house. When we say that X hurt Y by striking him, we mean that X's striking out at Y caused the injuring of Y.'

But this answer does not show that our concept of causation logically precludes talk about things causing events. For the sentence translations which are supposed to represent what we mean leave the notion of substances intact. Trees, stones, and people while acknowledged to be involved *in* events, are not themselves reduced to states and events. So it is open to the agent-causationist to say both that an agent's causing of his action is an event and to claim, without inconsistency, that the agent's causing of his act is the *agent's* causing of his act and not events within the agent. To put it another way, the agent-causationist need not deny that X's causing of harm to Y can be described in terms of a link between the event of X's striking out and the event of Y's being injured. But there is no incompatibility between his acknowledging this and his also claiming that if the event of X's striking out is an act, then this event cannot be further analysed into a series of smaller causally linked events.

The notion of agent-causation involves the idea that the agent exercises a causal power. Such a conception is, of course, at odds with the Humean conception of causation from which notions of power have been excised, leaving only the idea of regular succession. But since the Humean conception is itself recognized to be inadequate, it would be unwise to rely on it in order to criticize other conceptions of causation.

It might be claimed, however, that the notion of a causal power is conceptually linked with the idea of event-causation. This is what Davidson seems to be doing when he says that a causal power is 'such that an object that possesses it is caused to change in a certain way if a prior change takes place in the object'.[15] But this is not self-evident. It does not seem incoherent to suggest that an agent might exercise a causal power without having been caused to do so by a prior change.

I feel that none of the arguments which suggest that the doctrine of agent-causation is incoherent succeeds. However, there is an epistemological argument against agent-causation which we ought to consider: it is that the agent-causationist is unable to supply us with criteria for distinguishing between those situations in which agent-causation has occurred and those situations in which events within the agent have caused his behaviour.

There are two forms such an argument might take. It might be argued that there is no evidence that when agents act anything distinct from desire-and-belief-caused behaviour has occurred. In support of this one would have to show that whenever a decision or action occurs there is a preceding chain of events, consisting (at least partly) of desires and beliefs (or perhaps their neurophysiological realizations) which is causally sufficient for the agent's resulting behaviour, and which thus affords us no reason for thinking that a kind of causation has occurred which is different from causation by states and events within the agent.

But could one *show* this? Isn't it always open to the agent-causationist to say that although it looks as if these states are causally sufficient, looks could be deceptive? This would be a very weak response unless the agent-causationist could give us some reason, apart from mere logical possibility, for thinking that these states were not causally sufficient.

One way he might try to do this is by arguing that the appearance of causal sufficiency exists only from the perspective of the outside investigator (such as the psychologist or the neurophysiologist) and not from the point of view of the decision maker himself. From that internal point of view, it seems that there is no causal link between desire and decision, for we do not feel caused by our desires to make the decisions we do. Should this not be taken as evidence that we are not caused to do so? I argue later that it should not be taken as evidence for the absence of causation. But this prompts the question, why if the way something feels (from the inside) is not sufficient evidence of the way it is, should we assume that the way something looks (from the outside) *is* sufficient evidence for the way it is? The answer cannot be that the external point of view is one which is available to a number of people, while the internal point of view is available only to the individual, because all conscious individuals enjoy the internal point of view,[16] and all (or at least most) decision makers will have experienced the 'sense of freedom' in respect of their decision making. All of this suggests that in the first form, the epistemological argument cannot be wielded decisively either by the opponent or the advocate of agent-causation.

In its second form, the epistemological argument against agent-causation consists of the claim that there could never be evidence which established that agents caused their actions (or decisions) because any such evidence could be interpreted in ways which conflicted with this.

For example, suppose instead of an unbroken causal chain between desires and decisions, there was some kind of 'gap' just before the decision (or action). It might then be argued that this is evidence *for* agent-causation. Thorp in *Free Will* seems to be suggesting this when he says:

It is the events in the nervous system which would constitute the most detailed train of causally linked events leading up to action. If this train of sufficient causes is broken just before the action (or decision) then the proposed analysis of the alleged agent causality into event causality does not succeed. The events in the agent leading up to the action do not amount to sufficient conditions for the action. (pp. 100–1.)

But it could also be argued that whatever picture one has of a causal gap (or, as Thorp puts it, a 'broken' causal chain), it would be equally plausible to interpret the evidence of its existence as something which supports alternatives to agent-causation.

For instance, suppose that one pictures a state of affairs in which something is missing from the cluster of conditions which usually precede an action of a given type and yet action occurs. The agent-causationist might say that in such a case the action must have occurred because the agent caused it. But the same state of affairs could suggest either that the cluster of conditions which remained was sufficient to produce the action without the 'missing' condition or that the action which occurred was not caused.

Suppose, on the other hand, that what one had in mind when one imagined a causal gap was a state of affairs in which the cluster of conditions which often preceded actions was some-times not followed by actions. The agent-causationist might suggest that a plausible explanation of the fact that the con-ditions were often but not always followed by actions was that when there were actions it was due to the agent's having caused them and when there were not it was because the agent had not caused them.

But this is not the only way in which one could interpret such a situation. For we could explain the fact that the conditions were sometimes not followed by actions by saying that these conditions, although often causally productive, were not always causally productive. (Here I am relying on the argument in Chapter 3 that we can understand a cause as something which produces an effect, but which does not have to produce that effect.). So the existence of a causal gap would not give us a con-clusive reason to plump for agent rather than event causation.

Suppose, though, that the regular conjunction of event-types failed to occur *only in circumstances which involved the inten-tional behaviour of human beings*. Would this not be conclusive evidence of agent as opposed to event-causation? No, it would not be conclusive because we could interpret it as a case of inter-mittent causal productivity on the part of the states which usually preceded actions. But it would, I think, be more plaus-ible to claim it as evidence for agent-causation than for intermit-tent causal productivity.

This defence will probably not be of any practical help to the agent-causationist. For some scientists believe that indeterminism holds at the micro-level among the basic constituents of matter, so there is a good chance that the supposition, that regular conjunction might only fail in circumstances involving intentional action, would not be confirmed.

But the point about plausibility can be used to mount a general attack against the second form of the epistemological argument.[17] For that argument suggests that one can only legitimately accept something as evidence for a particular thesis if the evidence cannot be interpreted in other ways. But this is surely an unacceptable requirement since one can always find *some* alternative interpretation of evidence which has been taken, on the grounds of plausibility (and perhaps also economy), to be evidence for a particular claim. To insist that such evidence should bear no other logically possible interpretation would be to condemn us to perpetual uncertainty about everything. This might be gratifying for the confirmed sceptic, but it could hardly be comforting to the opponent of agent-causation, since it would mean that there could never be a legitimate reason to plump for event rather than agent-causation.

With the rejection of the second epistemological argument, we seem to be left with no way of decisively refuting agent-causation. On the other hand, apart from the appeal to the phenomenology of decision making, I do not know of any evidence which can be construed, more plausibly than not, as evidence *for* its existence. And since, as I argue later, the appeal to phenomenology does not work, it does not look as if there are any convincing reasons for accepting it. So once again, we have reached a stalemate.

But perhaps there is no need for the libertarian incompatibilist to invoke the doctrine of agent-causation. He does so, it will be remembered, because he accepts the assumption of his challengers that events which are uncaused are *ipso facto* events for which agents could not be morally responsible. I think this assumption ought to be questioned. I believe there is a case for saying that agents could be morally responsible for some kinds of uncaused events, namely those which consist in their choosing or deciding to do something or other.

I(*b*): We could be morally responsible for some uncaused events

Suppose, for the sake of argument, that there are such things as uncaused choosings and decidings. Why should this mean that agents are not morally responsible for them? As we have seen, the answer usually given is that uncaused events are 'accidental', 'random', 'chance' or 'fortuitous' and that their being these things makes it logically untenable to attribute responsibility for them to an agent.

But what is it about accidental or fortuitous events which is thought to preclude responsibility for them? I think it is assumed that such events could not be deliberately brought about by the agent, but would be like bolts from the blue; things which unexpectedly happened to him.

Now there are two worries in this assumption about uncaused events:

1. that they are events which happen to the agent, that is events in respect of which he is passive; and
2. that they are events which happen *unexpectedly* to the agent.

The first worry is not one which applies to deciding or choosing because, as suggested earlier, deciding and choosing are of necessity things which an agent *does* and not things which happen to him. Since they are of their nature active doings, they cannot be events in respect of which the agent is passive.

Someone might say "But a person could find himself deciding or choosing something in the same way he might find himself thinking about or desiring something." If this means that he could find a decision or choice occurring to him, as he might find a thought occurring to him or a desire growing in him, then for the reason given above this can be denied. If, on the other hand, it means that he might find himself making a decision or choice which is totally unexpected there are two things one can say in reply to this.

First, in one sense, the situation with which we are concerned cannot be one in which the making of a decision (or choice) is unexpected. For we are concerned with situations in which a person has been confronted by the knowledge that there is something he ought (morally) to do (or not to do). That is, he has been confronted by a situation which called for a decision (or choice) either to act in a way which he knew to be morally wrong or to act as he knew he ought to. Thus, there having been a decision (or choice) to flout the moral requirement is not so at odds with what might have been expected that it can be said to be like a bolt from the blue.

However, it might now be objected, that we need to distinguish between what might have been expected from the situation and what might have been expected from the agent. And, the objection would continue, it could be that the agent's making *that* decision was unexpected; that it was at odds with what might have been expected *of him*. Perhaps the agent was surprised to find himself deciding differently from the way in which he had decided in the past. If the decision were unexpected in this way for the agent, then would we not feel that he should not be held responsible for acting as the result of it?

This brings me to the second point which is that if the agent did find himself making a surprising decision or choice this would not automatically justify our exempting him from blame for acting as the result of it. For decisions and choices can be reversed and it can be argued that in acting on that decision (or choice) however surprising to him that he had made it, the agent was endorsing it. Furthermore, it would not follow from the fact that a decision (or choice) was uncaused that it was a surprising decision. An agent's decisions and choices might be consistent in type, although uncaused by previous events, or they might be consistent in type even though some were caused and some were uncaused.

To sum up: because of the nature of decidings and choosings the property of occurring-to-agents which is thought to militate against moral responsibility cannot be one which decidings or choosings have, whether caused or uncaused. The property of unexpectedness which is also thought to militate against moral responsibility does not necessarily militate against moral responsibility and, in any case, need not be a property which is possessed by uncaused decidings or choosings.

If I am right then there is no need for the U-condition advocate to defend the doctrine of agent-causation, because uncaused events are not *ipso facto* events for which we cannot be morally responsible.[18]

I(c): A threat to the claim that deciding is an event in respect of which the agent is active

The main force of the claim that uncaused choices and decisions could figure in events for which an agent is morally responsible comes from the assumption that both deciding and choosing are doings rather than happenings-to. But this assumption has been challenged in respect of decisions. In his book, *The Will*, Brian O'Shaughnessy argues that deciding-to-do is not an activity but an 'inactive event' which (usually but not always) emerges from an 'active' process of trying to decide.[19] (The terms 'active' and 'inactive' as applied to events are, of course, inappropriate. What O'Shaughnessy means, I assume, is that deciding-to-do is an event in respect of which the decision maker is inactive. But for the sake of convenience, I shall retain his terminology.) O'Shaughnessy divides events of deciding into two kinds, first, deciding whether something or other is the case and secondly, deciding to do something. The first sort of deciding he equates with an event of coming-to-believe and the second with an event of coming-to-intend. He argues persuasively that when one tries to decide whether or not some proposition is true, although the attempt to decide is an activity, the emergence of the 'cognitive commitment', that is the conviction that such and such is the case, is not itself an act; we do not 'will ourselves' to believe; the belief crystallizes independently of the will. He goes on to suggest that deciding-to-do is also an inactive event which emerges from the activity of trying to decide. And he bases this claim on the suggestion that trying to decide what to do is (often) the same enterprise as trying to decide whether, for when we are trying to decide what to do the uncertainty we are trying to resolve is an uncertainty about whether one course of action would be better in some way than another. O'Shaughnessy claims that once we have resolved the uncertainty about which course of action is better, we have resolved the uncertainty about which to do, so that the practical commitment in the form of a deciding to do (or coming-to-intend) emerges as the result of the 'cognitive crystallization' (the coming-to-believe). Thus the conclusion we are invited to endorse is that although coming-to-believe and coming-to-intend are distinct events, they are both the inactive emergences of the one enterprise of trying to decide.[20]

However, while I agree with O'Shaughnessy that we cannot end a process of deliberation with a 'short sharp act of willing belief', I am not convinced that we might not end it with what could be called an *act* of deciding-to-do.[21] Suppose, for instance, that an agent cannot make up his mind. Might he not, in order to end the uncertainty, simply plump for one option and would not this be an event of deciding in respect of which he was active? And, even in cases where the agent makes up his mind about which is the best course, can we not say that when on this basis he then decides what to do, this deciding is a separate and positive act of affirmation which one might imagine being accompanied by the thought, 'Right, I'll do that then.'?

But O'Shaughnessy has another suggestion which might be invoked in answer to this. He claims that there can be no order 'decide to do that' from which we are supposed to conclude that there can be no act of 'deciding to do that'.[22] He does not spell out the argument, but I imagine it would go like this: the order 'decide to do that' is senseless because it would be logically impossible to respond to it and it would be logically impossible to respond to it because there can be no action of deciding to do that.

There are two points which can be made in response to this: the first is that the reason it would be logically impossible to respond to this order is not one which entails that there can be no action of deciding. The reason it is absurd to order someone to 'decide to do that' has already been touched on in our previous discussion: deciding to do that involves the resolving of doubt about what to do and this doubt presupposes doubt about what the best course of action would be. The resolving of this latter doubt consists of a coming-to-believe. Thus the order 'decide to do that' would seem to be one which requires us to respond by first believing something and then committing ourselves to the course of action believed to be best. But we cannot (logically cannot) believe at will, so the command is absurd. Note, however, that the explanation of its absurdity would not undermine the suggestion made earlier that once we have come-to-believe one course of action would be better than another we could then actively decide to do that thing. The second point is that there can be logically appropriate orders to decide, namely orders like 'Decide (or make up your mind) by tomorrow.' Thus, if O'Shaughnessy's point about orders and acts relies on the assumption that it is a necessary condition of something's being an act that an order in respect of it be logically appropriate then deciding could be an act.

I(*d*): The distinction between deciding and choosing

But even if O'Shaughnessy were right about deciding, this would not mean that we had to abandon the earlier conclusion that some uncaused events could be ones for which an agent is morally responsible. For we are not bound to assume that all blameworthy offenders with whom we are concerned must be described as having *decided* to do something which they knew to be morally wrong. Not all offenders are uncertain about what to do before they act and many could more accurately be described as having 'chosen' to do something which they knew to be morally wrong, for the term 'choice' unlike the term 'decided' does not presuppose an uncertainty which must be resolved. A man can be said to have chosen to do something so long as he was aware of alternatives; he does not have to have been in the least attracted by the alternative he did not choose. Since there need be no indecision prior to the making of a choice, there is no reason to suppose that the event of choosing is an inactive emergence from the procedure of actively trying to choose. And one other consideration in favour of the claim that choosing is an event in respect of which the agent is active, is that there is no logical absurdity in the order 'Choose *that* one instead of that one.'

So far, I have argued that we could be morally responsible for uncaused deciding and choosing, but can events of deciding and choosing *be* uncaused?

Part II: Can there be uncaused decisions and choices?

There are two claims which, if true, have the consequence that no event of deciding could be uncaused. These two claims are (*a*) that the nature of deciding is such that any deciding must be for a reason; and (*b*) that doing something for a reason is a matter of doing that thing as the result of a cause (which involves desires and beliefs). I think that both claims are true.

II(*a*): Deciding must involve reasons

I shall discuss (*a*) first. Deciding is (necessarily) the resolving of doubt.[23] To decide is to make up one's mind about something, so any event of deciding must be preceded by uncertainty on the part of the decision maker. It is an event which one normally assumes to be the outcome of a process of trying to decide. But what could trying to decide consist in if not the consideration first of one option and then another? And it is surely the case that any agent who seriously does this must be searching for a basis on which to make his decision, that is a reason for deciding one way rather than another.

Furthermore, it seems plausible to say that an agent engages in the procedure of trying to decide because he has a desire to resolve the uncertainty he feels. Uncertainty is uncomfortable and discomfort, one assumes, gives rise to a desire to be rid of it. Such a desire can be said to serve as one's reason for trying to decide. Thus the doubt which is resolved by deciding provides the reason for the activity of trying to decide as well as a reason for searching for a reason to decide one way rather than another. It is hard to escape the conclusion that deciding must be deciding for a reason.

It might be objected that deciding need not be preceded by a process of rumination. A person can sleep on a problem and wake up the next morning having decided without its being the case that while asleep he was engaged in a procedure of weighing one consideration against another.[24] Since *ex hypothesi* such a decision would not have been preceded by a trying to decide, it might be thought that this sort of deciding-to-do-one-thing-rather-than-another is not based on any reason. But even if there is no reason to which one can point as the agent's reason for deciding to do this rather than that, it is hard to believe that his deciding anything at all was not prompted by a desire to end the uncertainty, a desire which prompted him to 'sleep on it' in the hope that things would be clearer in the morning. Thus it seems likely that deciding is always the result of a reason in the form of the agent's desire to resolve doubt. But one could also challenge the assumption that there is no process of deliberation preceding a decision on waking. Perhaps when asleep we are subconsciously weighing up the pros and cons of a course of action.

Have the arguments used here established that the claim that deciding must be for a reason is logically necessary? I am not sure whether there is a contradiction in the claim that one can resolve uncertainty (decide) for no reason, but I nevertheless believe it to be incomprehensible that the agent's doubt should not constitute his reason for trying to resolve it, for I find it an incredible thought that he should feel doubt and try to resolve it (decide what to do) without the two psychological phenomena (the feeling of uncertainty and the trying to decide) being connected. I would say that reasonless decisions are more than an empirical impossibility, and for want of a term for the kind of impossibility which amounts to inconceivability, but which may fall short of the sort of impossibility whose description is self-contradictory, I propose to fall back on the term 'logical impossibility' to describe reasonless decisions.

Choices can be reasonless

The arguments above apply to decisions. They do not apply to choices. For, as we noted earlier, choice unlike decision does not require (although it may be preceded by) uncertainty about what to do. I would suggest that it is logically possible for someone to have chosen to do what he did in full awareness that there was an alternative without having had any desire to do what he did or any desire not to do what he chose not to do. Such a choice could, I think, be called reasonless.

So if, as Davidson has powerfully argued, reasons *are* causes, then there could be one kind of uncaused event for which moral responsibility is logically possible, namely an act of choosing without reason.

Suppose for the moment that it is inconceivable that reasons should not be causes (I think Davidson's most powerful argument implies this). Then what would the implication be for the U-condition advocate of this conclusion coupled with the conclusions we have already reached about decisions and choices?

We must remember that in Chapter 3 we established that the U-condition advocate could reasonably argue that fulfilment of the U-condition was possible in two ways:

1. if the morally reprehensible decision or choice was the result of an uncaused decision or choice for which the agent was morally responsible; and
2. if the morally reprehensible decision or choice was itself uncaused.

But if decisions must (logically) be for reasons and if reasons must (logically) be causes, then fulfilment of the U-condition by either an uncaused decision or a choice for reasons is not logically possible.

So the U-condition advocate would have to modify his claim. He would now have to say that fulfilment of the U-condition could only be achieved by:

1. A morally reprehensible decision or choice which is the result of an uncaused choice for which the agent is morally responsible; or
2. an uncaused morally reprehensible choice.

But the U-condition advocate who is a *libertarian* could hardly be satisfied with this theory of blameworthiness for it would exclude many decisions and choices which by any account are morally reprehensible, for example those motivated entirely by greed or selfishness. This is because it implies that blameworthiness could only be attributed to someone for motiveless choices (2) or for decisions and choices which have themselves been caused by motiveless choices (1). It implies that no matter how reprehensible the reason for a decision or choice, that decision or choice could not be blame-conferring unless its origin could be traced to a choice which was made for no reason.

So it is in the libertarian U-condition advocate's interests to argue against the thesis that reasons are causes.

Now if he is to argue against this, then he must explain how desires can be relevant to (say) the decision making process without being causally efficacious. And he must do so not only for the reasons mentioned above but also beause, so far as we are aware, desires are so often 'there' preceding decisions, choices, and behaviour and it is generally assumed that they must play a role in the bringing about of these events and that the role they play is that of a motivating impulse (force, inclination) towards action.

But I believe that the arguments *for* the claim that there is a causal connection are very strong, that the arguments *against* it are very weak, and that the U-condition advocate has no hope of providing an alternative account which will be as satisfactory as a causal one. In what follows, I shall present my reasons for believing that a causal account is the right one. I shall begin (II(*b*)) with a summary of the traditional objections to the causal theorist's position and the answers which can be made to these objections. Then, I shall present the causal theorist's positive arguments for the reasons-as-causes thesis and will follow this by citing objections which can be made to his thesis as a thesis about the relationship between desires and *decisions*. I shall then offer a causal account of the relationship between desires and decisions which can meet these further objections. Finally, (II(*c*)), I shall examine a recent attempt to provide a non-causal account of the relationship between desires and decisions and shall argue that it fails.

II(*b*): The traditional case against the reasons-as-causes thesis and the response to it

Many of the objections which have been raised have largely relied on the assumption that reasons cannot fulfil those logical conditions which must be fulfilled by anything that is to qualify as a cause. Thus, it is argued that:

(*a*) causes must be events and desires and beliefs are not events but states;

(*b*) causing events must be distinct from the events they cause, but reasons are not distinct from actions;[25] and

(*c*) any causal sequence must be law governed, but the connections between reasons for action and actions are not law governed.

The first point can be resisted on two grounds:[26]

1. An agent's reason for acting could consist of the onset of certain desires and beliefs and the onset, or the coming to have these desires and beliefs, is an event.

2. Even as states, desires and beliefs could qualify as causally relevant to behaviour, in the same way that the weakened state of a bridge is causally relevant to its collapse. As states, desires and beliefs could be contributors to the efficient cause; they would be an indispensable part of the causal background without which some triggering event like the thought, 'Now is the right time to do this' would be ineffective.

The argument for (b) is that reasons are not distinct from actions because statements about the existence of reasons for action contain references to the actions. The obvious answer to this is that the fact that the descriptions of events are conceptually linked does not mean that the events themselves are not distinct.

Those who are worried by the fact that the descriptions of reasons often contain references to the actions they are reasons for seem to think that if there is a conceptual connection between descriptions, this connection must be one of logical necessity. And since there is no logically necessary connection between events they conclude that the events described in an explanation of actions which cite reasons cannot be causally connected. But their anxiety rests on two confusions, one is the mistaken belief that all conceptual connections must be logically necessary connections and the second is the mistaken belief that a logically necessary connection between descriptions of things is somehow projected onto what is described.

I turn now to (c), the claim that the connections between reasons and actions, unlike causal connections, are not law governed. I have argued in Chapter 3 that it is not logically necessary that causal sequences be deterministic, which implies that law governedness of the deterministic kind is not essential to the concept of causation. Of course, this still leaves the possibility that law governedness of an indeterministic (probabilistic) kind is essential to the concept of causation.[27] I do not think it is essential, but even if it were, one could argue that there is no reason why a sequence of events involving beliefs, desires, and actions should not be law governed.

It might be claimed that we could never know what such a law was for it would be impossible to know all the conditions which would have to be fulfilled before we could say that certain desires and beliefs would always (or usually) be followed by certain actions. But from the fact that we could never know what such a law was, it does not follow that there could not be such laws. They might be too complex for us ever to be able to state them, but there is no reason to assume that laws cannot be so complex.[28]

Another argument which is sometimes used by those opposed to the claim that reasons are causes is that a person can only know that one event causes another on the basis of inductive evidence (evidence of the past constant conjunction of certain event sequences); whereas he does not need to make any observations about past behaviour to find out what his reasons for an action are; he knows this straightaway.

One obvious objection to this is that what one knows about something is not a property of the thing itself so that it is not legitimate to argue that because one knows immediately what one's reasons are but does not know immediately that one event has caused another, our reasons cannot be causes.

In answer to this one could suggest that just as there are properties which are intrinsic to an object (event or substance) which permit us to be aware of it, visibility for example, it could be that there are properties intrinsic to an object which permit us to know of its existence straightaway, and perhaps causes lack this feature while reasons have it. However, one might argue that reasons are a distinctive kind of cause and that part of their distinctiveness lies in their being immediately knowable by the person who has them.

But a more promising argument is to deny that the knowledge conditions for reasons and causes are always different. We often take ourselves to be justified in believing that event sequences are causal on the basis of only one instance, and we also acknowledge that we can be mistaken about what out reasons for action are. So the only way of conclusively establishing what our reasons for a particular action were might be to look at other situations where we behaved in the same sort of way, which would be like confirming that one event caused another by looking at similar past event sequences.

Another way of bolstering the claim that knowledge conditions for reasons and causes are of the same sort is to invoke the causal theory of knowledge; the theory that someone's belief can only qualify as knowledge if it is causally connected in some appropriate way to that part of the world which the belief is about. For then one could say that just as it is a necessary condition for knowing that one event caused another, that the causal connection between those events was (in part) causally responsible for the belief that the connection was causal, so it is a necessary condition for knowing what our reasons for action were that the operativeness of those reasons was causally responsible for the belief that they were our reasons. (Of course this bare outline would have to be filled in with a mass of detail which is missing here and there could well be problems involved in doing so, for example how does the causal connection produce beliefs about itself?)

So the negative arguments against the reasons-as-causes thesis can be rebutted. But what are the positive arguments for it?

The positive arguments for the reasons-as-causes thesis

One argument of Pears's is that the only way to explain the fact (when it is a fact) that sometimes an agent who knows what he wants to do also knows that he will do it is to assume that there is a causal connection between wanting and doing.[29] I find this fairly persuasive.

A second argument for the thesis is this: many philosophers agree that part of what is meant by the claim that one event, A, caused another, B, is that if A had not occurred B would not have occurred. But we can say the same sort of thing about the connection between an agent's reason for acting and his action. We assume that an agent's having had a particular reason for acting was a necessary condition for his acting in that way at that time; which is to say that if he had not had that reason, he would not have acted in that way at that time. This is implied in statements such as, 'He acted as he did because he wanted to.'

This brings me to an argument of Davidson's which I find entirely convincing.[30] Davidson claims that only a causal picture of the relationship between desires, beliefs, and actions can do justice to the meaning of the 'because' in such statements. He argues that unless we assume that when someone acts for certain reasons there is a causal connection between reasons and action, we cannot account for the difference between:

1. the claim that when he acted, he had certain reasons for doing so; and
2. the claim that when he acted, he acted *for* those particular reasons.

The point is that it could be true that he had certain reasons for acting and yet false that he acted for those reasons. (He might have acted for other reasons.)

In other words, we can only make sense of the idea that those reasons were operative in bringing about his action, if we assume that they were *causally* operative.

I see this last argument as a conceptual one; as one which implies that it is inconceivable that a reason could be operative in action without being a cause. On this basis, I conclude that the claim that reasons are causes is not just empirical; I think of it as having logical force.

But while the positive arguments for the reasons-as-causes thesis are convincing in connection with action, we need further arguments for the claim that the connection between reasons and decisions is causal. First, because some of the arguments used by the causal theorists in connection with action do not seem applicable to the relationship between desires and decisions. One of these is Pears's claim that an agent knows what he will do because his desire causally produces his act. This cannot be applied to the desire-decision relationship because we do not know what we will decide before we deliberate and it might be thought that the reason we do not know is that our desires do not cause our decisions.[31]

Also, the image suggested by Davidson's account of what is involved in acting for a reason cannot be extended to deciding for a reason. The image suggested by that account is something like this: one has a desire for something and a belief that (say) ϕ-ing will fulfil it. This generates a desire to do that thing (to ϕ) and the onset of this desire causes the behaviour which constitutes an attempt to fulfil that desire. This won't do as an image of decision making because the desire which an agent decides to fulfil cannot straightforwardly be said to cause the decision to fulfil it. And this is to do with the fact that deciding is not simply a rubber-stamping procedure serving no purpose beyond that of carrying forward the motivational thrust of whatever desire happens to be present. One decides (often) *between* desires so the image of a simple causal sequence of desire-decision-action is not appropriate.

We also need further arguments about decisions in order to answer the objection that a causal theory is unable to account for the phenomenology of decision making (or choosing between alternatives). The full objection is that since we do not feel caused to decide in a certain way by our desires, we should take this as an indication that we might not be caused to decide (or to choose) by our desires.

In what follows, I shall present a causal account of the relationship between desires and decisions which meets these objections. It is an account which does justice to our belief that the relationship must be more complex than that suggested by Davidson's arguments about action, which explains why we do not feel caused to decide by our desires and, finally, why we have a sense of freedom in respect of our decisions.

A causal account of decision making

There are different kinds of uncertainty which an agent who is trying to decide might experience, for example:

1. He might not be sure which of two or more courses of action to take in order to get what he wants; or
2. he might have conflicting desires; or
3. he might be aware that (or unsure whether) there are reasons against doing what he wants to do. (This need not be a situation in which those reasons are other desires of his.)

In the first situation, he has to decide between the different ways of getting what he wants. In the second situation he has to decide which of his competing wants he should attempt to fulfil and in the third situation once he has established that there are reasons against doing what he wants to do, he must decide between his desire and these other reasons.

In all of the situations in which he is called on to decide what to do, his being prompted to undertake the attempt to decide is in part the result of the initial desires which exert a pressure for fulfilment and in part the result of a desire to relieve the discomfort of uncertainty. (See my earlier discussion on the uncertainty which is presupposed by decision making.)

Given Davidson's claim about the operativeness of reasons, we can conclude that it is only if the relationship between the desires mentioned and the attempt to decide is causal that we can make sense of the thought that it was because the agent wanted to end his uncertainty and thereby relieve (at least some of) the pressures on him that he began to deliberate about what to do.

Furthermore, it seems reasonable to suppose that the decision an agent actually comes to is (partly) the causal result of (*a*) what one might call a 'deliberation-guiding' desire, that is a desire whose content is something like 'desire to do whatever will yield the most satisfactory (or least unsatisfactory) result' and (*b*) a belief about how this can be achieved. In type-1 situations such a belief could be one to the effect that taking this course of action rather than that will best ensure fulfilment of the desire; in situations of type 2, the belief might be that acting on this desire rather than that will yield the most satisfactory result and the belief in type-3 situations might be that acting for *these* reasons rather than fulfilling the desire would be best. Note that the deliberation-guiding desire need not be a selfish one; whether it is or not will depend on what the agent takes to be 'the most satisfactory result'.

It might be thought that it is taking too much for granted to assume that there are deliberation-guiding desires. But I would suggest that it is highly unlikely that there are not. The uncertainty about action experienced by our agent is an uncertainty about which course of action would be best. But why should he be prompted by such uncertainty to begin to deliberate unless he is concerned to do what is best all things considered, and is it not reasonable to say that this concern is a kind of desire?

The important thing to note for our discussion at the moment is that in none of these three types of situation would it be correct to say that there was a straightforward relationship beween the desires to do (or to have) something (that is the desires which are the objects of deliberation) and the decisions to act on them such that it would not be misleading to say simply that the desire to do (or to have) something caused the decision to fulfil that desire. Of course the desire to do (or to have) such and such plays an essential role in the outcome, but its role is to initiate the deliberation procedure; it does not *immediately* prompt the decision.

To sum up: when one decides to fulfil a certain desire, one's decision is not straightforwardly caused by the desire one decides to fulfil; rather one's decision is caused by (*a*) the desire to resolve uncertainty which prompts the attempt to decide; (*b*) the desire to do what will yield the most satisfactory result; and (*c*) the belief that this (whichever desire it is decided to fulfil) will fulfil (*b*). The desire one decides to fulfil plays an essential part in the beginning of the deliberation process and in this respect is part of the causal picture, but it is not *this* desire which triggers the actual decision.

This helps to explain the phenomenology of decision making in the sense that it helps to explain why an agent feels a distance between himself as a decision maker and the desire he decides to fulfil. It is because the desire he decides to fulfil is not the immediate prompter of the decision, while the desires which prompt the decision to fulfil it are not themselves the subject of the decision.

However, it might be felt that in saying this we have not said all there is to say about what it feels like to decide and that what more there is to say militates against a causal account. The objection would go like this: you have purported to explain why agents do not feel caused to decide by the desires they decide to fulfil by positing other desires as immediate causal prompters. But one doesn't feel caused to decide by these so-called causally prompting desires, one does not feel caused to attempt to resolve uncertainty by the desire to do so, nor does one feel caused to decide by the desire to do whatever will yield the most satisfactory result. Why not accept appearances as an indication of reality and conclude that our not feeling caused by these desires is evidence that we are not caused to decide by them? Why not accept on the basis of the phenomenology that a reason for deciding is not a cause of deciding?

In answer to this, I begin by again invoking Davidson's insight that the operativeness of our reasons is best accounted for by a causal picture. But, even more pertinently, I reject the assumption that if reasons *are* causes, we must *feel* caused to decide (or to choose). Perhaps this assumption is based on an image of mental causation described by Professor Anscombe as that of 'pushing in another medium'.[32] But the 'pushing' image is not even appropriate for all purely physical causal sequences, for example that of a river's flowing towards the sea. And in sequences involving sentient beings where *some* mechanical image is appropriate (not necessarily a pushing one), it is not always the case that the experiences of those involved reflect the particular causal mechanism. Thus one might say that when someone falls to the ground, his falling is, in part, the causal result of the 'pulling' force of gravity, but he need not *feel* pulled towards the earth. Of course, (if he is conscious) he may well feel himself to be falling, but this is not the same thing as feeling 'pulled down' or 'caused to fall'. Furthermore, there are many connections involving psychological states which we acknowledge to be causal connections although they are not accompanied by a feeling of 'being caused to'. For example, the music excites me. I believe there is a causal connection between my hearing the music and my feeling of excitement, but I don't feel *caused* to be excited. I become angry at the sight of something. I believe there is a causal connection between my visual experience and my feeling of anger, but I do not feel caused to be angry. Of course, we sometimes do feel drawn towards or compelled by; we sometimes experience our desires as forces, but we do not always feel these things when we consciously react and yet often when we do not we still assume that our reactions have been caused.

In case there are lingering phenomenological doubts about treating reasons as causes, it is worth adding that there are times when we feel we have been caused to decide (pushed into deciding) or to choose and yet would not on this account deny that we have decided for reasons. For example, I might have to decide between competing desires and wish I did not because I want badly to fulfil both of them. It is likely that in such a situation I will feel that I have been caused to decide, and the unsatisfied desire will intensify my feeling that I *had* to make a decision, for it will remain (as O'Shaughnessy would say) as a 'force towards striving'[33] whose undrained energy will express itself in feelings of tension. Or, I might not want to choose what to do just now but believe that I must do so. I will in such a circumstance feel pushed into choosing but this does not mean that the choice or the action which succeeds it will be reasonless.

A final argument about the phenomenology of decision making: it is sometimes said that we have a 'sense of freedom' when we make decisions and choices. I believe that the sense of freedom is quite consistent with and can even be explained by the causal account of decision making.

I take the sense of freedom to consist partly in the belief which accompanies our awareness that there are competing claims on us, that neither (none) of these claims binds us in advance of our deliberations to honour it in preference to the others; partly in a feeling of distance between ourselves as decision makers and the desires (or other claims) which exert their pressure for fulfilment; and partly in a lack of awareness of the desire which accounts for the particular decisions we make, namely the desire to do the best possible thing in the circumstances (what I have called 'the deliberation-guiding desire'). It is understandable that we should not be aware of this latter desire, since it is an abiding presence, such a constant feature of our lives that we do not notice it. (One does not notice a constant pressure.)

Furthermore, as I have already argued, athough desires to act play a part in the beginning of the deliberation process and in this respect are part of the causal picture, the feeling of distance between the decision maker and these desires which he considers for possible fulfilment can be explained by the fact that the role played by these desires is mediated by the prompting of other desires (and beliefs) such as the deliberation-guiding desire and the desire to resolve uncertainty.

As for the belief that we are not bound in advance of our deliberations to choose one desire for fulfilment rather than another, *if determinism is true*, then this belief is false in one respect and true in another. It is false if it means that the way our deliberations will go is not determined, but it is true if it means that our decisions depend on our deliberations. In this sense the truth of determinism is compatible with the claim that our decisions are up to us (although they would not be up to us in the ultimate sense required by the U-condition advocate).

Furthermore, since, as I have indicated in Chapter 3, determinism could be false while it remained true that every event had a cause, one can see that even the belief that the course of our deliberations is not determined could be both true and yet consistent with a causal picture of such deliberations and their outcomes.

I hope it is clear that the compatibility between the sense of freedom and the causal picture is in no way undermining of the U-condition advocate's claim that a person whose decisions are the causal result of desires and beliefs is not morally responsible for those decisions or the behaviour which is their causal result (unless he is responsible for the desires themselves as the result of an earlier uncaused choice or decision).

II(*c*): Perhaps motives influence without causing

The arguments we have considered so far offer no hope to the U-condition libertarian who would like to feel that we are justified in blaming the vast majority of ordinary wrongdoers whose morally reprehensible decisions and choices have not been caused by some ultimate reasonless choice.

In his book, *Free Will*, Thorp provides an account of the relationship between an agent's motives and his decisions which might be thought to offer such hope. He argues that while desires influence the agent they are not (or need not be) the causes of his decisions.[34] This suggests that there could be a non-causal relationship between desires and decisions which both fulfils the U-condition and allows for the existence of reasons.

But the acceptability of Thorp's account depends on whether it can offer a plausible non-causal interpretation of claims such as 'X decided to ϕ because he wanted such and such' which does justice to the Davidsonian insight about the operativeness of reasons. I do not think that it does (or that it can) offer such an interpretation.

First some general remarks: the claim that motives are influences but not causes is, at first sight, both intuitively odd and intuitively appealing. It is odd because one feels that the influencing relationship must, at least, *depend* on a causal connection between the influencing object and the subject's awareness of that object and since this is so it is natural to assume that the influencing relationship itself consists in the subject's being causally affected by the object in such a way that he responds to it. It is natural to assume this because it is natural to think that if a causal explanation for the subject's awareness of the object is satisfactory, then it will also be satisfactory as an explanation of the response to that awareness, once one adds (causally) relevant factors such as affective dispositions.

Of course there is no logical compulsion to argue from the premiss that awareness of objects involves a causal component to the conclusion that the response to that awareness must also involve a causal component. So it is open to Thorp to say that even if the influencing relationship depends on a causal connection between the influencing object and the subject's awareness of it, this does not mean that the influencing relationship itself consists of a causal connection between awareness and response to awareness. And indeed, as we shall see, Thorp's arguments centre on what happens after the agent's awareness of his motives.

But if we are to be persuaded to drop the natural assumption that the influencing relationship is a causal one, then we need more than an argument to the effect that the denial of the assumption is logically coherent.

Now I said at the beginning that the claim that motives are influences but not causes is also intuitively appealing, and this might be thought to suggest that some of our beliefs about the influencing relationship are at odds with the natural assumption just mentioned. But this is not so. The intuitive appeal of the claim lies, I think, in our awareness that it would be wrong to interpret the sentence 'He was influenced by X to Y' by means of the sentence 'He was caused by X to Y.' But this is not incompatible with the claim that influences are causes. The claim 'He was caused by X to Y' can be construed as one which implies force or compulsion and we recognize that to be influenced is not to be forced. But, as has been pointed out many times, the claim that there is a causal relationship between a person's desires and his actions need not imply any claim about compulsion. To be compelled to do something is to be forced to do it against one's will. To feel compelled to do something is to feel that even if one wanted to one couldn't resist. But an unbroken causal chain of events between the desire and the decision to respond to it need not include any sequence in which what the agent does is against his will, nor any sequence in which the agent has a feeling of powerlessness such as the one described. Note how much more innocuous it sounds to say that desires cause our decisions than it does to say that we are caused by our desires to decide, particularly if we bear in mind the earlier discussion about the complexity of the causal processes involved in decision making.

I suspect that whatever appeal Thorp's claim has it is an appeal which is due not so much to his arguments for it, but to our tendency to confuse the claim 'Desires cause our decisions' with the claim 'We are caused (compelled) by our desires to decide.'

But I turn now specifically to Thorp's argument. He says:

It often seems irresistible to regard the mind as a sort of field in which there operate vector forces—the feelings, desires and motives to which we are subject . . . It is a part of the picture that the action we take is the simple resultant of the various forces which act on us. This is a model which gives rise to psychological determinism. Now in this model there would perhaps be some place for a distinction between influence and cause but it would be a shallow one. The cause of one's act might be identified as the strongest of the forces acting upon one, or the most unusual, or the one that is for some reason most interesting . . . and then all the others would be influences. But there would be no deep difference between the two—just a difference of strength or oddness; fundamentally all the forces work in the same way and on the same object.

The model that the libertarian will want to propose is such that the forces . . . do not ever meet in a point, and so there is no resultant. The agent is indeed aware of them and they influence him, but they do not cause him to do anything. Rather he causes himself to do what he does, and he does so in the knowledge of the forces that act upon him. (pp. 135–6.)

It is interesting that Thorp uses the rather loaded phrase 'they do not cause him to do anything' with its implication of compulsion. Is it possible that he too is confusing causation with compulsion?

It will probably be clear from the passage that Thorp is committed to the possibility of agent-causation and that he, therefore, has at his disposal a way of denying that desires are causes without denying causation altogether. But the reference to agent-causation is not to be seen as a merely cosmetic device— Thorp means us to understand that there is not a causal connection between the agent's being influenced by the forces and his causing himself to do what he does. We are not to take it that the agent is caused to cause himself to do something.

How then are we to understand the claim that the agent is aware of these forces, that they influence him, and that he then causes himself to do what he does, that is decide in a certain way (Thorp is concerned with decisions), *in the knowledge of* these forces? Thorp offers us no further elucidation, but in the discussion leading to the passage I have quoted, he says several things which, when added to his remarks in that passage, suggest that he might have had the following sort of picture in mind of the relationship between an agent's decision to act and his desires. The agent is aware of his desires as inclining him towards certain actions and is prompted by this awareness to consider them as candidates for fulfilment. Knowing that some desires are stronger than others and knowing that if he fulfils the weaker ones at the expense of the sronger ones he will experience more discomfort than if he fulfils the stronger at the expense of the weaker, he decides to fulfil the stronger ones.

This last bit of interpretation of Thorp's 'in the knowledge of' comment is, of course, not warranted by what he says in the quoted passage but is suggested by the discussion I have just mentioned which leads to that passage. For in that discussion Thorp compares people who find it hard to resist temptation with those who find it easy and he says that 'resisting temptation induces pain in the weak-willed . . . People dislike pain and they are likely (but not forced) to take avoiding action.'[35] Clearly, Thorp believes that our dislike of pain (discomfort, dissatisfaction) will influence our behaviour without causing it and for this reason I have thought it appropriate to include the agent's beliefs about what will happen to him if he does or does not fulfil certain desires under the heading of 'the knowledge in the light of which he decides'. But also, if we did not include some belief like this under the heading, there would be very little effective substance in the idea that an agent does what he does in the knowledge of the forces that act on him. For, without such content, that knowledge would amount to little more than the agent's awareness that he has desires which are inclining him towards certain actions and (perhaps) the awareness that some were stronger than others, but this would be insufficient to explain why he should decide to fulfil one desire rather than another. And we do want an account of deciding to do a particular thing *for a reason*.

There are certain things which it is tempting to read into this account but which we are forbidden to because they would introduce the idea of a causal connection which Thorp wants to eliminate. For instance, it is tempting to read into it the claim that the agent is moved by the thought of avoidable discomfort to decide to fulfil a certain desire. Clearly, we cannot understand the account in this way. Nor, returning to our earlier discussion of decisions, can we assume that it is acceptable to explain the agent's appearance, in this account, of being causally insulated from the desires he considers for fulfilment by saying that these desires are only the starting points of a complex causal process in which the proximate causes of his deliberation and deciding are other desires and beliefs. Obviously, we are not permitted to posit a deliberation-guiding desire or a discomfort-avoiding one as desires which prompt (cause) the agent to decide (choose) as he does; for Thorp is committed to the view that as decision makers we not only appear to be causally insulated from our desires but *are* causally insulated from them and furthermore that we are causally insulated from *all* desires, including presumably desires like the deliberation-guiding desire and the desire to relieve the discomfort of uncertainty. Thus, we can assume that on Thorp's view the agent's knowledge which he acts in the light of could include the knowledge that he had desires like those just mentioned. And since Thorp obviously believes that at any one time we can mentally stand back from all the psychological forces acting on us, then, given the existence of deliberation-guiding and discomfort-avoiding desires, he seems committed to the view that we can mentally stand back from these as well.

But such a thesis about decisions would have absurd implications. The claim that we can stand back from all desires and decide which to respond to implies that we can decide whether to respond to the desire to resolve the uncertainty which the need for a decision presupposes; that is it implies that the desire to resolve uncertainty does not prompt the decision making process but becomes instead the subject of another decision. And since any need for a decision presupposes uncertainty, it also implies that there is uncertainty about whether or not to resolve the uncertainty about acting. This in turn suggests that there is another desire, the desire to resolve the uncertainty about resolving the uncertainty which, if Thorp is right, we can mentally stand back from and decide whether to act on (by beginning deliberations) or not. But this need to decide in turn presupposes an uncertainty about whether to act on the desire to resolve the uncertainty about resolving the uncertainty and so on *ad infinitum*. This is surely absurd. The decision maker has at the most two decisions to make at any one time: first, which is the best course of action and secondly, what to do, not an endless series of decisions.

Suppose that we try to avoid these implications by denying that there are desires to relieve the discomfort of uncertainty and by suggesting that the decision maker, having stood back from all the remaining desires, decides to ϕ This too is unacceptable. For if we deny that there is a desire to relieve the discomfort of uncertainty, then I think we are committed to denying the existence of the discomfort and if we are committed to denying this then it is plausible to deny that there is any uncertainty since the discomfort is assumed to be generated by the uncertainty. And if we deny that there is uncertainty, then it does not make sense to speak of decisions.

All of these objections rely of course on the fact that Thorp has couched his thesis in terms of the relationship between motives and decisions. Perhaps if we were to re-express it in terms of choices it would appear more persuasive. How persuasive would it be re-expressed as the thesis that when an agent chooses to act in response to a particular desire, he chooses to act in the knowledge of his desire without being caused to do so by that desire?

What we need is an account of how the desire could act as the agent's reason for choosing without being the causal prompter of his choice.

I have repeatedly stressed that the causal thesis appears to offer the only hope of isolating those reasons which do not simply give a rationale for a person's act (or, in this case, his choice) but which are actually operative in bringing it about. It seems to me that if we are tempted to think that Thorp's thesis about influences can do as much it is because the notion of 'influence' has causal connotations. Thus, I would suggest that although we might imagine that we can picture to ourselves how it might be for an agent's desire to influence and in some non-causal sense to be operative in bringing about his choice, we are, in fact, bringing to that picture an unacknowledged belief that influences *are* causes and it is this unacknowledged belief which makes us accept that the influencing desire is *qua* influence operative.

Of course, the defender of Thorp's thesis is free to deny this. But if he is to convince us that the thesis about influences is not a causal thesis in disguise, then he must do more than simply deny that influences are causes. At the moment, we are simply asked to accept that influences are not causes and, by implication, that this thesis about non-causes can provide as satisfactory an account of the claim, 'He chose to X because he wanted to Y' as the causal account. But we have been given no reason to accept this beyond our simply being urged to do so and, as we have seen, there are good reasons for thinking that the causal account is the only satisfactory account which can be given.

So we should reject the claim that motives are influences but not causes.

Part III: Another argument for the claim that belief in the U-condition is incoherent

On the basis of the preceding arguments, we seem entitled to conclude that the U-condition can only be fulfilled by a reasonless choice, or a choice or decision which is caused by a reasonless choice.

However, it might be objected that a choice cannot be both reasonless *and* blameworthy, for if the choice is to be a proper object of moral assessment, it must be a choice for reasons.[36]

But this challenge can be rejected. It would be wrong to claim that all morally appraisable choices must be choices for reasons. I would suggest that while praiseworthy choices must be, blameworthy choices need not be. In Chapter 1, I argued that an agent could satisfy the M-condition for blameworthiness (the state of mind condition), if he acted in the knowledge that his act was wrong and did not have a reason for doing so which excused him. But the claim that you can satisfy the M-condition if your reason for acting is not excusing does not entail the claim that in order to satisfy it you must have a reason for acting. You do not have to have had *any* reason for acting in order to satisfy the M-condition. Your choosing to act in defiance of a moral rule knowing that this is what you are doing is enough. There is no logical requirement that the choice which fulfils the M-condition for blameworthiness must be prompted by a desire (and/or belief). On the other hand, the morally praiseworthy choice must be one which results either from a desire to do the right thing or, if one is a Kantian, from the belief that to act in this way is right, or from some other praiseworthy motive, for example the desire to alleviate suffering.[37]

For praiseworthiness, it is not enough that you are prepared to do the right thing; but to fulfil the M-condition for blameworthiness it is enough that you are prepared to do the wrong thing (you do not have to want to).

Reasonless blameworthy choices are logically possible. But are reasonless choices empirically possible? I shall argue that they are probably not.

Part IV: Reasonless choices are probably not empirically possible

Briefly, the argument is this: reasonless choices would only be empirically possible, if desires were not necessary for action. But desires are (probably) necessary for action. So reasonless choices are (probably) not empirically possible.

First, I must explain why the possibility of reasonless choices depends on the possibility of desireless action. Desires are psychological states which exert pressure for fulfilment and to say that they are necessary is to say that without the existence of such pressures for fulfilment the question of action would not arise for agents, that is it would not occur to them seriously to consider imminent action. (I add the qualifying words 'imminent' and 'seriously' to forestall the objection that in the absence of desires an agent might idly wonder to himself whether he would be capable of performing certain actions or what it would be like to do so.) So to say that desires are necessary is to say that without them agents would not choose to act.

Someone might say: 'Even if desires are necessary in this sense for choice, they need not be the reasons for choice. Perhaps agents can choose for no reason to act on their desires.'

But this suggestion is absurd. If desires are necessary, they are so as pressures for fulfilment. And it is because they exert such pressure, because they incline us towards their fulfilment, that we choose to act on them. This constitutes the motivating reason for choice. It is simply not possible that an agent's relationship with these inclining states should be such that he could reasonlessly choose to satisfy them.

So far, I have established that *if* desires are necessary for action, then reasonless choosing to act is not possible. But are desires necessary for action? Many would answer 'yes' unhesitatingly. There is a widespread, deeply-rooted belief that human beings cannot be moved to act unless they have certain desires. If we combine this with the plausible assumption that human beings cannot act unless they are moved to act, this entails the conclusion that desires are necessary for action. The widespread belief has recently been challenged by Nagel and McDowell who deny (or appear to deny) that desires are essential for motivation. In IV(*a*), I shall argue that these challenges fail. In IV(*b*), I shall argue that unmotivated action is (probably) not empirically possible. Hence the conclusion that desires are (probably) necessary for action.

IV(*a*): Are desires essential for motivation? The challenge by Nagel and McDowell

John McDowell says this: 'It seems to be false that the motivating power of all reasons derives from their including desires.'[38] And Philippa Foot in 'Reasons for Action and Desires' writes:

Yet surely we cannot deny that when a man goes shopping today because he will be hungry tomorrow he wants or has a desire to avoid being hungry? This is true, but an analysis of the use of such expressions as 'want' and 'has a desire to' in such contexts shows that these 'desires' cannot be the basis of the reason for acting ... What we have here is a use of 'desire' which indicates a motivational direction and nothing more. One may compare it with the use of 'want' in 'I want to φ' where only intentionality is implied. (p. 204.)

Although Foot believes that *moral* motivation must involve desires and McDowell denies this, both agree that reasons for action[39] need not always include desires and both quote in support of this a particular passage from Thomas Nagel's *Possibility of Altruism*, a passage in which he claims that it is only trivially true that desires must underly all acts:

That I have the appropriate desire simply follows from the fact that these considerations motivate me; if the likelihood that an act will promote my future happiness motivates me to perform it now, then it is appropriate to ascribe to me a desire for my future happiness. But nothing follows about the role of the desire as a condition contributing to the motivational efficacy of those considerations. (pp. 29–30.)

Philippa Foot endorses Nagel's claim because (as she sees it) he does not misrepresent the experience of prudential reasoning by positing the presence of a consciously entertained prudential desire whenever a prudent man is moved to act; and McDowell endorses it because its illustration of the possibility of prudential motivation without desires points to the possibility of moral motivation without desires.

McDowell claims that it is possible for a man to be moved to act solely by his view of the circumstances confronting him, that is that the sort of psychological state which could be cited as a full explanation of his action is one which can be characterized as a perception. Nagel too seems to believe that cognitive states can motivate on their own. (Nagel (p. 28) presents as his target the claim that cognitive states *cannot* motivate on their own.)

The picture of motivation which both Nagel and McDowell wish to reject is the Humean one which suggests that a thought (or perception or belief) cannot move a man unless it is relevant to some pre-existing desire of his.[40] According to this, a person's acting in his own interests could not be explained by merely citing the perception that acting in that way would be in his interests; we should have to cite the presence of a desire to further his interests in order to explain why the perception has the effect it has. And, *a fortiori*, a person's acting in someone else's interests could not be explained by merely citing the belief that his action would be beneficial to that other person. We should have to cite the presence of a desire in respect of that other person (perhaps a concern for him) to explain why his belief had this effect.

Because Nagel's arguments against this are often appealed to by other philosophers, I shall start by examining them in some detail. But I don't feel able to embark on this examination by simply stating what I take Nagel's arguments to be because, as will become apparent, what he has to say is susceptible of different interpretations. For this reason, I shall begin by quoting a number of relevant passages from *The Possibility of Altruism*:

The assumption that a motivating desire underlies every intentional act depends, I believe, on a confusion between two sorts of desires, motivated and unmotivated ... many desires like many beliefs are *arrived at* by decision and after deliberation. They need not simply assail us, though there are certain desires that do, like the appetites and in certain cases, the emotions ... The desires which simply come to us are unmotivated though they can be explained. Hunger is produced by lack of food but is not motivated thereby. A desire to shop for groceries after discovering nothing appetizing in the refrigerator is on the other hand motivated by hunger. Rational or motivational explanation is just as much in order for that desire as for the action itself.

The claim that a desire underlies every act is true only if desires are taken to include motivated as well as unmotivated desires and it is true only in the sense that *whatever* may be the motivation for someone's intentional pursuit of a goal, it becomes in virtue of his pursuit *ipso facto* appropriate to ascribe to him a desire for that goal. But if the desire is a motivated one, the explanation of it will be the same as the explanation of his pursuit. Although it will no doubt be generally admitted that some desires are motivated, the issue is whether another desire always lies behind the motivated one, or whether sometimes the motivation of the initial desire involves no reference to another unmotivated desire.

Therefore it may be admitted as trivial that, for example, considerations about my future welfare or about the interests of others cannot motivate me to act without a desire being present at the time of action. That I have the appropriate desire simply *follows* from the fact that these considerations motivate me; if the likelihood that an act will promote my future happiness motivates me to perform it now, then it is appropriate to ascribe to me a desire for my own future happiness. But nothing follows about the role of the desire as a condition contributing to the motivational efficacy of those considerations. It is a necessary condition of their efficacy to be sure, but only a logically necessary condition. It is not necessary either as a contributing influence, or as a causal condition.

In fact if the desire is itself motivated, it and the corresponding motivation will presumably be possible for the same reasons. Thus it remains an open question whether an additional, unmotivated desire must always be found among the conditions of motivation by any other factor whatever. If considerations of future happiness can motivate by themselves, then they can explain and render intelligible the desire for future happiness which is ascribable to anyone whom they do motivate. Alternatively, there may be another factor operating in such cases, one which explains both the motivational influence of considerations about the future and the motivated desire which embodies that influence. But if a further unmotivated desire is always among these further conditions, it has yet to be proved.

If we bring these observations to bear on the question whether desires are always among the necessary conditions of *reasons* for action, it becomes obvious that there is no reason to believe that they are. Often the desires which an agent necessarily experiences in acting will be motivated exactly as the action is. If the act is motivated by reasons stemming from certain external factors, and the desire to perform it is motivated by those same reasons, the desires obviously cannot be among the conditions for the presence of those reasons. This will be true of any motivated desire which is ascribable to someone simply in virtue of his intentional pursuit of a goal. The fact that the presence of a desire is a logically necessary condition (because it is a logical consequence) of a reason's motivating, does not entail that it is a necessary condition of the *presence* of the reason; and if it is motivated by that reason, it *cannot* be among the reason's conditions. . . .

when we examine the logical reason why desire must always be present we see that it may often be motivated by precisely what motivates the action. An alternative basis for that motivation must therefore be discovered. (pp. 29–31.)

While some things are clear others are unclear in these passages. It is clear that Nagel is claiming that although a desire is attributable to any agent whenever he is motivated to act, we are not to assume that this desire is always the source of the motivation. But it is not clear what kind of desires are supposed to be included in the list of the 'always-attributable'. Are we to take it that when Nagel says desires are always attributable he means that when a person acts there will either be an unmotivated desire *or* a motivated one? This seems to be suggested in the first sentence of the second paragraph. Or are we to take it that he thinks of the always attributable desires as motivated desires? This fits in with what he says in other passages. And there is a further problem of interpretation: it is not clear what Nagel thinks motivated desires are. Some of his remarks suggest that he sees them as the effects of motivation, causally generated by other motivating psychological states (which may, but need not, include other desires) and causally generating action. I shall call this 'Thesis I'. Other remarks, however, suggest that he believes motivated desires are not actual states which are present in the causal chain leading from motivation to action, but are, as one commentator puts it, simply 'logical ghosts'[41] with no causal role whatsoever. I shall call this 'Thesis II'.

Thesis I: Desires need not be the sources but can be the effects of motivation

That Nagel thinks of motivated desires as later psychological states in the causal chain which precedes action is suggested by a number of things, for instance, he speaks of them as being 'arrived at by decision and after deliberation'; he suggests that they would be explicable by the same psychological states as those which explain the action; he talks of desires as always having to be 'present'; and says that 'the claim that a desire underlies every act is true'. The Thesis I interpretation is also supported by those of Nagel's remarks which imply that any motivated desire could be described as 'the desire to perform a certain act'. This is suggested by Nagel's claim that a motivated desire can be explained by citing the same psychological states as those which explain the action. Secondly, it is suggested by the fact that his example of a motivated desire in the first paragraph quoted, namely the desire to shop, is an example of a desire to perform a certain act. And finally, it is indicated by his remarks in the penultimate paragraph: 'if the act is motivated by reasons stemming from certain external factors and the *desire to perform it* is motivated by those same reasons . . .' (my emphasis).

All of this suggests that the picture of motivation which Nagel is arguing for is one in which cognitions generate desires to act which in turn generate actions. And the difference between this and the Humean picture Nagel wants to reject is that in *this* picture the cognition can be effective in generating a desire (to act) without needing to be based on an earlier desire.

So, according to the Thesis I interpretation, Nagel believes that desires of some kind must underly all actions, that these could be motivated desires, and that motivated desires are the effects of a motivational source which need not include desires.

Why should Nagel think that desires of some kind must underly all actions? His remarks suggest two different and irreconcilable answers. Some of what he says suggests that he might have been influenced by a conception of what it is to act which involves the notion of trying, or striving towards a goal. If you think of an action as a trying (or a striving) then it is natural to assume that if someone were prevented from acting as he intended to, he would feel frustrated or thwarted. And if a feeling of frustration really is an inevitable response to being prevented from acting as one intends to, then this seems a compelling reason for assuming that whenever there is an act, there must always be a desire to act. (Remember that O'Shaughnessy describes desires to act as 'forces towards striving'.) One might say that to be moved to act is, in part, to feel an inclination towards striving.

This reading of Nagel is suggested by two of his remarks, first, his speaking of the 'desires which an agent necessarily experiences in acting' and secondly, his claim that they 'will be motivated exactly as the action is'. I do not think that one *necessarily* experiences *any* desires in acting, but Nagel could have been thinking of the feeling of frustration one would have if prevented from acting. Such a feeling would imply the presence of a desire to act and a desire to act is just what would fit Nagel's description of the state which is 'motivated exactly as the action is'. This is consistent with the Thesis I interpretation since it suggests that the motivated desires Nagel has in mind are desires to act. If this reading of Nagel were correct, then we could say that he is committed to the claim that the desires which must underlie all actions are desires to act.

But it is hard to tell whether this is a correct reading, because other remarks of Nagel's suggest an interpretation which is totally at odds with it, the interpretation I have called 'Thesis II'.

Thesis II: The Logical Reducibility Thesis

According to this, Nagel is claiming that statements to the effect that someone has had a certain motivated desire are logically reducible to statements that he has been moved by certain cognitions to perform a certain act. This interpretation suggests itself most powerfully to two passages, the one which I quoted at the beginning of this discussion:

That I have the appropriate desire simply *follows* from the fact that these considerations motivate me; if the likelihood that an act will promote my future happiness motivates me to perform it now, then it is appropriate to ascribe to me a desire for my own future happiness. But nothing follows about the role of the desire as a condition contributing to the motivational efficacy of these considerations. (pp. 29–30.)

And the penultimate paragraph:

the presence of a desire is a logically necessary condition (because it is a logical consequence) of a reason's motivating . . . (p. 30.)

The Thesis II interpretation of logical reducibility fits in well with Nagel's claim about the triviality of attributing desires, but it casts a different light on his claim that desires underlie all actions. Viewed from this new perpective that claim would seem to mean that whenever someone has been moved to act, it follows as a logical consequence that he had a desire because that is all that having a motivated desire means. This is drastically different from the interpretation suggested earlier, namely that desires to act are always present as forces which generate action and which are in turn generated by preceding states. Here the motivated desire is not viewed as a force at all, but, as suggested earlier, as nothing more than a logical ghost.

Furthermore, the candidates for motivated desires which, on this interpretation, Nagel assumes to be trivially attributable (in the sense that claims about them are logically reducible) are not, as on the Thesis I interpretation, desires to act, but desires *for* things, for example the desire for my future happiness and the desire for the happiness of others. This is clearly indicated in the passage about the triviality of citing certain desires with which I began the discussion and part of which I have just requoted.

I think it is impossible to impose one interpretation on these passages because it is impossible to reconcile the different claims contained within them. But we can assess the two main (and

irreconcilable) theses separately in the hope of reaching a conclusion about the claim that desires are necessary for motivation.

Thesis I: If we accept that whenever there is an act there must
always be a desire to act present as a force towards striving,
then we must accept that desires are necessary constituents of
the motivating states which lead to action, even if they are not
necessary as sources of motivation. (In fact, if we accept Thesis
I, we accept that desires are necessary for action full stop, and
there is no need to proceed to the second part (IV(*b*)) of this
argument.) But should we accept Thesis I? The argument about
the feeling of frustration which would be experienced if one
were prevented from acting seems persuasive but I have one
reservation about it which I shall discuss at the end.

Thesis II: If we accept that sometimes claims about desires
are logically reducible to claims about being moved to action by
certain cognitions, then since this implies that there could be
action without desires needing to be present as causal forces, if
Thesis II can be substantiated, we are entitled to conclude that
desires are not necessary for motivation.

Is Thesis II true? As we have seen, the sort of desires which
Nagel claims to be trivially attributable are desires like the
desire for the happiness of others, or for the agent's own happiness. But is it right to suggest that claims like 'X has benevolent
desires towards others' are *ever* simply reducible to claims like
'X has been moved by the thought that an act of his will be helpful to someone to perform that act'?

One objection which is immediately prompted by this claim is
that the suggestion of reducibility as it stands cannot accommodate what is an easily imaginable situation in which it could
be true that someone has been moved to (say) alleviate the suffering of another by the thought that his act would alleviate
such suffering and yet false that he was concerned for the person. For such a thought might only have motivated him because
he wanted gratitude or admiration. So it could not be claimed to
be a sufficient condition of the attributability of a particular sort
of desire that someone has been moved by a particular sort of
thought.

In the light of this, it might be thought that the thesis of logical reducibility would be acceptable if we were careful to stipulate that the claim that someone had a particular desire was logically reducible to the claim that he had been moved *solely* by a particular thought or perception.

But this brings me to another objection: we believe that the citing of a particular desire explains why a person has been moved by a certain thought (or perception) and we take it that we can explain why a person has not been moved by a certain thought or perception by citing the absence of such desires. But if the presence or absence of desires can legitimately be cited as explanations of a person's being moved or not moved, then the claim that such desires exist or do not exist cannot be logically absorbed into claims that a person has or has not been moved.

But is it always legitimate to cite desires as explanations? What justification is there for assuming that a desire is always present when someone is moved by a perception (or belief) to act? After all, agents are not always aware of having particular desires when they act. An argument which seems to be implied by some of McDowell's remarks in 'Are Moral Requirements Hypothetical Imperatives?' is that it would be a travesty of what happens when a moral agent responds to the thought that an act is required of him, to represent his experience of seeing a requirement in the situation which confronts him as one of being aware of a desire which motivates him to act as morality requires (see p. 19).

Of course, the fact that one is not aware of something is not conclusive evidence for the claim that it does not exist. Nevertheless, these claims about how things appear contain an implicit challenge to those who endorse theses which go against the appearances; the challenge is to demonstrate why we should not accept the appearances as true reflections of reality. So, if a response to a situation as perceived seems to be one which does not involve a desire, what right have we to assume that there must be one?

One way of answering this is to cite cases in which appearances are shown to be deceptive. A man reacts to the colour green by rushing out of the room. He appears to have been moved to act solely by this perceptual feature. But we find his behaviour inexplicable. Why should seeing green make him rush out of the room? Then we are told that green has certain emotional associations for him, due to a traumatic past experience involving the colour, associations of which he is not aware but which nevertheless influence him. Such a case undermines the appeal of appealing to appearances.

But, it could be argued, we might not always be able to point to past emotional traumas when desires seem to be missing and when we cannot, isn't it simply dogmatic to insist that desires must be present?

However, there is another way of answering the claim that we should conclude on the basis of appearances that cognition can motivate on its own. This involves making one concession to the advocate of cognitions without conceding that cognition alone is responsible for motivation. The concession is the acknowledgement that there need not always be a prior occurrent desire whenever someone is moved by a cognition. But this concession is accompanied by the insistence that there must always be a prior affective dispositional state, one which we might label 'a standing desire'.[42]

So we can concede that a faithful rendering of an agent's experience could be one which described it purely as a case of his feeling compelled to act by what he sees, while at the same time maintaining that he is only compelled by what he sees because he is affectively constituted in a way which gives rise to the disposition to react to the cognition as he does.

The challenge then to the suggestion of reducibility would be that when we attribute self-concern or concern for others to a person we are attributing to him a dispositional state which explains, because it is causally responsible for, his being moved by certain beliefs or perceptions to (want to) perform certain acts. This dispositional state (standing desire) can be said to be the affective element which provides the causal background or standing condition (or field) within which the cognition (thought, perception, belief) plays its causally efficacious role.

The concession, that the affective element need not be an occurrent desire but could instead be a dispositional state, allows for a much more realistic picture of what self-concern or concern for others might be than that which would be afforded if the discussion about them were confined to talk of occurrent desires. Furthermore, when we reflect on the ways in which self-concern or concern for others manifests itself we come to see how misguided any reductive move would be which construed them simply as episodes of being moved to act by particular cognitions.

This is not just because, as has already been urged, we see such states as explaining these episodes, but also because we take it that they explain a number of other facts as well, not just the fact that someone is moved by certain cognitions, but the fact that he even has certain cognitions; not just the fact that he acts in certain ways as the result of what he sees or thinks, but the fact that he has certain feelings as the result of what he sees or thinks. The person who is not concerned for others will fail to notice when their interests are threatened, while the person who is concerned will be disposed to view situations in the light of their possible relevance to others. (I am reminded of a remark by David Wiggins in a seminar several years ago: 'The affection focuses the mind on features of reality which would not otherwise have been of any interest.') The person who is concerned for someone else will have thoughts and feelings which the person who is not concerned will not have: he will wonder how she is faring; whether she is thriving, and he will feel either pleased or sad as a result of his conclusions.

This response to the reductive move relies on three assumptions:

1. that, however things appear to be, there must always be some further element which explains why a person reacts to his cognitions as he does;
2. that this further element, whether occurrent or non-occurrent, is appropriately thought of as a desiring state; and
3. that this same element can be used to explain a number of other facts: why a person has certain cognitions, why he has certain occurrent desires and feelings.

But what justifies these assumptions? Here is one suggestion: different people will often react differently to the same (kind of) cognitive state, for example one person will be moved by the sight of suffering to try to alleviate it while another will not be, and their different reactions can often be correctly explained by citing different occurrent desires. So the natural thought is: since we know that different occurrent desires are responsible for different reactions in many cases, it seems reasonable to suppose that something similar must be at the root of all cases of different reactions; a state which, while not always occurrent, is nevertheless like a desire. And if it is reasonable to suppose that a desiring state is present in all cases of *different* reaction, it is reasonable to assume that desiring states play an essential role in *all* reactions to cognitions. The suggestion continues: another thing we know about occurrent desires is that one desire can be responsible for a variety of different phenomena. For instance, a hungry man's desire for food will account for his thinking about food, his desire to do things in order to get food, the fact that he notices the presence of a restaurant in a street full of different shops, and the fact that he feels upset when he finds that the restaurant is closed. Since we know that one occurrent desire can account for this variety, it seems reasonable to say that one dispositional state could account for such a variety if that dispositional state is a desiring state.

But is it sufficient to say that because occurrent desires can be cited in these explanatory ways, the dispositions we appeal to in their absence, in order to explain the same sorts of things, should be described as desiring states? It might be thought that, since we invoke these dispositions to explain the existence of and reaction to cognitions as well as the existence of certain desires and feelings, the dispositions have as much right to be called cognitive as they have to be called desiring. On the other hand, it could be argued that there is no reason to think of them as either cognitive or desiring, but simply as states which give rise to both cognitions and desires.

However, there is another argument for the claim that these dispositions should be thought of as desiring, and not cognitive, which I find intuitively appealing. We can see why an occurrent desire would generate feelings, thought and other desires, and why it would explain a tendency to notice some things and not others. This is because a desire is an inclining state, a state which exerts a pressure for fulfilment, and it is easy to understand why such a state would give rise to the other states. But it is not easy to see why a state which did not incline its possessor towards fulfilment would do this and cognitive states do not exert pressure for fulfilment.

But to this it can be objected that some cognitive states do exert a pressure for fulfilment. I have suggested that different reactions to the same cognition are best explained by citing different desires and also that desires have a better claim than perceptions to be thought of as the underlying explanatory states because desires are inclining and perceptions are not. But there is an argument of McDowell's in favour of perceptions which can meet both of these points.

First, McDowell's argument suggests that the different reactions of two agents to the same cognition ('same' in the sense that both can be said to see the same situation) can be explained by citing *cognitive* differences between them. For he claims that the two agents might react differently to a situation which both would describe in the same morally neutral way because one sees it as a reason for acting and the other does not.[43] Secondly, a perceptual state which can be described as 'seeing a situation as a reason for acting' could very well be a state which exerts a pressure for action.

Pace McDowell, I feel that 'the state of seeing a situation as a reason for acting' is most plausibly explained by citing either an underlying affective disposition or an occurrent desire. It seems very unlikely that such a 'perceptual' reaction is basic, or that its explaining cause consists solely in other *cognitive* states.

Nevertheless, I think there is a kind of inclining cognitive reaction some of whose instances could very well be basic. I refer to such enriched cognitive states as finding something (or someone) attractive, appealing, beautiful, delightful, or pleasing. Often there will be no explanation for our finding something attractive apart from the fact that we just do, and this is no explanation. (In this respect, it can be true that 'there is no accounting for taste'.)

But while such states don't always need underlying desires to explain them, it seems plausible to assume that if they issue in action it is only because they generate desires to act in specific ways. Thus, my finding something attractive might generate a desire to possess it or to continue to gaze at it, but in the absence of these generated desires, I will not do anything. So even these states are not exceptions to the rule that cognition alone cannot move someone all the way to action. But they *are* exceptions to the Humean claim.

It is time now to review the challenges to the claim that desires are necessary as motivators of action and to see how it has fared against them. We have seen that Nagel's Thesis I, the claim that while desires are not always the sources of motivation, they are always present as desires to act, is not really a challenge since it implies that desires to act are necessary. On the other hand, the logical reducibility thesis (Thesis II) is a genuine challenge since if it were true some claims about desires could be reconstrued as claims about being moved to act by perceptions or beliefs.

Now in treating the logical reducibility thesis as a genuine challenge, I have assumed that it was inconsistent with the claim that desires to act are necessary for action. This is not an inevitable move, since it would be possible to hold that claims about desires *as the sources of motivation* are logically reducible to claims about being moved to act by perceptions, and also to hold that involved in being moved to act by perceptions are desires to act. This might be thought an attractive option since it would accommodate the intuitively appealing thought that there must be some kind of inclining state which precedes action, for if the agent were to be prevented from acting as he intended to, he would feel frustrated.

But the logical reducibility thesis with which I have been concerned is assumed to be one which implies that there can be actions which are not preceded by *any* kind of desire. That such a thesis would deny the omnipresence of desires to act (states of inclining towards action) might seem a good reason for rejecting it, to those persuaded by the argument about feelings of frustration. But I do not think the latter argument is conclusive, since it seems unable to account for the possibility that an agent who has reluctantly committed himself to some course of action might actually feel relieved at being prevented from undertaking it. (More about this presently.)

The main argument for the reducibility thesis seems to be the argument from appearances, the claim that it often appears that agents are moved to act solely by thoughts or perceptions, coupled with the claim that differences in action can be explained as being entirely the results of differences in perception. (Both points are attributable to McDowell.)

Against this, I have presented an argument to the effect that while the antecedents of action need not always include occurrent desires, they must include what one might call 'affective-inclining' dispositions, dispositions which explain not just an individual's behavioural reactions to perceptions, but also a number of other events which we take to be linked with the way in which he reacts to perceptions, that is events which involve his feeling certain things, his thinking certain things and his perceiving situations in the way he does.

It seems to me that one of the best reasons for accepting the thesis of affective-inclining dispositions and rejecting the reducibility thesis is that the former offers a model which is intuitively plausible and of far greater explanatory power than that which is offered by the claim that actions can be explained as entirely due to the way in which agents perceive situations. After all, the preferred thesis is capable of explaining why agents perceive situations as they do.

But as we have seen, such dispositions cannot always explain why agents perceive or react to perceptions as they do because there are some enriched cognitive states, such as finding someone attractive, which are themselves inclining, and whose inclining force may not be explicable in terms of some further, underlying, inclination.

And yet, since these states will issue in action only if they generate desires, they do not constitute a challenge to the claim that desires are necessary for motivation.

But what about the cases of reluctant action where one cannot posit generated desires to act? Could these be examples of desireless action? I doubt it. I think that in such cases the agent will have been prompted by antecedent desires. Why might someone decide to do something which he very much does not want to do? One possibility is that he feels it is his duty, another is that he is under some kind of coercion. In the first instance, it seems reasonable to suggest that he has been prompted to decide to act by the desire to satisfy the urgings of his conscience. Citing such a desire would enable us to give a very satisfying explanation for his feeling relieved at being prevented from acting. The explanation would be that he is relieved not just because he does not have to do what he does not want to do, but also because his failure to do his duty is not something he needs to berate himself for.

In the second instance, the desire which prompts reluctant action could be the desire not to anger his coercers. If he is then prevented from acting by forces beyond his control, he might feel relieved both because the intended act was distasteful to him and because he feels that his threateners will not blame him for the failure of their plans.

I conclude, therefore, that so long as we understand the term 'desires' as one which covers affective-inclining dispositions *and* occurrent desires (including the desire to act in certain ways), the belief that desires are necessary for motivation survives the challenges by Nagel and McDowell.[44]

But to have established that the belief survives these challenges is not equivalent to establishing that all action requires desires. The most that the argument against Nagel and McDowell can be said to show is that if action is motivated, then a desiring state must be part of that motivation. To reach the conclusion that all action requires desires, we need the further claim that all action must be motivated.

IV(*b*): Is unmotivated action possible?

One kind of action which might be thought to be unmotivated is acting on a whim, because it seems to be an example of acting without reason. I do not think that such action is reasonless, but even if it were it could not be called desireless. For someone who acts on a whim does so because the thought of acting in a certain way appeals to him; and this suggests that the thought generates a desire to act. This suggestion is supported by a belief that if one were prevented from acting on a whim one would feel thwarted. It is because acting on a whim involves an appealing thought that I doubt that it is an instance of reasonless action. There might seem to be no explanation for the fact that the thought of acting in a certain way appeals to an agent and thus in this sense no reason for its appeal, but the fact that it did appeal *is* the reason for his action, not, perhaps, a justifying reason, but certainly the motivating reason. If this is correct, then acting on a whim is not unmotivated acting.

This suggests that one would only be justified in describing an action as desireless if it were undertaken by someone who was incapable of being moved by any thought, that is someone who was incapable of caring about anything even to the extent of feeling a momentary enthusiasm for it. I say this because unless one knew that an agent was incapable of even a momentary

enthusiasm, one could not rule out the possibility that his behaviour was an example of acting on a whim, and thus the
result of a desire.

Is it possible for someone to be incapable of being moved by
any consideration and yet still act? As I can see nothing in the
concept of action itself which renders the idea incoherent, I can
see no reason for denying that it is logically possible. But is it
empirically possible?

The only relevant evidence I can think of is our knowledge of
those who are severely depressed. And this suggests that their
inactivity is linked to indifference:

The chief symptoms of depression are passivity and dejection. The
individual experiences an overwhelming inertia; he feels unable to
make decisions, to initiate activity, or to take an interest in anything or
anyone . . . In the most intense state of depression the patient is bedrid-
den and indifferent to all that goes on. He refuses to speak or to eat,
and he has to be fed intravenously and completely cared for by
others.[45]

Is it not overwhelmingly likely that the depressed person's inactivity is *due* to his indifference, and does this not constitute a
case for saying that it is not possible for someone who is incapable of being moved to act, to act? While the evidence just
quoted strongly suggests that it is not possible, I do not think it
can be regarded as conclusive.

But we are, I think, entitled to conclude on the basis of the
evidence that it is highly unlikely that unmotivated action is
possible and, therefore, highly unlikely that desireless action is
possible.

This means that we cannot *absolutely* rule out the possibility
of reasonless choices, but I think the U-condition advocate
would be foolish to pin his hopes on this; first, because even if
there were reasonless choices, this would not necessarily mean
that they were causeless: the thesis that reasons are causes leaves
open the question of whether lack of reason indicates lack of
cause; and secondly the most the U-condition advocate would
be entitled to claim if he insisted on clutching at this very tiny
straw is that it is just, barely, possible that there are entirely
motiveless choices. But where would this get him? Given our
previous arguments, it would allow him to say that blameworthiness *might* be empirically possible for agents who make

motiveless choices and for agents whose decisions and choices are caused by motiveless choices. But this is so very remote from anything which would allow us to feel justified in blaming ordinary moral offenders, that it is simply not worth considering.

Conclusion

I have argued that blameworthiness as conceived by the U-condition advocate is logically possible but (probably) not empirically possible.

Since the U-condition advocate's conception of blameworthiness is one to which we are committed by some of our intuitions (see Chapter 4), this means that we are committed to a requirement for just blaming which cannot be satisfied. Should we then abandon this commitment? This is a question I shall try to answer in the next two chapters.

6

What should we do about our commitment to the U-condition?

It has been established that the U-condition for blameworthiness (probably) cannot be fulfilled. As we saw in Chapter 4, our commitment to the belief in this condition is a consequence of our commitment to the belief that offenders who are motivated by states for which they are not responsible do not deserve to be blamed. It follows that if and when we blame people for flouting moral requirements we are doing something which is unjust.

Should we not then give up blaming? One answer, which might be seen as suggested by some of Professor Strawson's arguments in 'Freedom and Resentment', is that the question is absurd because we cannot give up blaming. Strawson claims that we are prone to a number of reactive attitudes such as anger, resentment, gratitude and love, and that our proneness to such attitudes is an ineradicable part of our natures. He implies that our moral practices of praising and blaming reflect feelings which are the natural outgrowths of such attitudes. This would mean, for instance, that moral indignation is the natural outgrowth of ordinary anger. Strawson further suggests that we could not give up the moral reactive attitudes without giving up the ordinary reactive attitudes: 'as general human capacities or pronenesses they stand or lapse together'.[1] But, according to Strawson, we are not, in any case, able to give up either kind of attitude: 'It is not in our nature to (be able to) do so.'[2]

Now it might seem to follow from the claim that we can't give up moral indignation that we would not be able to give up the practice of blaming which expresses it. But this is not an immediately obvious consequence. Even if we are bound to have such feelings it does not follow that we are bound to express them. Perhaps we could stop ourselves from expressing those feelings which give rise to the desire to condemn or punish. In answer to this, it might be said that the strain of not expressing the feelings we are bound to have would become intolerable and that we would be incapable of suppressing them for long.

But even if this is so, it does not follow that all blaming and all punishment would be bound to continue. To assume that it does is to imagine that blaming is always the immediate result of intense feelings and that punishment is an immediate response to blame. But there is no uniform and unvarying relationship between feeling and blame, blame and punishment. Blaming can consist in an outburst against someone which is the immediate result of a surge of emotion or in a calmly premeditated rebuke which is preceded by hardly any (or no) emotion at all. Punishment is often a delayed reaction to the awareness that someone has done something wrong and where there is a decision to punish, the decision is not always preceded by strong feelings.

The issue is further complicated by the fact that blaming is not always a practice which *expresses* attitudes, but can itself consist in the holding of attitudes, as it does when someone blames himself or 'feels guilty'. Feeling guilty can embrace the disturbing belief in one's own wrongdoing, a kind of self-directed rebuke and a feeling of shame. In the case of this kind of blaming, unlike the case where one blames others, there is no distance between awareness and feeling, feeling and rebuke. Each element is an inseparable part of the whole. And because this self-directed attitude is often an immediate response to the awareness of what one has done, the possibility of giving it up is much more remote than the possibility of giving up the rebuking of others. On the other hand, there is more likelihood of our giving up premeditated rebuke and punishment than there is the kind of rebuking (or punishment) which is a spontaneous reaction to intense feeling.

So it would not be absurd to say that some blaming and some blame related activities could be stopped. But this still leaves us with the disquieting thought that the blaming and punishment which results from strong feelings could not be stopped.

But are we bound to continue to have such feelings? The answer depends on what the question means. If it means, 'Are human beings bound, in virtue of their natures, to have moral feelings?' than I think the answer is 'no'. If it means, 'Would those who have strong moral feelings continue to have them despite their acknowledging that no one deserves to be blamed?' then I think the answer is 'yes'.

I do not think that having moral feelings is an ineradicable part of human nature. There are human beings who do not react morally, psychopaths for instance, and if only such human beings reproduced themselves and brought up their offspring then it is possible that in time no human being would react morally. This fantasy (or nightmare) does not depend on the belief that the propensity for moral feelings is transmitted genetically. It depends on the belief that those who, like the psychopath, are unable to care about others would be unlikely to foster any other-regarding attitudes in their children.

Of course, even in such a world people would still have feelings but these would be, almost exclusively, feelings about themselves. The propensity to react angrily to situations which are perceived as frustrating or threatening to oneself is, I am sure, an ineradicable part of human nature. The propensity to react with moral indignation to situations involving (say) the cruel treatment of others is not. So I do not agree with Strawson that non-moral and moral reactive attitudes 'stand or lapse together'.

But I think that to the extent that we have strong moral feelings about certain things, we would continue to feel intensely even if we fully acknowledged that no one deserved to be blamed or punished.

For instance, many of us have strong anti-feelings about the torturing of innocent (and even non-innocent) people. We are likely to react to the knowledge that innocents have been tortured with a mixture of horror and anger. I find it hard to believe that these feelings would not survive the acknowledgement that the torturers do not deserve to be blamed or punished.

I can imagine someone saying 'Ah, but these feelings would no longer be moral. Moral horror would be replaced by horror, moral indignation by ordinary indignation.' But I think that this response is wrong.

Moral reactive attitudes differ from non-moral ones in being justifiable by appeal to moral principles[3] but these principles need not concern blameworthiness. I stress the word 'justifiable' because I don't think it is essential to an attitude's being moral that it be *prompted* by any thoughts about moral principles, or even that the person who has the attitude should be able to articulate what the principle is. It is sufficient for it to be moral that it be the kind of attitude which *could* be justified by appeal to a moral principle. Of course to be this, the attitude must have a content, which could be articulated by the attitude holder, which lends itself to such justification. But this content need involve no more than the thought that such and such has been done and that this is a bad thing.

To return to the reaction to torture example, the anti-feeling qualifies as moral if it is prompted solely by the thought that someone has tortured an innocent person. It need not be accompanied, or prompted by, or involve the thought, 'People should not be treated like that.' But it is because the principle 'People should not be treated like that' could be invoked as a justification for the anti-feeling that this anti-feeling qualifies as moral. Note that the principle makes no mention of what should happen to those who violate it, but it is a moral principle none the less.

Now it might be said that since we think of moral principles as principles whose violation renders the agent liable to blame, appeal to any moral principle must involve notions of blameworthiness. Later in this chapter, I shall be discussing a closely related issue the upshot of which is that, except where moral principles are *about* blameworthiness, their moral content does not essentially depend on the connection between these principles and thoughts about blameworthiness.

I have argued that intense moral feelings could survive the full acknowledgement that no one deserved to be blamed or punished. And it seems plausible to say that we would find it very hard not to express these feelings. This means that we might continue to react to offenders in a punitive or condemning way despite the acknowledgement that they did not deserve punishment or condemnation.

Should we then give up the belief that it is unjust to blame those who do not fulfil the U-condition? It seems to me that such a question could only be motivated by some sort of confusion about what it is to have beliefs about justice and injustice. For it implies that a belief in what constitutes injustice could be deliberately dropped simply because it makes things awkward for us.

But if it were true that we could not stop ourselves from blaming in certain situations, then the realization that in doing so we are bound to be unjust would not lead to the disappearance of our belief about the injustice of such blaming; the hope of avoiding injustice would disappear, but the belief about what constitutes it would not.[4]

A consequentialist might argue that where we have a choice we should not give up blaming and that where we do not we should not worry about it because blaming can be justified by its beneficial consequences. To many the suggestion that blaming be retained because of its consequences would be abhorrent simply because they would not feel that anything could justify the violation of a principle of justice.[5]

But the consequentialist could reply that the price of not acting on his suggestion is probably one which most of us would not be willing to pay. For to give up moral condemnation would be to give up an essential device for inculcating and reinforcing those values we adhere to, while to give up punishment would be to endanger our safety.

I think that our commitment to the idea of desert is too strong for us to be able to stop worrying about the blaming we cannot give up. This need not disturb the consequentialist who might reason that since we cannot give up our reactions to certain situations, they will continue to have their beneficial effects despite our worries. But what about the first part of his suggestion, that we do not give up what we can give up?

I have claimed that it would be easiest to give up premeditated blaming and punishment; blaming and punishment which is not the immediate result of strong feeling. Now one could argue that deliberately to persist in treating offenders in ways which we no longer felt to be deserved would be to detract from the efficacy of such treatment in promoting the beneficial consequences envisaged by the consequentialist. For part of its efficacy must depend on our believing that the treatment is deserved. How could we, given our commitment to justice, wholeheartedly commit ourselves to continuing to do something unjust? Surely our rebukes would become half-hearted, the decision to punish would be taken uneasily.

On the other hand, we might find that the knowledge that our treatment of offenders was not justified by desert actually improved the moral quality of this treatment and in some cases its efficacy. For it would stop us from indulging in the more odious kinds of condemnation, those which smack of self-righteousness and smugness. If we fully accepted that none of us is responsible for being the sort of people we are, then we would find it impossible to adopt the tone of moral superiority which must provoke a great deal of resentment in offenders. Such resentment hardly bodes well for the future, so any device for controlling behaviour which can avoid provoking it will be more effective in promoting beneficial consequences.

But must we accept that we have no choice but to continue to do something which reflection reveals to be unjust? I have argued that we cannot give up our belief in what would constitute a just blaming simply because, as the world is, there can be no just blaming. But if it could be shown that the belief about the injustice of blaming was incoherent, this would be a completely acceptable reason for giving up that belief or, if we could not give it up, for ignoring it. In the first of his John Locke lectures on free will, Dennett suggests that the incompatibilist claim that blaming would be unfair in a deterministic world is incoherent. He does not argue much for this claim, offering in support of it only the following remark: 'of course, if there is no real freedom, there is no fair or unfair, there are no triumphs and no catastrophes.'[6] It looks as if Dennett thinks that the incompatibilist is logically committed to a very extreme thesis, the belief that if determinism is true and agents are not free then there can be *nothing* of value. But there is no reason to think that the incompatibilist is (or need be) committed to such a thesis. There is also no reason to think that the incompatibilist is committed to a position in terms of which there cannot be fair and unfair treatment. There are many situations in which it is appropriate to speak of fair and unfair treatment to which the issue of determinism is completely irrelevant, situations in which the criteria for fair treatment are based on criteria of desert which are not moral. For instance, we hold that it would be fair to distribute food to all those who are hungry and unfair to discriminate between the hungry on any basis other than need; and an incompatibilist is not precluded from using terms like 'fair' and 'unfair' of situations like these.

But of course to answer Dennett satisfactorily, we have to

show that the incompatibilist is entitled to use terms like 'fair' and 'unfair', 'just' and 'unjust' of situations in which the issue of *moral* desert is relevant. But why should it be thought that he is not entitled to do so? There is no obvious incoherence in the belief that blaming is unjust in a deterministic world because it is undeserved and its corollary, the belief that the just thing to do is not to blame in such a world.

Perhaps the argument for its being incoherent is this: to say that an act is 'unjust' is to say (in part) that it is wrong. To say that an act is 'wrong' is to say (in part) that it is one for which the agent deserves to be blamed. So the incompatibilist is committed by his belief in the injustice of blaming to this claim: since in the world as it is no one deserves to be blamed, anyone who does blame deserves to be blamed for doing so.

But are the connections between injustice and wrongness, wrongness and blameworthiness as tight as this argument suggests? Could one not defend the incompatibilist by saying that 'unjust act' simply means 'act which violates the requirements of justice', while 'wrong act' simply means 'act which violates the requirements of morality'?

I think that the connection between wrongness and injustice is as tight as the argument suggests. To do something unjust is to do something wrong (although of course it is not simply this). But the connection between wrongness and blameworthiness is neither as tight as the argument suggests, nor as loose as the attempted defence of the incompatibilist suggests. It does not follow from the claim that one has done something wrong that one deserves to be blamed for it. The offender might have acted inadvertently or been suffering from a psychotic delusion. So doing the wrong thing is not enough for blameworthiness. But while the connection between 'morally wrong' and 'blamable' is not one of full entailment, there is some logical connection. It is part of our common understanding of 'doing the wrong thing' that this makes one a prima-facie candidate for blame. 'Wrong acts' are 'acts for which an agent deserves blame, if he also fulfils certain other conditions.' Now the incompatibilist we are envisaging accepts that one of these other conditions cannot be fulfilled. So his belief that it would be unjust (and therefore wrong) to blame amounts, logically, to this: if you were to blame anyone you would be doing something to him which he does not deserve because no one can satisfy all the conditions for blameworthiness, and in doing this you would be doing something which would itself deserve blame, if it were not for the fact that since no one can deserve blame, you cannot either.

There is no incoherence here, but the discovery that this is what the incompatibilist's belief logically amounts to might be thought to undermine his position in a more subtle way. The argument I have in mind is this: the thought of injustice arouses strong feelings in many of us. We are often upset when we hear that others have been unjustly treated, outraged when we think that we have been and disturbed by the suggestion that we ourselves might be the perpetrators of injustice. These feelings are based on the belief that injustice is full-bloodedly wrong. And even when we acknowledge that injustice is sometimes excusable or even justified, we think of it as the kind of thing which *can* be fully-bloodedly wrong. It is this belief in the full-blooded wrongness of injustice which explains the strong impact on us of the incompatibilist's suggestion that blaming is unjust.

But we can now see from the logical exposition of that suggestion that the reason for concluding that blaming is unjust is at the same time a reason for concluding that injustice can never be full-bloodedly wrong. And this suggests that we should therefore feel less strongly about injustice than we do and thus less strongly about the incompatibilist's case. It is in this sense that the discovery of what his case logically amounts to is undermining of it. It diminishes its impact.

Now one thing which could be said in reply to this is that while the impact of the incompatibilist's case might be diminished in one respect, it might be strengthened in another. For the discovery that something we have always felt very strongly about is not something we need to feel very strongly about could have quite an impact of its own.

But I think that one can tackle the imagined argument head on: it is true that many of us react to injustice in a way which suggests that we think of it as full-bloodedly wrong, but I suspect that the idea we have of its full-blooded wrongness is rather vague; I doubt that we have any specific thoughts about the reasons for this. So it would be incorrect to suggest that our strong reaction to injustice is actually motivated by the thought that we can be blamed for being unjust.

'Still', someone might object, 'once we are convinced that we can't be blamed for anything, we will agree that one of the elements of full-blooded wrongness is missing and our feeling about injustice will be correspondingly weakened.'

I think that even if this thought were to have a weakening effect on our feelings, it would not make them significantly weaker because there are other elements associated with the idea that something is morally wrong which would continue to produce a strong emotional response. To see how one could be aroused by the idea of wrongness in full awareness that individuals do not deserve condemnation and punishment, imagine (as earlier) the reaction we would have if we had been told that someone had been physically tortured. We would think this very wrong and I suggest that we would continue to think this and to feel strongly about it even if we accepted that no one could be justly blamed for it. We would not conclude that the inflicting of pain in this way was not full-bloodedly wrong because the conditions for blameworthiness could not be met.

But all this shows, someone might say, is that we react strongly to thoughts of physical harm; this does not mean that the thought of injustice, particularly the abstract thought of injustice, would have such an effect.

I suspect that if we were asked to list acts which were morally wrong, the first kind of act which would spring to mind would involve physical injury to someone else. But perhaps it is precisely because we associate moral wrongness with physical harm that abstract concepts like 'moral wrongness' and 'injustice' often have the power to arouse strong feelings.

But also as our conception of what constitutes damage to someone enlarges to include emotional as well as physical damage, loss of dignity and self-esteem, as well as physical pain and disfigurement we come to accept that people can be injured by being made to feel inferior, ashamed, and unworthy, and if we are then told that they are being made to suffer these things undeservedly, we feel, I think, as upset (or nearly as upset) about this as we do about unprovoked physical harm.

We think of the wrongness of such treatment as consisting in its being the undeserved inflicting of harm, and I cannot see why the belief that it is very wrong would not survive the thought that no one can be blamed for inflicting it. To insist that it would not is to forget that the predominant element in the idea of an act's wrongness concerns the kind of thing which is being done to the victim. The idea that wrong acts are acts for which their agents can be blamed is subordinate to this other element.

So injustice is not thought of as wrong because it is the kind of thing for which you are blamed; rather it is thought of as the kind of thing for which you can be blamed because it is thought of as wrong, and it is thought of as wrong because of its possession of other features.

Conclusion

We are left with two unresolved tensions, first, the tension between the realization that in some cases we have no choice but to continue to react punitively to offenders (because our moral feelings are quite strong) and the belief that it is unjust to do so; secondly, the tension between our desire to continue to blame for the sake of its consequences and the belief that blaming is unjust. I can think of no way of resolving these tensions, but in the concluding chapter I shall propose something which will, I hope, help to make them less uncomfortable.

7

A compatibilist principle for just blaming

Because we are committed to the U-condition for blameworthiness and because the U-condition cannot be fulfilled, we are forced to conclude that blaming is unjust. This makes things uncomfortable for us since, for reasons discussed in the last chapter, we are committed to blaming.

This discomfort cannot be obliterated, but it might be possible to ease it. One way of easing it would be to accept that we are also committed to a compatibilist condition for blameworthiness whose fulfilment would preclude fulfilment of the U-condition. In Chapter 4 I suggested that we might be committed to such a condition, and I shall briefly summarize the main points of that discussion. We believe that deprived and non-deprived offenders should be treated differently. This sense of difference could be explained by the supposition that we believe in a principle of retributory balance, a principle which is connected with the idea that wrongdoers must pay for what they have done, but which stipulates that they must not pay either more or less than their offence warrants. In terms of this principle we would conclude that an offender who has suffered as part of the process of becoming the sort of person who fulfils the M-condition has already paid something in advance for his offence and in virtue of this deserves to pay less for his wrongdoing than someone who has not suffered (or suffered less) but has committed the same sort of offence.

So the principle of retributory balance generates a payment-in-advance-condition for blameworthiness. Unlike the U-condition which is a condition for blameworthiness *tout court*, the payment-in-advance-condition is a degree of blameworthiness condition. It comes into play only after an offender has already been judged to be blameworthy, its role being to determine how much an offender should suffer for his wrongdoing. Although it might be thought that belief in this degree of blameworthiness condition is not incompatible with belief in the U-condition (for one is concerned with degrees of blameworthiness and the other with blameworthiness), in fact the two beliefs are incompatible. For fulfilment of the payment-in-advance-condition requires a world in which M-states of mind are caused by states and events for which the offender is not responsible. Thus acceptance of this as a condition for blameworthiness commits one to the belief that it is just to blame offenders whose decisions and choices are caused in this way.

We are now in a position to see how if we did endorse the payment-in-advance-condition this would help to quell the uneasiness about the injustice of blaming: endorsement of the payment-in-advance-condition would commit us to the belief that the conditions for just blaming can be fulfilled in a world where people are not responsible for the desires which motivate their decisions and choices. What would these conditions be? Presumably, they would be the old compatibilist conditions, (*a*) that the agent did something wrong; and (*b*) that he did it as the result of an M-state of mind. But they would be morally bolstered by the addition of the requirement that any suffering experienced by the offender as a result of his becoming someone who fulfils the M-condition should be regarded as payment towards the price he is morally obliged to pay for his wrong doing. Now, unlike the U-condition, all of these conditions are empirically fulfillable.

Since we would be committed, via the sense of difference to the belief that the requirements for just blaming can be fulfilled in a world where the U-condition cannot be, we would have an acceptable reason for continuing to blame despite the fact that to do so would be to violate our U-condition belief about just blaming. It would be acceptable because, unlike the consequentialist rationale for continuing to blame, it does not ignore the demand of justice for *deserved* blame and punishment; instead it would be supported by the thought that the only requirements for just blaming which we can fulfil are those which preclude fulfilment of the U-condition requirement.

So the proposal would be that we accept that blaming can be justified non-consequentially and compatibilistically.

But this proposal is only acceptable if we do endorse the payment-in-advance-condition and, as we saw in Chapter 4, the

U-condition advocate has fairly strong grounds for suggesting that the sense of difference does not commit us to such an endorsement.

Perhaps, though, the case for such an endorsement could be strengthened by showing that there is an analogous principle for praiseworthiness which we would be willing to endorse. I shall call this 'the principle of compensation for effort' and will show that a commitment to this principle is incompatible with commitment to a U-condition.

The two conditions for praiseworthiness

It is plausible to assume that the sort of intuition which motivates commitment to a U-condition for blameworthiness would also motivate commitment to a U-condition for praiseworthiness. I mean the intuition that it is unjust to praise/blame someone who is not responsible for his motivating states. A U-condition for praiseworthiness would be satisfied whenever an agent's choosing to fulfil a moral requirement was not caused by anything unchosen by him.

But of course this is not sufficient for praiseworthiness. The agent must also have been motivated by a certain state of mind. Let us call this the 'R-condition'. The R-condition for praiseworthiness would be satisfied whenever an agent chose to fulfil a moral requirement because he wanted to do the right thing or the benevolent thing or because he had seen that to act in this way was to do the right thing or the benevolent thing. The claim that there is an R-condition for praiseworthiness does not need arguing for. We would all agree that a praiseworthy act is necessarily one which is undertaken for reasons of the kind mentioned above.[1]

But if fulfilment of the R-condition is necessary for praiseworthiness doesn't this mean that commitment to a U-condition for praiseworthiness is incoherent? For fulfilment of the R-condition requires that the right choice be made for certain reasons, while it was established in Chapter 5 that, among other things, since reasons are causes, fulfilment of the U-condition depends ultimately on the possibility of reasonless choices.

If it were only logically possible to fulfil the U-condition by an uncaused (and therefore reasonless) choice, then commitment to a U-condition for praiseworthiness would be incoherent. But, as we have seen, the U-condition can be fulfilled by a choice for reasons so long as that choice is caused by a reasonless choice. Thus an agent could make a reasonless choice to be motivated in future morally problematic situations by states of mind which fulfil the R-condition for praiseworthiness, such as the desire to do the right thing. His ultimate choice because reasonless would not be praiseworthy, but future choices would be. It might be argued that unless the original choice was praiseworthy, it could not give rise to praiseworthy choices. This is certainly what Kant felt.[2] But I do not see why a praiseworthy choice could not have as its originating antecedent cause a choice which was not praiseworthy. As I claimed in Chapter 3, praiseworthiness is different from blameworthiness in this respect, and as we have seen from Chapter 5, this is not the only respect in which the two differ.

But while the U-condition for praiseworthiness is not logically impossible to fulfil, it is probably empirically impossible to fulfil (if the arguments in Chapter 5 are correct).

This means that in so far as we are committed to a U-condition for praiseworthiness we are committed to the view that people do not deserve to be praised for doing the right thing. Does this mean that praising people would be unjust in the same way that blaming them would be? Not quite. The claim that it would be unjust to praise cannot be a straightforward counterpart to the claim that it would be unjust to blame and it is worth seeing why this is so before we continue with the main argument.

The injustice of praising and blaming

There are two ways in which one can be unjust by treating someone as he does not deserve:

1. One can be unjust to the person by treating him in the undeserved way; or
2. one can be unjust to others by not treating them in the same way, when there is no justifying basis for treating them differently.

Whether one is unjust in the first or the second way will

depend on whether the treatment meted out to the undeserving person is considered pleasant or unpleasant. When a person has been singled out for undeserved blame we feel that *he* has suffered an injustice. But we also feel that he has suffered an added injustice in being singled out from his fellows for such undeserved treatment, that is he has not only been treated unjustly by being blamed, he has been treated unjustly in relation to others. And we would feel that he has suffered this added injustice even if we believed that no one deserved blame.

On the other hand, when a person has been singled out for undeserved praise, we do not normally think that an injustice has been done to him, but we do feel that others who have not been praised have suffered an injustice, even if they too do not deserve praise (more so, of course, if they do deserve praise). Since our idea of what constitutes unjust treatment depends in part on the sort of treatment which is in question, we can see that in a world where no one deserved praise or blame, we could avoid responding unjustly to any agent in respect of his actions if we either desisted from both praise and blame, or we praised all agents. If, however, we were to blame all agents, although we would not have treated any agent unjustly in relation to his fellow agents, we would have treated each agent unjustly.

The unfairness inherent in our having the desires we do

To return to the main argument, I think it is plausible to attribute to anyone who endorses the U-condition for moral responsibility, the belief that in a world in which motivations are caused by unchosen states and people are praised and blamed, some agents are at an unfair advantage in relation to other agents because they have the sorts of desires which lead them to fulfil moral requirements, while others are at an unfair disadvantage in having the sorts of desires which lead them to flout moral requirements.

One can imagine the U-condition advocate reasoning like this: in a world in which motivations are caused by unchosen states, agents in morally problematic situations who fulfil the M-condition for blameworthiness do so because they are not moved enough by the thought that something is morally required of them to fulfil the requirement, while agents who do not fulfil the M-condition in these situations do so either because they are moved enough by this thought (in which case they might fulfil the R-condition for praiseworthiness) or because they are moved by morally neutral thoughts.

But for an agent to be moved enough depends on his having desires which will prompt him to attempt to fulfil the moral requirement (when he becomes aware of it) and his not being moved enough can be explained by his not having such desires or his having strong desires to perform acts which flout moral requirements.

It is not unreasonable to assume that the motivating desires which prompt moral action are distributed unequally, as are the desires which prompt immoral action, so that some people have more 'good' desires than others and some have more 'bad' desires than others. But this inequality in the distribution of 'good' and 'bad' desires is unfair because neither those who have 'good' nor those who have 'bad' desires can be said to deserve to have them. The differences are arbitrary, they have no justifying basis.[3]

In reply to such reasoning, it might be said that to speak of a man's not deserving to have certain desires is to misuse the concept of 'desert' for what can be said to be deserved must be something which is considered pleasant or unpleasant (reward or punishment, benefit or burden) and desires which are 'good' in the sense that they are conducive to moral action are not necessarily pleasant to have, while desires which are 'bad' in the sense that they are conducive to immoral action are not necessarily unpleasant to have.

The U-condition advocate could protest that although the having of such desires might not itself be pleasant or unpleasant, the consequences of having such desires are. For behaving well brings rewards such as praise, respect and esteem, while behaving badly brings punishment, shaming condemnation, the loss of respect, etc. It is in this sense, he might say, that those who have 'good' desires can be said to have an advantage lacked by those who do not, an advantage which is no more deserved than is the disadvantage of having 'bad' desires.

One can object by pointing out that in our world being good does not automatically bring rewards for the rightdoer and can bring suffering for him, while being bad does not automatically bring suffering to the wrongdoer and can bring benefits. Furthermore, it can be said that the mere having of bad desires does not inevitably lead to immoral action and thence to condemnation.

To this last point, the U-condition advocate will reply that a man will only not act to fulfil his 'bad' desires if he is moved enough to attempt to fulfil some moral requirement and he will only be moved enough if he has certain 'good' desires, and his having or not having these desires is a matter of luck.

Also, he might say, while it is true that the mere having of 'bad' desires may not lead to bad action if there are other desires to counter them, those who have 'bad' desires will find it more difficult to be good than those who do not and it is unfair that they should have to contend with a burden which those without such desires don't have as Feinberg says in *Doing and Deserving*:[4]

If Jones's chronic desire to do something harmful is as powerful as, but no more powerful then, normal people's desires to do socially acceptable things, then we think of Jones's desire as a kind of unfair burden. It is no harder for him to restrain, on individual occasions, but he must be restraining it *always*, one slip and he is undone. He is really quite unlucky to have this greater burden and danger. (pp. 289–90.)

But it can be argued against the U-condition advocate that in our world there are, at least in theory, approved mechanisms for compensating offenders who feel that their 'bad' desires are a burden, so that any unfairness could, to some extent, be rectified. This is so for the following reasons: having 'bad' desires will only be felt to be a burden if the desirer sees them as impelling him on a course he would, all things considered, rather not take (or if he sees them as preventing him from taking a course he would prefer to take). But if he does see them in this way then the chances are that he will have attempted not to act on them and this attempt could be one which exonerates the agent from blame, even if it is a failed attempt. For any agent who has attempted to comply with a moral requirement by struggling against a desire which has proved too much for him can be said to have offended *because* his desire was irresistible. And in Chapter 2 it was established that, in some cases, people who act because of the irresistibility of their desires do not fulfil the M-condition for blameworthiness.

So the reply to the U-condition advocate's claim about the unfairness of having the burden of bad desires is that in so far as they are felt as burdens, they are probably desires which the agent will have struggled not to act on, and if he does struggle not to act on them and fails, he will not fulfil the M-condition. If he does not fulfil the M-condition, he is not blameworthy even in a world in which fulfilment of the M-condition is considered sufficient for blameworthiness. Thus the unfairness of his having the burden of bad desires would to some extent be compensated for by his not being blameworthy.

The U-condition advocate would probably say that there is still an unfairness here. For the agent who struggles against his bad desires and escapes blameworthiness does so because he is lucky enough to have 'good' desires. If he didn't have these desires he would not struggle and would fulfil the M-condition. But since his having or not having these desires is not something for which he is responsible, the agent who does not struggle and who on this account fulfils the M-condition is at an unfair disadvantage.

But the U-condition advocate's response to those who struggle to comply with moral requirements is disquieting because it runs counter to a widespread, powerful and deep intuition about such struggles. This can be seen most clearly when we consider the struggle to be good which is motivated by desires which fulfil the R-condition.

The struggle to be good

I have suggested that if a man struggles to comply with a moral requirement and fails, then, at least, he escapes blameworthiness. But it could also be said that in some instances such a person actually deserves to be praised. If the struggle to comply with the moral requirement has been motivated either by benevolence or duty, then even if the agent fails to achieve his aim of compliance with the requirement, he deserves praise because in trying to fulfil the requirement for the right reasons he has achieved moral worth. The failed attempt to conform to a moral requirement can be a morally worthy act.

Now this is a particularly satisfying thought since there are so many situations in which an agent's unsuccessful efforts are not rewarded and about which we feel a certain uneasiness. For instance, when a student works hard to pass an examination and fails, we feel that he deserves *something* for his efforts although we acknowledge ruefully that according to the rules he does not merit a pass mark. But in the moral sphere the struggler can pass the test by merely struggling, for to try to be good is to achieve goodness and by virtue of this to deserve praise.

However, the U-condition advocate is committed to saying that if the person struggling to be good is not responsible for having the sorts of desires which induce him to struggle, then he deserves no praise for his act. One can imagine someone protesting, 'But . . . it isn't a matter simply of luck; it *is* a matter of effort.'[5] And the U-condition advocate replying: 'Very well, then, it is a matter of effort; without exerting the effort you may not overcome the deficiency. But whether or not you are the kind of person who has it in him to exert the effort is a matter of luck.'[6] But this reply, with its allusion to the familiar incompatibilist anxiety, falls strangely flat. Although this anxiety is capable of striking a responsive chord in many of us when raised about those whose achievements come easily to them, it fails to strike a responsive chord when raised about the effort-maker. The U-condition advocate's question—'How is it possible that a man should deserve praise for his acts when his acts are caused by desires for which he is not responsible?'—is liable to elicit from many of us the response, 'It is not possible.' But if for the word 'acts', the word 'struggles' were substituted instead, many of us would be tempted to answer that in this case, it is certainly possible.

Why should this be? Struggles are no more and no less act-like than other acts. And yet, the struggle has a response-provoking quality which is not shared by acts which are not struggles. We have a special feeling about the struggler and effort-maker which we don't have about those whose achievements come easily to them.

I would suggest that this special feeling is a matter of our viewing the effort-maker as someone who in making the effort has incurred a cost for which he deserves to be compensated. The view that praise is something which is due to a man as compensation for his well-motivated efforts would explain our resistance to the U-condition advocate's worry that the agent is not responsible for the desires which motivate him. On such a view of what it is to deserve praise, it would not matter that the effort-maker had done nothing to deserve the desires which prompted him to make the effort, it would be enough that he had made the effort. There would be no unfairness to those who had not made an effort in praising those who had.

But if praise for moral right-doing is to be viewed solely as compensation deserved for well-motivated efforts, then we must abandon any thought of its being due to a person who is benevolent or dutiful without effort, that is we must reject the traditional view that it is sufficient for praiseworthiness that a person's right doing is undertaken for the sake of duty or benevolence. Praiseworthiness would also require that his right-doing was an effort for him.

It might be thought that this means we have to endorse the principle that men are only praiseworthy if they have had to struggle against a disinclination to fulfil moral requirements. But it does not mean this. For the struggle to be good need not involve a struggle against oneself. It could, for instance, involve making an effort to overcome some physical obstacle in order to help someone, or in order to do something else which is considered morally worthwhile.

The thought that praise for moral right-doing should be reserved for those who have struggled (or made an effort) to be good is one which might appeal to philosophers who believe that a just society is one in which burdens and benefits are distributed equally and who argue on this basis that since the effort to contribute to society involves the incurring of a burden, that effort ought to be rewarded (even if it does not succeed). Such philosophers maintain that the agent who contributes without effort does not deserve to benefit as a matter of justice but they do not deny that there may be other grounds on the basis of which the effortless contributor can be judged an appropriate candidate for reward, for example that of utility.[7]

But why should we accept the principle that praise is deserved only by rightly motivated strugglers and deny that it is deserved by agents who do right effortlessly from benevolence or a sense of duty? There are other views of praise which are less restrictive and which, in being able to accommodate the effortless but well-meaning right-doer, are more in keeping with traditional intuitions.

Thus, if we accepted the view that praise should be seen as something like a 'payment deserved for goods received' (the 'goods' in this case being moral goods), this would enable us to say that both non-effort-making and effort-making right-doers deserved it.

However, this would leave out the person struggling to be good who failed to perform an act which benefits someone else; for although he would have produced something morally worthy, he would not have produced anything which could be said to have been 'received' by anyone. And surely any acceptable notion of praiseworthiness must be one which allows us to say that the failed struggler can be praiseworthy.

Perhaps then praise could be viewed as 'payment deserved for goods produced (well-meaningly)'. This would enable us to accommodate the traditional view that all well-meaning right-doers deserve praise without excluding the person struggling to be good who fails.

But I think that it would be better to reject the traditional view and to instead revise our conception of praiseworthiness so that it covers only those who have made an effort to be good. For only such a modification to our beliefs about praiseworthiness would render them immune to the worries of the incompatibilist since, as I have shown, these worries should only arise in connection with those whose good actions come easily to them.

But how much should our conception of praiseworthiness be revised? It might be thought that the revised conception should be one which applies only to those whose struggles to do the right thing are rightly motivated. This would mean that it would retain the traditional requirement of a certain sort of motive, for example benevolence or duty.

But there is a case for suggesting that the revision in our conception of praiseworthiness should be even more drastic than this, that it should include all strugglers to do the right thing, whatever their motives.

I say this because only such a conception would enable us to include those individuals who have been so grossly emotionally deprived that they have never been able to develop a sense of concern for others, and who are unlikely, therefore, to have benevolent motives (or dutiful ones). But such individuals could well be motivated to do the right thing (as most of us are at some time) by the desire for affection, or approval, or the fear of punishment.[8]

What I am proposing is so drastic that I know many will find it unacceptable. Nevertheless, I think it comes much closer to satisfying the demands of justice than the previous proposals.

But in holding that only those who have to struggle (for whatever reason) to be good deserve praise, am I not unduly depriving those whose good actions come easily to them? I do not think so. People who are naturally and easily benevolent, thoughtful and kind are usually liked; they often provoke gratitude, affection and even love. To be found likeable or pleasing to others is an immensely rewarding experience. It would be no hardship, I think, to many of those who provoke such reactions to be excluded from the domain of those who are considered *morally* praiseworthy. (This is not to suggest that moral strugglers might not also be likeable, but those who have to make an effort to do the kind or unselfish thing are probably less liked than those who do not.)

Conclusion

The principle of compensation for effort and the principle of retributory balance are analogous in several respects. Each involves the idea of cost and payment. Each can be applied in a world where agents' states of mind are caused by factors for which they are not responsible and each represents a condition which can be fulfilled both logically and empirically. In the case of blameworthiness, this is the payment-in-advance condition, in the case of praiseworthiness the condition that some effort must be made.

Each principle also seems consistent with our sense of what is just. It is just that people should be compensated for their efforts; it is just that people should not pay more than their offence warrants, and if they have already paid something in advance, then it is just that they should not pay as much as those who have not.

Because these principles (at least to some extent) satisfy our sense of justice, they could be used to underpin a compatibilist approach to moral responsibility which is superior to the traditional compatibilist approach in terms of which all that matters is what the agent has done and what his state of mind was when he did it. Knowing, as we now know, that emotional deprivation in childhood can be responsible for states of mind which lead to harmful behaviour, the traditional compatibilist approach to blameworthiness appears inadequate. Feeling as we do that those who struggle to achieve deserve something in the way of compensation which is not deserved by those whose achievements come easily to them, the traditional compatibilist approach appears inadequate in respect of praiseworthiness.

But while the different approach recommended is superior to the traditional approach, there remains the worrying possibility that we are not really committed via the sense of difference to a payment-in-advance condition.

The arguments in favour of our being so committed are:

1. that the idea has an intuitive appeal; and
2. that we would endorse an analogous condition for praiseworthiness.

But the intuitive appeal of the first idea is balanced by the intuitive appeal of the U-condition advocate's rival explanation for the sense of difference. And also, it could be that what has the intuitive appeal is not so much the idea that *we are committed via the sense of difference to a payment in advance condition*, as the idea of the payment-in-advance condition itself. As for the second argument, although it is satisfying to have a unified theory of moral responsibility, the fact that if we did endorse both conditions we would have such unity, is not a strong argument for our actually being committed to both.

Those who find the U-condition advocate's explanations more convincing will conclude that we are committed wholly to the U-condition for blameworthiness. Since, however, the explanations only relate to blameworthiness, it would be possible at the same time, and without inconsistency, to endorse the new compatibilist condition for praiseworthiness.

Furthermore, although someone committed only to the U-condition for blameworthiness cannot endorse the payment-in-advance condition as one which is relevant to *deserved* blame and punishment, he might be willing to endorse its adoption as a *faute de mieux* step. The sort of view I have in mind is one which, while acknowledging that there can be no just blame or punishment, is nevertheless convinced (perhaps by the arguments in Chapter 6), both that we cannot give up reacting punitively and condemningly when strong moral feelings are aroused and that if we could give these up, the price in lost security would be too high. Such a view would then embrace an analogue of the payment-in-advance condition as something which should be added to the traditional compatibilist approach in order to ensure at least some kind of justice for wrongdoers.

It seems to me that, whether or not one believes that there is a compatibilist *justification* for blaming, our only hope of *justice* lies in adopting the payment-in-advance condition.

But while this approach offers the only chance of justice, it is not without its problems. I shall end by briefly discussing some of these and tentatively suggesting some solutions.

First, one has to explain how the payment-in-advance condition would enable us to deal justly with the problem cases which, as we saw in Chapter 4, generate a commitment to the U-condition. But this is not very difficult since, as we found when discussing these cases, it can be said that offenders whose morally reprehensible states of mind are the result of brain damage, brain tumours, etc., have paid a price in virtue of their having acquired the states of mind in these ways. So appealing to the payment-in-advance condition for these cases would justify the belief that problem-case offenders should be treated less harshly than those whose states of mind are not the result of such factors. And this, while not completely satisfying our sense of justice, since we believe the offenders in these cases are not blameworthy *at all*, would nevertheless be a just solution and it is, in any case, the best we can do.

A more serious problem is this: the belief that the offender must pay for what he has done seems to involve the thought that the victim of his action should be compensated for the wrong done to him. But if the payment-in-advance condition were invoked then offenders with certain backgrounds would be deemed to deserve to pay less[9] for their offending than others and this would mean that the compensation to victims would vary not just with the varying gravity of the offence but with the varying backgrounds of the offenders. And it seems unjust that the victim should receive less compensation simply because the persons who offended against him are deemed to have paid something in advance. After all, the price paid in advance has not been paid to the victim.

One answer to this is suggested by an argument of Ted Honderich's in his book *Punishment*. Honderich argues that part of what it means to say that a person deserves to pay for a particular offence is that his punishment will bring satisfaction to the person or persons he has offended against. But he adds that the satisfaction should be seen as the satisfaction of the victim's grievance and that the grievance should be seen as something whose size will vary with 'the extent to which the offender may be regarded as responsible for his action'.[10] Honderich also claims that grievances should be seen not just as injuries but as feelings, in particular as desires for satisfaction. It would be consistent with this view to suggest that the amount of punishment which would be required to satisfy the victim's desire will depend on the victim's belief about the offender's background. The thought would be that, if the victim believes that the offender has become an offender because of circumstances which involved suffering for him, then the victim would be satisfied if the offender were punished with less harshness than his offence might otherwise be thought to warrant. But this suggestion is not satisfactory for two reasons, first, because it links the question of punishment with what the victim believes to be the case and this could lead to injustice; and secondly, because it is not certain that all victims would be influenced by knowledge of the offender's background. I think that if the grievance of a victim is something whose size varies with the responsibility of the offender, then it should not be equated with the victim's desire for satisfaction. But then it becomes unclear in what sense the grievance of the victim is a grievance *against the offender*.

Perhaps the belief that compensation is due to the victim could be distinguished from the belief that the offender must pay for what he has done. An indication that these beliefs are recognized as independent is the existence of the Criminal Injuries Compensation Board whose function is to award compensation to victims of violence out of public funds. The fact that the scheme for compensating victims of crimes of violence operates separately from the procedures for trying and sentencing those who have committed these crimes could suggest that punishment of the offender is not viewed as a way of compensating his victim and this in turn could suggest that payment for an offender's crime is viewed as payment for a wrong done which is independent of the suffering caused to the victim.[11]

On the other hand, it might be argued that the scheme can be seen as an expression of the belief that punishment of the offender is not enough compensation for the victim who deserves something more tangible to make up for what he has suffered. More important, though, than what the feelings might actually be which have prompted the scheme is whether a moral case can be made for separating the question of what is due from the offender for his wrong and what is due to the victim who has been wronged. There is need for more work here, but it is beyond the scope of this book.

It might be objected that I have placed too much emphasis on those moral wrongs which are the subject of the criminal law and that in doing so I have distorted the discussion of blameworthiness by focusing too much on punishment. I think it is difficult to discuss blameworthiness without some reference to punishment. What can it mean to deserve to be blamed if not to deserve something which is unpleasant? Someone might say: 'This need not be punishment, but simply a rebuke.' But is not the strong rebuke a form of punishment? I think that the idea of punishment for blameworthiness is not confined to legal contexts. But it is useful to be able to refer to the legal institution of punishment because it so starkly represents the kind of beliefs about a wrongdoer's just deserts with which we are concerned. This is because it is (partly, but deeply) rooted in the idea of just retribution, an idea which crucially depends on the notion of moral desert.

This brings me to another problem for the payment-in-advance condition. When a terrible crime (wrong) has been committed, it is difficult to discern in our response to the offender a belief about what he deserves which is separate from our abhorrence of what he has done. And it might seem to follow from this that in these cases there is no independent

notion of what the offender deserves in terms of which the payment-in-advance condition would be relevant.

I think that to come to such a conclusion would be a mistake.
In cases of terrible wrongs, our initial response to the offender
is, no doubt, a simple mixture of horror, revulsion and rage. But
this is not a sufficient basis for concluding that we believe that
the question of what he deserves is answerable solely by reference to our feelings of horror.

Of course, in such cases, it is possible (and sometimes prob-
able) that reflective beliefs about what the offender deserves will
play no role at all in decisions about the treatment to be meted
out to him. The desire to satisfy public outrage or to give
expression to public abhorrence or the need to protect society,
these might all contribute to the offender's receiving a sentence
which in terms of the payment-in-advance condition he does not
deserve. This does not mean that we do not, or that we ought
not to endorse such a condition. It simply means that in these
cases ideals other than the ideal that justice should be served
have prevailed.

Appendix
Freedom, Moral Responsibility, and Motivation in the Critique of Practical Reason

I shall examine an argument in Kant's *Critique of Practical Reason* for the claim that the existence of the freedom to act independently of natural causes is a necessary condition for the existence of morality. This argument is different from the one which is usually discussed of Kant's, namely the argument which assumes that the freedom to act independently of natural causes is a necessary condition of moral responsibility; and before examining it, I shall indicate how it differs from the more usually discussed argument about moral responsibility and the bearing it has on the freewill–determinism debate.

The core of the usually discussed argument can be found in the *Critique of Pure Reason*, in Kant's solution to the Third Antinomy. There Kant tried to reconcile what he took to be two conflicting doctrines, the claim that determinism is true and the claim that it is justifiable to praise and blame agents for their actions. It is clear that Kant was an incompatibilist: he saw determinism as a threat to moral responsibility. And he also believed that the principle of causal determination is constitutive of experience. So he concluded that it was only possible for praise and blame to be justified if human beings were not just members of the causally determined world of nature, but also members of a non-causally determined, non-spatio/temporal 'noumenal' world, a world which was in some way linked with the world of nature. Kant felt that by establishing the possibility that men were members of such a world, he had established the possibility of their freedom and that by establishing the possibility of their freedom, he had established the possibility of moral responsibility.

But Kant's proposed solution is rightly regarded as unsatisfactory. For one thing, his claim that human beings are moral agents by virtue of their membership of the noumenal world gives us no reason to assume that we can hold them morally responsible for what they do in this world; particularly since, according to Kant, in the natural world all human actions are causally determined. For another, it is not clear how agents in the natural world could be identified with agents in the noumenal world which is *ex hypothesi* a non-spatio/temporal world. Also, the doctrine of 'noumenalism' involves incoherencies like non-temporal 'choices' and 'acts of will'.

Of course, the unsatisfactoriness of Kant's solution cannot be used as an argument against his incompatibilist intuition that there is a conflict between unqualified determinism and moral responsibility. If Kant is wrong about this, then his wrongness must be established on different grounds. On the other hand, in the Third Antinomy, Kant does not *argue* for his incompatibilist intuition; rather, he more or less assumes that the freedom to act independently of natural causes is a necessary condition of moral responsibility[1] and the compatibilist can legitimately criticize him for this absence of argument.

In the *Critique of Practical Reason*, Kant does provide an argument for the incompatibilist intuition, but it is an indirect one. It is indirect because Kant does not argue for the claim that the justifiability of blame for the flouting of moral requirements (or of praise for fulfilling them) would be threatened by determinism; instead he argues that unless the absence of causal determination is possible, *there can be no moral requirements*.

Now, this second claim, which Kant does not always clearly distinguish from the first, is more fundamental than the claim that if determinism is true it is not justifiable to praise or to blame agents. Nevertheless, it presents just as much of a challenge to the compatibilist belief that praiseworthiness and blameworthiness are compatible with determinism. For if there can be no requirements then, of course, there can be no praise or blame for their fulfilment or non-fulfilment. Thus if Kant's belief could be substantiated that the requirements themselves depend on freedom from causal determination, then the incompatibilist intuition that determinism poses a threat to moral appraisal would be vindicated.

But, for the purposes of this discussion, the most important respect in which Kant's argument differs from that in the *Critique of Pure Reason* is in the reason for which freedom is held to be necessary. In the *Critique of Pure Reason*, it is assumed to be necessary in order to ensure that agents could have acted otherwise. This is the familiar, traditional, incompatibilist belief about moral responsibility. But in the argument we are considering the claim that morality requires the falsity of unqualified determinism is thought to follow from the claim that morality requires the existence in human beings of a desire-independent ability to act. And the power of this latter claim lies in its appearing to follow from the incontrovertible assertion that there are moral requirements.

I shall argue that the claim that morality requires the falsity of determinism does not follow from the claim that it requires the existence of a desire-independent ability to act and thus that Kant fails to establish that morality and determinism are incompatible.

But this still leaves the argument about desires intact and, although Kant does not realize it, this argument, even when detached from the claim about determinism, has an important bearing on the debate about determinism. For it implies that the existence of moral requirements depends on the falsity of a belief about human motivation which is widely thought to be true—the belief that human beings could never act unless they had certain desires. So if the argument about desires succeeds and the belief about human motivation is true, then there are no moral requirements. And if there are no moral requirements, then the age-old debate between the compatibilist and the incompatibilist about the relationship between moral responsibility and determinism is superfluous.

The elements of Kant's argument are to be found mainly in the first chapter of the second *Critique*.[2] While many of the elements are immediately accessible, some of them are submerged in the sense that they are not explicit assertions but can be said to follow from what is explicitly asserted. Because some of the elements are submerged and because they are not presented by Kant in the order in which I shall present them, I cannot be certain that this is the argument he saw himself as offering. At the least, it can be said that it is an argument he would have been committed to endorsing since it follows from much of what he says in the first chapter. For this reason, I feel it is justifiable to refer to the argument as 'Kant's argument'.[3]

My examination of Kant's argument will proceed in three stages. In Stage I, I present a bare outline of the argument (*a*), followed by (*b*) a more detailed presentation and finally (*c*) a criticism of it. In Stage II, I examine those elements of the argument which survive the initial criticisms of (*c*). It is at this stage that I argue that the claim about determinism does not follow from the claim about desires. In Stage III I discuss the claim that morality requires the existence in human beings of a desire-independent ability to act and the belief that human beings cannot act without desires. (I call this belief 'the psychological thesis'.)

For those who want to see at a glance what happens to Kant's argument as it proceeds through each stage, I have added a description in outline form at the end of the Appendix.

Stage I

(*a*) A bare outline of the argument

1. There are moral requirements.
2. Moral requirements are essentially unconditional, universal, necessary and *a priori*.
3. No requirements based on the desires and inclinations of agents could have the nature of moral requirements, that is they could not be unconditional, universal, necessary and *a priori*.
4. If men could not fulfil moral requirements, there could not be moral requirements (ought implies can).
5. To fulfil moral requirements, men must act independently of their desires and inclinations.
6. All and only acts caused by desires and inclinations are causally determined.
7. Therefore, to act independently of desires and inclinations men must be free from causal determination.

Conclusion: Agents' freedom from causal determination is a necessary condition of the existence of moral requirements.[4]

(b) A more detailed presentation of the argument

1. *There are moral requirements*

Kant speaks on page 117 of 'the moral law of which we become directly conscious' and he says on page 120 'We may call the consciousness of this fundamental law a fact of reason'. Of course, these claims refer to the supreme moral requirement, the requirement that we act only on maxims which we can will as universal laws. But implicit in the recognition of this supreme requirement is the recognition that there will be a multiplicity of moral requirements which are generated by it, a host of true statements about what we ought and ought not to do in different situations.

2. *Moral requirements are essentially unconditional, universal, necessary and* a priori

They are unconditional in the sense that the truth that agents ought to perform a certain action (say ϕ) does not depend on the presence in those agents of any particular desires or aims (pp. 106, 107, 117, 119, 120, 121, 123). They are universal in the sense that they apply to all agents in relevantly similar situations (pp. 105, 106, 107, 115, 120, 123–4). A statement on page 107 which partly captures both of these points is the following: 'rules are objectively and universally valid only when they hold without any contingent subjective conditions which distinguish one rational being from another.' When Kant says that moral requirements are 'necessary' he means two things by this. First, he means that they are categorical (p. 106), that is that they are unconditional and that they command absolute obedience. Thus, he describes the moral law on page 119 as commanding that: 'We absolutely must proceed in a certain manner. The practical rule is therefore unconditional, and hence it is conceived *a priori* as a categorically practical proposition by which the will is determined absolutely and immediately.'

Kant calls such 'categorical' necessity 'objective necessity' and contrasts it with 'subjective necessity', the necessity a rule has for those for whom following it is a means to some end they desire (pp. 107, 114, 126). But Kant also uses the term 'necessary' to mean 'non-contingent'. Thus, on page 106 he says: 'the necessity is wanting which—if it is to be practical must be in-

dependent on conditions which are pathological and are therefore only contingently connected with the will.' And on page
113, he denies that a universal desire for happiness and a universal agreement on what would constitute it could be the basis of
a moral law because (he says) such unanimity would be contingent.

Finally moral requirements are *a priori* in the sense that they
can be known without consulting experience (p. 114). Kant says
on page 114 'practical laws ... must be known by reason *a
priori*, not by experience ...'

*3. If moral requirements were based on the desires of agents,
they could not be unconditional* (pp. 113–4, 122, 123), *universal*
(pp. 113, 122, 123, 125), *necessary* (pp. 107, 113, 114, 123, 124,
125, 126) *and* a priori (pp. 108, 113).

For then the truth of statements expressing them, that is the
truth that agents ought to do such and such, would depend on
the truth of the claim that agents had certain desires and inclinations. And if the truth of moral ought statements did depend on
the truth of claims that agents had certain desires or inclinations
then those statements could not have the particular features
which distinguish moral from non-moral requirements. For instance, since claims about the existence of certain desires and inclinations are contingent, any claims based on them could not
be necessary. Kant says at page 97: 'It is a clear contradiction to
try to extract necessity from a principle of experience and to try
by this to give a judgement true universality.' There are a
number of other passages in which Kant makes the point that
desire-based rules could not have the logical features of moral
requirements, but I shall quote just one:

Even supposing, however, that all finite rational beings were
thoroughly agreed ... still they could by no means set up the principle
of self-love as a practical law for this unanimity itself would only be
contingent. The principle of determination would still be only subjectively valid and merely empirical, and would not possess the necessity
which is conceived in every law, namely, an objective necessity arising
from *a priori* grounds (p. 113).

On the basis of these remarks, we are justified, I think, in assuming that Kant would have endorsed the following interim conclusion: *The truth value of claims that agents ought morally to*

perform certain acts is independent of the truth value of claims
that agents do/do not want to perform those acts.

4. The truth of the claim that agents ought morally to perform certain acts depends on the truth of the claim that agents can perform those acts

Of course, Kant does not put it like this, but he says enough to
indicate that this is what he believes. Thus, on page 120, he
claims that principles of morality can only apply to those capable of acting according to principles and, on page 126, that
agents must be capable of knowing how to fulfil requirements if
these requirements are to apply to them. But on page 119,
Kant's endorsement of the 'ought implies can' principle is at its
most explicit. He says there of an imaginary agent: 'He judges,
therefore, that he can do a certain thing because he is conscious
that he ought ...' I want to pause for a moment to consider
what has been established. Since (by step 3) it can be true that
agents ought morally to perform certain acts even if it is false
that they want to perform those acts, and since (by step 4), it can
only be true that agents ought to act if they can act, and since
(by step 1), it is true that agents ought to perform certain acts, it
follows that agents must be able to act even if they do not want
to act. It must be true that agents can fulfil moral requirements
whatever they happen to desire.

If we assume for the moment that premisses 1 to 4 are acceptable, the argument so far can be said to have established only
that human agents can act independently of their desires in
order to act morally, it has not established that men have to act
independently of their desires in order to act morally. From the
fact that the moral 'ought' applies whatever you desire, it does
not follow that it cannot be fulfilled as the result of a desire. To
claim that it did follow would be to confuse questions of justification with questions of motivation, that is to confuse claims
about what justifies the statement that an act is morally required
with claims about what it is that motivates an agent to fulfil a
moral requirement.

But Kant need not be seen as guilty of this confusion. For he
also holds that immanent in all moral requirements is the re-
quirement-to-act-independently-of-desires. He says of the
moral law on pages 117–9 not just that 'reason presents it as a

principle of determination not to be outweighed by any sensible conditions, nay wholly independent of them', but also that 'we can become conscious of pure practical laws . . . by attending to the necessity with which reason prescribes them and *to the elimination of all empirical conditions which it directs*. Thus, in addition to the claim that the moral requirement is unconditional in nature we have Kant's claim that

5. *The moral requirement commands an unconditioned response, a response unconditioned by desires and inclinations*

(See also Chapter 3, pp. 165 and 178.) It commands all agents to act (in part) by first setting aside desires and inclinations.

6. *All and only acts caused by desires and inclinations are causally determined*

(Remarks which add up to textual evidence that Kant believed this can be found on pp. 107–8, 109, 111–2, 114, 116, 122, 133, 166, 187.) Kant believed that the will was determined exclusively either by desires and inclinations or by pure reason. He also believed that it was only desires and inclinations which could be called empirical determining influences (pp. 107–8, 109, 114, 116, 187). On the basis of these beliefs and his belief that in the empirical world all events were causally determined, he seems to have concluded that acts were causally determined iff they were determined by desires and inclinations. (On page 122, Kant speaks of 'the physical law that we should follow some impulse or inclination.')

7. *Therefore, to act independently of desires and inclinations men must be free from causal determination*

(See pages 122 and 165.) Kant assumes that he has demonstrated that the fact of freedom follows from the fact of morality. And he assumes that the agent who sees that he is bound by a moral requirement must also see that he is free. On page 119 he says: 'He judges, therefore, that he can do a certain thing because he is conscious that he ought, and he recognises that he is free, a fact which but for the moral law he would never have known.' The conclusion that freedom follows from morality is at the same time a conclusion that: the existence of freedom (from causal determination) is a necessary condition for the existence of morality. As Kant says on page 88: 'Freedom is the *ratio essendi* of the moral law.'

(c) Criticism of the argument

One of the most contentious premises is step 5, the claim that we are always morally required to act independently of desires, that is that any requirement does not just consist in an injunction to do something, but consists in an injunction to do something *desirelessly*. One's immediate reaction to this is to deny it and to insist that our awareness of a particular moral requirement is an awareness simply that we ought to do something or other, and not an awareness that we ought to disregard desires and inclinations in order to do it. It is tempting to assume that Kant has simply confused the claim that the moral law commands action unconditionally with the claim that it commands unconditioned action, action unconditioned by desires. But there are hints in the first chapter of the *Critique of Practical Reason* that Kant felt he could support step 5. For he explicitly endorses the belief that all desires are self-regarding (pp. 108–12), and that *qua* creatures of nature, human agents are necessarily and always motivated by self-love (p. 112). Such beliefs would be prima-facie reasons for assuming that to be motivated by a desire is *ipso facto* to be motivated in a way which is inimical to the fulfilling of a moral requirement. And it might seem to follow from this that in order to fulfil any moral requirement we must disregard desires. But even if the foregoing were true, this still would not license the conclusion that any moral requirement *is* always a requirement to disregard desires. Indeed, Kant himself could be said to have a reason for not accepting the claim that underlying all moral requirements is the requirement to disregard desires. For this claim is incompatible with the belief that it is possible to act in accordance with the moral law, but not for the sake of it; that it is possible for one's actions to have 'legality' but not 'morality' (see p. 164, Ch. 3). One's intuitive understanding of this claim is that it is possible for an agent to do the right thing from a selfish motive. But if doing the right thing consists (in part) in disregarding one's desires and inclinations, then this is impossible. It would seem impossible to do the legal thing without doing the moral thing.

However, it might be held that if to be motivated by a desire is *ipso facto* to be motivated in a way which is inimical to the fulfilling of a moral requirement (as suggested above), then in order to fulfil any moral requirement agents must disregard desires. And since the ability to fulfil moral requirements is a condition of their applicability, the ability to disregard desires would be a condition of their applicability. Kant would still be entitled to this conclusion although he would not be able to claim that the requirement consisted in a requirement to set aside desires.[5] But is there any reason to accept that to be motivated by a desire is *ipso facto* to be motivated in a way which is inimical to the fulfilling of a moral requirement, once we have rejected the claim that the requirement consists in a requirement to disregard desires? Even if, for the moment, we accept Kant's claim that all desires are self-regarding (a claim which is inconsistent with his acknowledgement elsewhere that men can be moved by benevolent desires), it would be perfectly possible for someone to be moved by a self-regarding desire to fulfil a moral injunction such as 'Help others'. Of course his motive would not be moral, but his action would constitute a fulfilment of the moral requirement.

What I have just said might seem to contradict one of Kant's most insistent claims, that to act morally is necessarily to act-for-the-sake-of-duty. But if this means that only action-for-the-sake-of-duty *can fulfil a moral requirement*, then as we have seen there is reason not to accept this claim. Nevertheless, we can distinguish between an act which is 'moral' in Kant's terms, that is one undertaken for the sake of duty, and an act which fulfils the moral requirement. The argument we are examining is an argument which begins from premises about the nature of the moral requirement and moves to claims about the nature of the will which is needed to fulfil such requirements. We have seen that there is reason to reject the claim that the requirement consists partly in a requirement to be motivated in a certain way. If therefore, requirements are purely requirement-to-act, then there is prima facie no reason for denying that agents can fulfil these requirements as the result of all sorts of motives, selfish desires and inclinations included. This does not mean that we have to reject Kant's claim that only morally motivated action is praiseworthy, this is consistent with our intuitions about such things,[6] although many do not accept Kant's doctrine that benevolent desires cannot be part of such a motivation.[7]

But in addition to acknowledging the possibility of benevolent desires and then discarding them as sources of moral motivation, as we have seen, Kant also, and inconsistently, claims that all desires are self-regarding. In rejecting this belief, we find further reason to reject Kant's belief that to be motivated by a desire or inclination is *ipso facto* to be motivated in a way which is inimical to the fulfilment of moral requirements.

It is not just Kant's fifth premiss which presents problems. The second and fourth premisses contain elements which are inconsistent with one another. Thus if, as is claimed in premiss 4, the truth value of 'ought' statements depends on the truth value of 'can' statements, then statements expressing moral requirements cannot be known *a priori* (as claimed in premiss 2), because our knowledge of what particular agents can do is empirical.

It might be objected that to say this is to overlook the fact that, despite appearances, moral requirements do not enjoin agents to succeed in bringing about a particular state of affairs, but to try to do so (see Chapter 2). And, the objection would continue, while it is true that we don't know *a priori* whether people can succeed in doing things, we do know *a priori* that people can try to do certain things, and in knowing this *a priori*, we can know *a priori* that the moral ought applies to them.

But the claim that we know *a priori* that people can try to do certain things seems to me false. The ability to try to do certain things depends both on an agent's motivational propensities and his capacity to envisage a way of bringing about a state of affairs which he can engage in. We do not know *a priori* that any particular agent has the right motivational propensities or the capacity to envisage how he might try.

It might be further objected that nevertheless Kant was right in thinking that there are things we know *a priori* about moral requirements; for instance, we know *a priori* that moral requirements must be universalizable. This might be true, but it does not count against the claim that knowledge of whether individual requirements apply to individual agents cannot be *a priori* if applicability depends on ability. Furthermore, statements about an agent's abilities are contingent: so, if moral 'ought' statements depend on 'can' statements for their validity, then they cannot be 'necessary' in one of the senses in which Kant thought that statements expressing moral requirements are necessary, that is in the sense that they are not based on any contingent claim. I shall assume at this point that the fourth premiss is true and that Kant's second premiss must be revised to avoid contradiction. Deprived of its fifth premiss, and of those elements in the second premiss which render it inconsistent with the fourth, what elements remain of Kant's argument and can these remaining elements be used to support any conclusions about freedom?

Stage II

We are left with the following claims:

1. that there are moral requirements;
2. that these requirements are unconditional and universal;
3. that if these requirements depended for their legitimacy on the presence of desires and inclinations in potentially responsive agents they could not be unconditional and universal;
4. that all agents to whom the moral requirement applies, that is to whom the 'ought' statement is rightfully addressed, can comply with that requirement;
6. that all and only acts caused by desires and inclinations are causally determined;
7. that to act independently of desires and inclinations is to manifest one's freedom from causal determination.

Now to examine these premisses. The first premiss needs neither explanation nor justification, it is both self-explanatory and true. It seems also to be true that moral demands are unconditional, in the sense that their legitimacy as moral demands does not depend on our having any particular desires or inclinations. But it might be objected that there could be occasions when what constitutes a person's moral duty depends on what he happens to desire. One can envisage situations in which it might be morally wrong for someone to perform a certain action *because* he lacks or has certain desires and inclinations.[8]

For example, it might be wrong for a person who has an in-eradicable aversion to sights of physical disfigurement to seek work with those who have been physically disfigured; or it might be wrong for someone who values intellectual ability above all else to become a teacher of the mentally handicapped. For having these particular likes and dislikes could militate against their treating the patients or pupils in their care with humanity and kindness. Thus, it seems we have sometimes to take account of our desires and inclinations in order to decide what our moral duties are.

But this point does not threaten the general claim about the unconditionality of the moral requirement. The examples rely for their force on the principle that we ought not to harm others. The person who values intellectual ability above all else would run the risk of harming his mentally handicapped pupils by being unable to respond to them with genuine liking or affection. But his duty not to harm them is not a duty which is conditional on his having or lacking a particular desire—that duty *is* unconditional. The relevance of his inclinations is not that they determine whether or not he ought to fulfil the basic moral principles. Rather, his knowledge of his inclinations can help him to gauge how best to conform to those principles.

It also seems to be true that moral demands are universal in the sense that what is a requirement for one person in certain circumstances is a requirement for all persons in relevantly similar circumstances, and the notion of 'a relevantly similar circumstance' does not include the idea that agents who are morally bound by the requirement must have similar desires. This third premiss appears to be a negative restatement of the second premiss, but it contains a hidden assumption which the second premiss does not contain, namely that men differ in their desires and inclinations. Only this can explain why it should be thought that the basing of moral assumptions on human desires would itself deprive these requirements of their universality. However, the assumption that men do so differ is plausible. The fourth premiss also seems to be true. Premisses 1 to 4 taken together appear to rule out the possibility that a man's ability to conform to the moral requirement could depend on his having any particular desires or inclinations.

We take it that the agents to whom moral demands are

addressed often can fulfil them. If, as the argument suggests, this ability does not depend on their having desires and inclinations, then it follows that such agents can act independently of their desires and inclinations. Let us assume for the moment that this conclusion is justified. Even so, there is some way to go before we can reach the conclusion expressed in the seventh premiss that the ability to act independently of desires and inclinations is a manifestation of freedom from causal determination. This claim depended on premiss six, the claim that all and only acts caused by desires and inclinations are causally determined. But why should we accept this? There is nothing in the doctrine of determinism *per se*, in the doctrine that every event is causally necessitated, which implies that all acts are caused by desires and inclinations. The doctrine of determinism would be consistent with the claim that agents are moved to act solely as the result of their perceptions or beliefs. An agent's causally determined and determining motivational states could consist in a perception of the moral requirement or in the thought that something was morally required of him and in his decision to act as the result of this perception or thought. Such an agent would fulfil Kant's criterion for true morality; he would be moved to act solely for the sake of duty, solely because such action was morally required of him, and his fulfilment of the requirement would take place within the natural world governed, if Kant is right, by deterministic laws. (See my further comment at the end of the Appendix for a more detailed look at Kant's beliefs about moral motivation.)

At this point Kant might invoke a curious and rather bad argument in the *Critique of Practical Reason* in order to object to the claim that an act which is motivated by the thought of duty could be causally determined. The argument goes like this: since the form of law is not an appearance, not an object of experience, the *idea* of the form of law is also not an appearance. Therefore any will which is moved by the thought that its maxim can be universalized (can have the form of law) is a will which, in being moved by something which is not an appearance (in this case, the thought containing the idea of the form of law) is not causally determined and, therefore, free (see pp. 116, 166).

There is an obvious criticism of this, which is that, since the idea of the form of law occurs in time, it must be an 'appearance', an item in experience. And if, as Kant believes, all appearances are subject to deterministic laws, then the thought or perception of the moral requirement could constitute the sole determining cause of an agent's action.

And this means that even if Kant is right that morality requires the existence in human beings of a desire-independent ability to act, *it does not follow from this* that it requires the falsity of unqualified determinism.

So Kant does not succeed in establishing that if unqualified determinism is true, there can be no moral requirements. But his argument still leaves us with a worrying problem. For it implies that if a widely held belief about human motivation and a very plausible belief about human action are true then there can be no moral requirements as we conceive of them. The widely held belief is that men cannot be moved by thoughts alone, but need some desire or inclination, some 'passion' as Hume would have put it, to move them to action. The very plausible belief is that men cannot act unless they are moved to act, that is that all action requires motivation. These two beliefs entail the claim that desires are necessary for action. I shall call this 'the psychological thesis'.

(Before I go on to discuss the problem which the psychological thesis poses, I want to stress how independent that thesis is from the doctrine of determinism. Just as the psychological thesis could be false and determinism true, in the case where action is motivated by cognition alone, so determinism could be false and the psychological thesis true. Thus it might be true that human beings can be moved to act only if they have certain desires and false that every act is *determined* by desires or determined by anything else. For (as I argue in Chapter 3), there is no *a priori* justification for assuming that all causes are necessitating. Also, necessary conditions are not sufficient conditions.

I turn now to the problem which is posed by Kant's argument and the psychological thesis.

Stage III

This arises in the following way. The psychological thesis, in conjunction with the ought implies can principle, is in conflict with Kant's claim that moral requirements are unconditional. This is because according to the second and third premisses of Kant's argument, moral requirements are unconditional in the sense that the truth of moral 'ought' statements is independent of the truth of any claims about the desires or inclinations of agents; and according to the fourth premiss of Kant's argument moral 'ought' statements do depend for their truth on the truth of the claim that agents can act to fulfil them. But, according to the psychological thesis, the ability of agents to fulfil moral requirements depends on their having certain desires. Thus a contradiction arises between the claim that the moral 'ought' statements are not conditional on the truth of claims about desires, and the claim that they are conditional on the truth of such claims (via the assumption that ought implies can).

Now it might be thought that there is a rather quick way of disposing of this argument. And this would be to object that the ability to act does not depend on desires. Someone who endorsed this objection might point out that it is considered quite acceptable to say things like 'It is not that he lacks the ability, he just doesn't want to'; and that we would think it absurd if someone were to say 'He couldn't do it because he didn't want to do it.'[9]

But against this, it can be argued that it would seem equally absurd to say, 'Although he could not have been moved to respond to the moral requirement, he could nevertheless have responded to it.' And the absurdity of this claim lies in the suggestion that someone's ability to be motivated to do something is not relevant to his ability to do it. So if motivation is essential for action and if desires are essential for motivation, then it follows that the ability to act does depend on the presence of desires.

One traditional objection to this sort of claim is that it confuses what is necessary for the *existence* of an ability with what is necessary for its exercise. Thus, it is argued, while desires might be necessary for the exercising of the ability to act, they are not necessary for the existence of the ability to act.

But to concede that desires are necessary for the exercising of the ability to act is to concede that without desires there is no possibility of action and if there is no possibility of action without desires then an agent cannot act without them. So the impossibility of action without desires would be enough to support the claim that, given the four premises of Kant's argument, there is a threat to the belief that the moral ought is unconditional.

In any event, the claim that the existence of the ability to act does not depend on desires can be objected to on the grounds that it seems to refer exclusively to physical abilities and to ignore what one might call 'psychological abilities'. A physically healthy but severely depressed person who cannot be induced to get out of his chair is 'able' to get out of his chair only in the sense that there is nothing physically wrong with him and there are no external physical impediments to his doing so, but is he not psychologically unable to do so? It does not seem inappropriate to say that the apathy he suffers from, an apathy which leaves him wanting nothing (except perhaps to die), has rendered him incapable of wanting to do anything and therefore incapable of acting. (See the brief discussion of the severely depressed at the end of Chapter 5.)

So, given the ought implies can principle, we seem still to be left with the conflict between the belief that moral requirements are unconditional and the claim that they cannot be if it is true that desires are essential for action.

In Chapter 5, I argued that desires are essential for motivation. I then went on to argue that, while evidence relating to very depressed people suggests that unmotivated action is not empirically possible, the evidence cannot be regarded as conclusive. So the arguments there support the conclusion that it is highly likely that the psychological thesis is true; that it is true that desires are necessary for action, but they do not entirely rule out the possibility of desireless action.

This leaves me with a choice. I can ignore the fact that there is no conclusive ground for suggesting that such action is empirically impossible, stress the likelihood, given the evidence, that it is impossible and confine the rest of the discussion to the implications for morality (given Kant's argument) if all action must be motivated. Or I can ignore the likelihood that it is impossible, stress the fact that I have no conclusive ground for rul-

ing it out, and discuss the implications for morality if it is possible. Or, finally, I could discuss the implications for morality of
each of these hypotheses. This is what I propose to do.

In other words, I shall consider two questions: first suppose it
is true that all actions must be motivated, then, given Kant's
argument, what follows? and secondly suppose it is true that
some action can be unmotivated then, given Kant's argument,
what follows?

As we shall see, the truth of either of these claims, in conjunction with Kant's argument, would have extremely disturbing
implications. Let us take the possibility of unmotivated action
first. The arguments at the end of Chapter 5 suggest that if it is
possible, it is so only for agents in whom all feeling is dead.
Since this is so, the upshot of its possibility would be a travesty
of what Kant wanted. For given Kant's conclusion that desireless action is necessary for morality, it means that the existence
of morality depends on the existence of agents who cannot be
moved by any consideration. And any agent like this who acted
in accordance with a moral requirement would be someone who
only happened to do so. The possibility of such haphazard
moral action is hardly what Kant wanted to serve as the basis
for morality. He wanted moral requirements to be motivational
influences. (See my further comment at the end for more on
Kant's views about moral motivation.)

Suppose, on the other hand, that all action must be motivated. Then since, as has been argued, being moved to act requires desires, there are no moral requirements, if Kant's
argument is correct.

So it looks as if our best hope of avoiding either of these disturbing implications is to find something wrong with one or
more of the four premisses which generate the conclusion that
morality requires a desire-independent ability to act. It is time,
therefore, to re-examine them and since the first premiss seems
incontestable, this leaves the second, third and fourth premisses.

All of these premisses concern statements like, 'Agent X
ought morally to do such and such'. Taken together, the second
and third premisses assert that the truth of such a statement is
independent of the truth that agent X does/does not have the
desire to do such and such; while the fourth premiss asserts that
it is only true that agent X ought morally to do such and such if

he can do it. But what does it mean to say that an agent (X) ought morally to do something when this is understood as a claim which relates to a specific situation? I think this involves two thoughts:

1. that agent X is in a situation in which a specific moral response is demanded; I shall call this 'claim 1'; and
2. that the moral response demanded by the situation can legitimately be demanded of him (X). I shall call this 'claim 2'.

For claim 1 to be true all that is required is that X be in the vicinity, within viewing or hearing distance, when an occasion for morally obligatory action presents itself. This would be sufficient to make it appropriate to say that he was 'in' a situation which involved a moral requirement. For claim 2 to be true more is required than that X be 'in' a situation which demands a moral response. For it to be true that the response demanded by the situation can legitimately be demanded of him, X must have both the capacity to see that something is morally required of him and the capacity to respond appropriately. Claim 2 also involves another claim, that if X does not respond as required he deserves to be blamed for not doing so.

Returning to premisses 2, 3 and 4, these can now be restated as follows. Premisses 2 and 3 become:

The statement that X is in a situation which contains a moral requirement is true whether or not X has desires which would induce him to fulfil that requirement.

I shall call this 'the first implication' of premisses 2 and 3.

The statement that the response demanded by the situation can legitimately be demanded of X is true whether or not X has desires which would induce him to fulfil that requirement.

I shall call this 'the second implication' of premisses 2 and 3. Premiss 4 (which clearly relates only to Claim 2 above) becomes:

The statement that the response demanded by the situation can legitimately be demanded of X is true only if X can fulfil the requirement.

The first implication of Premisses 2 and 3 is obviously true.

But whether or not the second implication is true depends on whether action must be motivated. If all action must be motivated then, given the argument at the end of Chapter 5, the capacity to fulfil the moral requirement which is mentioned in premiss 4 depends on the agent's having some desire or affective disposition. So, given premiss 4, the second implication of premisses 2 and 3 would be false. On the other hand, if action can be unmotivated, then the capacity to fulfil the moral requirement does not depend on the agent's having any desires. In this case, the second implication of premisses 2 and 3 could be true.

It might be objected that the possibility of unmotivated action of the kind envisaged would not make the second implication true for such action would not be a response to the agent's knowledge that something was morally required of him. Indeed, the whole point about such action is that it would not be a *response* to anything. However, it could be argued that it is arbitrary to insist that the word 'response' be included in the description of the second implication. If we substituted the word 'act' for the word 'response' than the second implication would be compatible with the claim that action could be unmotivated and if unmotivated action is possible, then the second as well as the first implication of premisses 2 and 3 would be true.

Turning to premiss 4, this, as restated, involves the following two thoughts:

(*a*) that it is only appropriate to demand that someone act morally if he can and

(*b*) that it is only legitimate to blame someone for not acting morally if he could have acted morally.

Thought (*a*) expresses what we might call the 'exhortative' or 'response-inducing' role of some moral ought statements; while (*b*) expresses the blame-conferring role of some moral ought statements, for example, statements like 'You ought to have done such and such' said in a reproachful way.

Thought (*a*) seems true. It would be inappropriate to say to someone that he ought to do something if he could not do it because one means to induce him to do it by speaking. Obviously, therefore, it would be inappropriate to say to someone who could not be motivated by any consideration that he ought to do something since the purpose of saying this to him would be thwarted by the fact that he could not be moved by your saying it. And this suggests that to endorse 4 (*a*) is to be committed to denying that moral action can legitimately be demanded of someone who is immoveable even if such a person is able to act without being moved. So Kant's argument is partly responsible for implying that the existence of moral requirements might depend on the existence of people who can act without being moved to act and yet the fourth premiss of that argument suggests, at the same time, that moral requirements do not apply to such people. This leaves us with the following options:

1. to accept both the argument and the claim that unmotivated action is possible and to conclude that the possibility of unmotivated action is needed to ground the possibility of morality for those who *can* be motivated; or
2. to reject the claim that unmotivated action is possible; or
3. to reject the argument.

To adopt option 1, would be to accept that those who make morality possible are not the subjects of moral requirements, and this is surely unacceptable, indeed absurd. As for option 2, I have already argued that while it is likely that the claim about unmotivated action is untrue, I have no conclusive grounds for saying this.

This leaves option 3, to reject Kant's argument. The case for rejecting Kant's argument can be made if we can make a case for rejecting premiss 4 (*b*), the claim that it is only legitimate to blame someone for not acting morally if he could have acted morally. This is, of course, the traditional claim about moral responsibility that it is a necessary condition of an agent's deserving to be blamed that he could have acted otherwise.

In Chapter 2, I argued that this claim was false. If that argument is correct, then we can reject premiss 4 and thus Kant's argument and the disturbing conclusions which it appears to warrant.

Conclusion

At the beginning of the Appendix, I said that Kant's argument

for the claim that determinism is incompatible with the existence of moral requirements could be seen as an indirect argument for the claim that it is incompatible with moral
responsibility.

We have seen that Kant fails to establish that morality requires the falsity of unqualified determinism, but, as I indicated
at the beginning, the argument about human motivation which
he mistakenly thought would lead to that conclusion has an independent bearing on the debate between the compatibilist and
the incompatibilist about the relevance of determinism to moral
responsibility. For if that argument were to succeed then,
granted the truth of the claim that desires are necessary for
action, there could be no moral requirements as we think of
such requirements and so any debate about moral responsibility
would be pointless.

I have argued that desires are most probably necessary for
action, but it might be thought that the small possibility that
they are not necessary is enough to justify the belief in the existence of moral requirements and, therefore, the debate between
the compatibilist and the incompatibilist about moral responsibility. But even if we were to ignore the reasons I have already
cited against endorsing this possibility, given its unlikelihood it
is surely far too tenuous a basis on which to pin the belief that
morality, and thus the possibility of moral responsibility, exist.

The only strong ground for believing that the debate about
moral responsibility is not pointless is a demonstration that
Kant's argument has failed. Such a demonstration has been provided in the first three chapters of this book, where I have considered the role of the could-have-acted-otherwise claim in the
debate and have argued that there is not a could-have-acted-
otherwise condition for moral responsibility. It is this which
constitutes the case for rejecting Kant's premiss 4.

A further comment on Kant's argument

Some of the conclusions I have reached in the discussion of
Kant's claim that morality requires a desire-independent ability
to act presuppose my earlier discussion in Chapter 5 of Nagel's
thesis that desires need not be the sources of motivation.

It will be remembered that Nagel offered two alternatives to the Humean belief that desires are the bases of all motivation, the logical reducibility thesis according to which claims about desires in action can be restated as claims about being moved to act by cognitions (Thesis II); and the thesis that while a desire must always be present when action occurs, the desire need not be the source but could instead be the effect of the agent's having first been moved by a cognition (Thesis I).

There are some striking analogies (and disanalogies) between Nagel's Thesis I picture of motivation and Kant's beliefs which are worth considering for the added insights they will give us into Kant's views about motivation and the bearing these have on the argument we have just discussed.

Kant believes that feelings or inclinations (he tends to use the words interchangeably) must always be part of the motivating psychological states which lead to human action (see pp. 166, 177, 187). This he takes to be a consequence of the fact that human beings have sensible (as well as rational) natures. But like Nagel and unlike Hume, Kant does not hold that in all cases of human action, the feeling or inclination must be present *before* the cognition can do its work. On the contrary, he believes that in all cases of truly moral action—and *only* in cases of such action—feeling is produced by cognition, namely awareness of the moral requirement. To use Nagel's way of speaking, Kant believes that when someone acts morally both the act and the feeling which leads to the act are motivated by awareness of the moral requirement. Kant says:

While the moral law ... is a formal determining principle of action by practical pure reason ... it is also a subjective deter-mining principle, that is, a motive to this action, inasmuch as it has influence on the morality of the subject and produces a feel-ing conducive to the influence of the law on the will. There is here in the subject no *antecedent* feeling tending to morality. For this is impossible, since every feeling is sensible and the motive of moral intention must be free from all sensible con-ditions. On the contrary, while the sensible feeling which is at the bottom of all our inclinations is the condition of that impression which we call respect, the cause that determines it lies in the pure practical reason; and this impression therefore on account of its origin must be called not a pathological but a practical effect . . . Thus the respect for the law is not a motive to morality, but is morality itself subjectively considered as a motive . . . now it is to be observed that as respect is an effect on feeling, and therefore on the sensibility of a rational being, it presupposes this sensibility and therefore also the finiteness of such beings on whom the moral law imposes respect; and that respect for the law cannot be attributed to a supreme being, or to any being free from all sensibility and in whom therefore this sensibility cannot be an obstacle to practical reason. This feeling (sentiment) which we call the moral feeling is therefore produced simply by reason. (pp. 168–9.)

It is clear that Kant's picture of motivation resembles Nagel's Thesis I in its belief (*a*) that an inclination of some kind must underly all human action, and (*b*) that the inclination need not be the source but could be the effect of a motivational source which consists purely in cognitions.

But it differs from Nagel's in at least two respects. First, Kant believes that cognition can only be the motivational source of truly moral action (that is action which is motivated solely by the thought of duty), and Nagel does not suggest that moral action alone is motivated by cognitions. Secondly, the desires and cognitions Nagel discusses are supposed to be ordinary desires and cognitions, at least in the sense that they are supposed to be a part of the every day natural world. But for Kant, the feeling of respect (or reverence) which is produced by moral awareness and the awareness which produces it are not ordinary. In the passage just quoted, Kant says that the moral feeling is produced simply by reason. And reason for Kant is a faculty which places human beings in some sense 'outside' and transcendent of the natural, sensible world including their own natural selves. (He seems to have regarded the exercise of reason as something which is not causally determined and which does not 'take place' in space or time (see B575, the *Critique of Pure Reason*.) And since Kant also holds that recognition of the moral law is necessarily involved in being rational, he is committed to the view that we are free in virtue of our awareness of moral requirements.[10] This helps to explain why Kant believes that reverence is very different from ordinary feelings and inclinations: 'Yet although reverence is a feeling it is not a feeling received through outside influence, but one self-produced by a rational concept and therefore specifically distinct from feelings of the first kind all of which can be reduced to inclination and fear.'[11]

But despite Kant's belief in the 'specialness' of this feeling, he sees it as one which plays the same kind of role as other inclinations, namely that of a motivating force towards action within the sensible world. For while the cause which determines it is not sensible, reverence *is* sensible (remember that in the *Critique of Practical Reason* he says, 'the sensible feeling which is at the bottom of all our inclinations is the condition of that impression which we call respect'). Later in the passage from the *Groundwork* which I have just quoted, he says that reverence is 'analogous' to fear and inclination. And in the *Critique of Practical Reason*, he makes clear his view of it as a motivating force towards moral action and against countervailing inclinations when he says that it is a motive which is necessary since 'the being requires to be impelled to action by something because an internal obstacle opposes itself'.

So the Kantian picture of truly moral motivation which emerges is this: the reason-produced feeling of reverence is because *reason*-produced, the effect of a non-natural and therefore non-determined awareness of the moral law but, because it is a *feeling* and thus a part of human beings as members of the sensible world, it is able to do battle with other feelings.

What bearing do Kant's views about motivation have on his claim that morality requires a desire-independent ability to act and hence on the argument we have just considered? I have pointed out that Kant regards the claim about desires and the claim that morality requires freedom from causal determination as necessarily linked, that is he believes that we can only be free from our desires if we can be free from causal determination. Kant might have thought, therefore, that if he could show that moral motivation has its source in a cognition which is not determined, then he would have thereby demonstrated our freedom from causal determination, and hence our freedom from desires and thus the existence of morality.

But I have argued that the claim that morality requires a desire-independent ability to act and the claim that it requires freedom from causal determination are not necessarily linked and furthermore that it is the first claim and not the second which represents a threat to the existence of moral requirements. For if it is true that morality requires a desire-independent ability to act and if it is also true that desires are necessary for action (the psychological thesis), then there can be no moral requirements as we conceive of them (that is as requirements which are unconditional).

So Kant's views about motivation could only be of help in countering this threat if they implied that desires were not necessary for action. But they do not imply this. Instead they imply that acting in accordance with moral requirements is conditional either on the existence of ordinary desires and inclinations (in which case such action would be in our terms 'moral' but in Kant's terms merely 'legal'), or on the production of a feeling of reverence, and since Kant views reverence as a kind of inclination (in that he sees it as a sensible moving force towards action) he is committed to the view that some inclination or inclination-like state is necessary for human action.

Outline of Kant's argument in the first chapter of the *Critique of Practical Reason*

I. *The argument*

1. There are moral requirements.
2. Moral requirements are essentially unconditional, universal, necessary and *a priori*.
3. No requirements based on the desires and inclinations of agents could have the nature of moral requirements, that is they could not be unconditional, universal, necessary and *a priori*.
4. If men could not fulfil moral requirements, there could not be moral requirements (that is the truth of the claim that agents ought morally to perform certain acts depends on the truth of the claim that agents can perform those actions); ought implies can.
5. To fulfil moral requirements, men must act independently of their desires and inclinations; the moral requirement commands an unconditional response.
6. All and only acts caused by desires and inclinations are causally determined.
7. Therefore, to act independently of desires and inclinations, men must be free from causal determination.

Conclusion: The existence of freedom (from causal determination) is a necessary condition for the existence of morality. 'Freedom is the *ratio essendi* of the moral law'.

II. *Surviving elements of arguments after initial criticisms*

1. There are moral requirements.
2. Moral requirements are essentially unconditional and universal.

3. If requirements depended for their legitimacy on the presence of desires and inclinations in potentially responsive agents they could not be unconditional and universal.
4. All agents to whom a moral requirement applies, that is to whom the 'ought' statement is rightfully addressed, can comply with that requirement.
6. All and only acts caused by desires and inclinations are causally determined.
7. Therefore to act independently of desires and inclinations men must be free from causal determination.

III. *Final surviving argument*

Premisses 1 to 4. These generate the conclusion that the existence in human beings of a desire-independent ability to act is a necessary condition for the existence of moral requirements. And this presents a challenge to 'the psychological thesis', the claim that human beings are so constituted that they cannot act unless they have certain desires.

Notes

Introduction

1. There is a non-traditional compatibilist approach advocated by Frankfurt in terms of which the blameworthy offender would also have to identify, by means of his second order desires, with the morally reprehensible desires which move him. (See his 'Freedom of the Will and the Concept of a Person', 'Identification and Externality', and 'Three Concepts of Free Action'.) But since this approach would not ease the anxiety which motivates incompatibilism, I have not discussed it.

2. See Bowlby, *Child Care and the Growth of Love*, pp. 41–2.

3. Another actual kind of case which looks problematic for the compatibilist is one in which wrongdoing is the result of upbringing in families where no stigma is attached to certain sorts of crime. (G. Strawson has mentioned this.) But I have not mentioned this kind of case here for two reasons. First, because the compatibilist would have at least a prima-facie basis for thinking that his position can accommodate such cases, since they involve wrongdoing which, because it is *ex hypothesi* not seen as wrong does not seem to be the result of morally reprehensible states of mind. And because, as I shall argue in ch. 1, the traditional compatibilist holds that such states of mind are necessary (as well as sufficient) for blameworthiness, this seems to suggest that the 'no-stigma' upbringing cases are not problematic for him after all. (But whether such cases are actually problematic for the compatibilist depends on whether the kind of moral ignorance which they involve really does disqualify them from being cited as examples of action which is motivated by morally reprehensible states of mind. In the Addendum to ch. 1, I argue that such states of mind do not always have to include knowledge that the intended act is wrong.)

   The second reason for not mentioning 'no-stigma' upbringing cases, when I do mention cases of emotional deprivation, is that (as I shall argue) emotional deprivation has a special relevance to the issue of blameworthiness which is not shared by the 'no-stigma' cases. This is because such deprivation involves suffering for the deprived person, prior to his becoming a wrongdoer, and there is no prima-facie reason for thinking that the inculcation of an anti-law-abiding attitude *per se* involves suffering during the inculcation process. (The moral significance of suffering prior to wrongdoing is discussed in ch. 4 and mentioned briefly later in this Introduction.)

4. See e.g. P. F. Strawson, 'Freedom and Resentment' *passim*, and esp. p. 24; and also 'P. F. Strawson Replies', pp. 264–5.

5. Throughout this book I have used the terms 'wrongdoer' and 'offender' interchangeably.

Chapter 1

1. See e.g.: Watson's Introduction to *Free Will*, pp. 2–5, and the papers by Chisholm, Aune, Lehrer, and van Inwagen in this collection; Moore, *Ethics*, ch. 6; Thorp, *Free Will*, esp. ch. 2; van Inwagen, *An Essay on Free Will*, esp. ch. 3, 4; Bennett, 'Accountability', pp. 16–19; and the papers by Edwards, Hospers, Chisholm, and Pap in Hook (ed.), *Determinism and Freedom in the Age of Modern Science*. These suggestions represent a very small sample of the vast literature on this topic.

2. As I am using the term 'morally reprehensible' it means something like 'morally objectionable'; it should *not* be taken to mean 'morally blameworthy'. For further discussion of M-states of mind see the addendum to this chapter.

3. The phrase 'kinds of' needs to be added to avoid attributing to the incompatibilist a position which violates the principle that different token (i.e. particular) events must (logically) have different token causes.

4. Most incompatibilists would say that what is morally required is that the agent should have been able to *decide* or to *choose* to act otherwise despite the presence of those desires and beliefs which led to the original decision (or choice). See Thorp, *Free Will*, pp. 4–7.

5. 'Absolute' as opposed to what one might call the 'conditional' could-have-acted-otherwise condition which is favoured by those compatibilists who say that an agent is morally responsible for his act so long as it is true that he *would* have acted differently *if* he had had *different* desires.

6. As we shall see in ch. 4, the compatibilist might argue that fulfilment of the M-condition is not sufficient for blameworthiness if the M-state of mind has been abnormally caused. But to introduce discussion of this now would be unnecessarily confusing, particularly since I argue in ch. 4 that the compatibilist justification for this won't work. The important point in the context of the present

discussion is that the compatibilist believes that only the *kind* of cause matters and since this is so, he can consistently maintain that the question 'Could X have willed otherwise?' does not arise.

7. This is what Frankfurt does. See the next chapter.

8. See Kripke, *Naming and Necessity*, pp. 39–53, 110–15.

9. Paul Snowdon, in his capacity as an independent adviser for OUP, has pointed out that some philosophers believe metaphysical necessity involves much more than origin. At various points throughout the book I shall refer in footnotes to remarks made by Paul Snowdon in that capacity.

10. A utilitarian might disagree.

11. Foley, 'Compatibilism', pp. 421–8.

12. It is legitimate to view this as an account of the could-have-willed-otherwise claim since Glover identifies the terms 'will' and 'intention' on p. 66. But because I shall be quoting from his book it will be less confusing if I use the term 'intention' throughout my discussion.

13. It has been pointed out by Paul Snowdon that the compatibilist opponent whom I am addressing would endorse the 'ought implies can' principle but would object to the claim that this implies anything about what the agent could have done or willed in the *actual total circumstances*. I agree that the compatibilist would object, but I do not feel that he has a legitimate basis for doing so, unless his objection stems from the belief that the C-claim is reducible to the M-claim. But if this is not the reason for his objection then I cannot see what grounds he has for ruling out this 'strong' interpretation of the could-have-acted-otherwise claim.

   It might be thought odd that I have invoked the 'ought implies can' principle as part of an argument whose ultimate aim is to show that there is no C-condition for moral responsibility. However, at this stage in the argument, I am deliberately adopting the point of view of someone who believes in an independent C-condition, while at the same time trying to interpret that condition in a more plausible way than it has usually been interpreted by traditional compatibilists.

   In the Appendix I distinguish between two roles for moral 'ought' statements, the response-inducing role and the blame-conferring role, and I suggest that when such statements are used for the first purpose, 'ought' *does* imply 'can', but not when used for the second purpose.

14. *Responsibility*, p. 66.

15. Ibid, 136.

16. It might be thought that Glover could answer this criticism, in

view of his claim that:

> not all intentions are seen as internal to the person blamed. Sometimes a person's intention is one that he does not identify with, or endorse, and is one that he would prefer to be without . . . Then it appears that he is not capable of altering his intention, and this lack of capacity may well exempt him from blame. (p. 66)

Thus, it might be suggested that Glover has allowed for the committed-to-the-death idealist, for such a person would identify with his intentions and they would therefore be seen as internal to him and, by virtue of this, as intentions with which he should be identified for purposes of praise and blame. But (I think) it is clear from the passage quoted that Glover believes that not identifying with one's intentions is *evidence for their unalterability* and that it is the unalterability of the intentions rather than the agent's feelings about them which, for Glover, is relevant to the question of moral responsibility. (Frankfurt would argue that it is not the alterability or unalterability of the intentions which is morally important but whether the agent identifies with them. See n. 1 to the Introduction.)

17. 'Self-Creation', *Proceedings of the British Academy*, p. 457.

18. Something should be said about the phrase 'the ability and opportunity to will otherwise'. I take it that someone's ability to will an act depends partly on his having the relevant concepts and partly on his being so affectively constituted that he can be moved to undertake the act. In so far as I can give a sense to the term 'the opportunity to will', I assume that an agent would have such an opportunity if the thought of acting this way had occurred to him.

My use of the term 'will' is intended to be an innocuous as possible. It should not be seen as a use which necessarily presupposes the view that willings are *distinctive* mental activities, separate from decidings or choosings, which precede all actions. As I have used the term 'will', it could be replaced by 'choose', or 'decide', or 'resolve'. Of course, even in allowing this much flexibility for the term, I am not being completely neutral. For, as I am using it, 'willing' stands for something which *precedes* action. But some philosophers (O'Shaughnessy, Hornsby, McGinn) see willings as tryings, i.e. actions already under way.

19. The claim that such a person's state of mind would be morally reprehensible should not be confused with the claim that he would deserve to be blamed for the resulting act. We might be reluctant to blame someone whose abhorrent convictions had been inculcated in childhood and who had never been exposed to a different way of seeing things. The compatibilist who believes that

an M-state of mind is sufficent for blameworthiness would either have to say that such a person was blameworthy or deny that his state of mind was morally reprehensible.

20. A counter-example suggested by Paul Snowdon seems to imply that either the M-condition does not need to include beliefs which are even remotely connected with acknowledged moral principles, or that the M-condition is not necessary for blameworthiness. He says:

> 'Aren't there some offences which the offender does not realize, as he acts, he is committing? For example, a surgeon doing a complex operation is careless or thoughtless. He will not consider as he is so that he *is* being careless. He can be blamed for the outcome. What sort of M-condition applies to him?'

Despite appearances I think that this example does not undermine either the claim that the M-condition is necessary for blameworthiness, or that it must include some belief about the nature of the intended act which would indicate to any normal and morally knowledgeable person that such an act was wrong. Thus, I would suggest that if the surgeon had no inkling at all that he was acting carelessly, then he would not fulfil the M-condition and so would not be *morally* blameworthy. This does not mean that he ought not to be found professionally incompetent and, perhaps also, legally and professionally liable for such incompetence. But it is hard to believe that a surgeon would have no inkling that he was acting carelessly. Surely, if he had managed to survive the long and demanding training needed to become a surgeon, then he would either be aware enough of what he was doing to know that he was not paying sufficient attention (in which case if he continued he would fulfil the M-condition), or his lack of attentiveness would be due to some physical or emotional trauma so powerful that it (temporarily) robbed him of the ability to monitor his own performance (in which case he would not fulfil the M-condition).

21. This description will be amended in ch. 2.

22. I do not mean that the content of his belief is "my act satisfies a morally neutral description", but rather "I am doing such and such" where "such and such" does not involve any explicitly *moral* notions.

Chapter 2

1. Van Inwagen, *An Essay on Free Will*, pp. 162–82. (See also his 'Ability and Responsibility'.)

2. I have slightly modified the abbreviation which van Inwagen uses for the Principle of Alternate Possibilities in 'Ability and Responsibility'.

3. Frankfurt, 'Alternate Possibilities and Moral Responsibility', p. 829.

4. Ibid. 838.

5. 'Three Concepts of Free Action', pp. 113–25.

6. I owe this objection to Derek Parfit.

7. Even this amended description should continue to be regarded as an abbreviated version of the more adequate description referred to in the addendum to ch. 1.

8. Is impulsiveness an exception to this? Paul Snowdon suggests that it might be. We think of impulsive action as action without thought and yet as action which is intentional and morally assessable. (But to say that someone has acted without thought is not to say that he had no time for thought, which is what I would say about the person whose desire takes him by storm.) I think that impulsive action can be characterized as deliberate action which has been preceded by hardly any deliberation. Since I think of such action as deliberate, I don't feel it is inappropriate to say that the impulsive agent has 'chosen' to act, but it might be inappropriate to say that he has 'decided' since deciding presupposes uncertainty and a weighing up of reasons for and against. (Cf. my discussion of deciding and choosing in ch. 5.)

9. Hilgard, Atkinson and Atkinson, *Introduction to Psychology*, pp. 460, 462.

10. Van Inwagen does not use the term 'could-have-acted-otherwise condition' but it is clear that it is this condition he is arguing for.

11. *An Essay on Free Will*, p. 165.

12. Ibid. 167.

13. Ibid. 171.

14. I suspect, though, that the principle owes its initial air of plausibility to our being naturally inclined to interpret 'failing to perform a given act' as in (a).

15. *An Essay on Free Will*, pp. 164–5.

16. For any bringing about of a state of affairs by an agent must be his *particular* bringing about of it and Frankfurt's arguments are concerned with an agent's moral responsibility for his particular bringing about of states of affairs.

Chapter 3

1. Nozick, *Philosophical Explanations*, p. 291.

2. Thorp, *Free Will*, p. 27. On p. 24, Thorp's remarks indicate that

he is aware that there is a distinction between the claim that a decision has been necessitated and the claim that it has been necessitated by something beyond the agent's control. But, unlike me, (i) he thinks that it matters that the decision has been *necessitated* by something beyond the agent's control, while I believe that what matters is not that it has been necessitated, but that it has been *caused* by something beyond the agent's control (see the later discussion in this chapter); and (ii) he subsumes the second anxiety under the anxiety about the powerlessness to decide otherwise, whereas I believe that these two should be distinguished.

3. Thorp insists that there is a could-have-decided-otherwise condition for moral responsibility (ibid. 4–7).

4. Perhaps when Kant insists that the agent's choice of his moral nature must be 'free' he is expressing his commitment to a could-have-chosen-otherwise condition as well as a commitment to something like the U-condition.

5. Wisdom, *Problems of Mind and Matter*, p. 123.

6. The reason I stress that the decision must be uncaused by *previous events and states* is that some incompatibilists believe that decisions could be caused by the decision-maker himself *as opposed to* events and states within him. I discuss agent-causation in ch. 5.

7. pp. 20, 31, 34, 40, 42, 43, 46, 65–71.

8. I owe the term 'psychological connectedness' to Derek Parfit who uses it, in his work on personal identity, to cover direct psychological links such as those between a person's experience and his (or his surviving self's) memory of it, or someone's intentions to act in a certain way and her (or her surviving self's) subsequent actions. (See the next footnote for *some* elucidation of the notion of a 'surviving self'. For full elucidation see Parfit, *Reasons and Persons*.)

9. Parfit describes a logically possible situation in which a person splits and the resulting halves are psychologically (and physically) continuous with the original whole. We are logically debarred from claiming that either of the surviving halves is identical with the original person, but we are not logically debarred from saying that each surviving half might inherit the responsibility of the original person. (Parfit, *Reasons and Persons*, pp. 323–6.)

10. This second objection has evolved from thoughts which were prompted by a different, although connected, point raised by Paul Snowdon. He suggested that my argument—that if X is responsible for deliberately acquiring morally objectionable desires, he is morally responsible for acting as the result of them—might trade on neglecting an ambiguity which can be brought out by dis-

tinguishing between 'X is responsible for the results of his original decision, which include his present actions' and 'X is responsible for the present action which resulted from his original decision':

Consider the following case. I deliberately and knowingly make myself go mad—in that condition I do G. Am I responsible for doing G? It seems that when I did G I was not responsible for my actions. However I am responsible for putting myself into a condition which was dangerous. So I am responsible for the results. So, even if I am in one sense responsible for the action (and its results) I was not, as I acted responsible.

This is a very interesting case, but I have two objections to Paul Snowdon's conclusions. First, if madness does make me *not* responsible for my actions, then it also makes me *no longer* morally responsible for my original choice. One can lose the capacities or qualities which make one responsible. So it is not true, as he suggests, that I *now am* blame-conferringly responsible for putting myself into a condition which was dangerous. Rather, I *was* responsible but I am no longer so. Thus the case is not really one which illustrates an ambiguity.

Secondly, I would suggest that the case is either (*a*) not really relevant to my argument or (*b*) the implications which Paul Snowdon draws from it can be denied. It is not relevant to my arguments if by 'madness' he means the sort of psychotic delusions suffered by paranoid schizophrenics. For such people, when in the grip of their delusions, are *ipso facto* not being motivated by M-states of mind. So if this is the sort of madness which was chosen in the original M-state, then the original choice does not satisfy one of the conditions for responsibility-spreading, namely that the subsequent decisions and choices should be characteristic of M-states.

If, however, he means to include among the mad, those psychopathic agents who can be aware that there are things which are considered wrong but are not moved by this awareness to avoid wrongdoing, then I would suggest that such 'madness', if the result of an original M-state choice, would not exonerate the agent from responsibility for his present choices.

Having said all this, however, I can think of an imaginary case, incorporating the essential elements of Paul Snowdon's case (including the 'madness' element), the implications of which are problematic for me.

According to one legal definition of insanity, an agent could qualify as "mad" if he were so severely disturbed that he did not know that what he was doing was wrong. And another legal definition of insanity proposed by the American Law Institute suggests that someone is insane if 'as a result of mental disturbance or defect he lacks substantial capacity . . . to appreciate the wrongfulness of his conduct.' (Hilgard, Atkinson, and Atkinson, *Introduction to Psychology* p. 488.) Finally, in a recent article, 'Sanity and the Metaphysics of Responsibility', Susan Wolf suggests that someone could qualify as not fully sane if he were unable to appreciate that the way in which he was acting was morally wrong. (She acknowledges that her use of the term 'insane' is specialized and contentious.)

Unlike the first two definitions which suggest that one would have to be incapable *and* that the incapacity would have to be due to a disturbance or defect of some kind, Wolf seems to imply that the incapacity *is* the defect. I don't wish to comment on this difference, nor on the contentiousness of the suggestion that insanity could consist in mistaken moral beliefs, but want instead to describe a case in which the agent would satisfy all the definitions.

Imagine an agent who makes an uncaused, deliberate, and effective choice to be drastically changed so that his original moral beliefs about rightness and wrongness are reversed, guaranteeing that in the future he will think that wrong things are right and will be motivated by his new perceptions of 'rightness' to act wrongly (only of course he will now think of it as acting 'rightly'). In his original state the agent knew that his choice would lead to wrong actions. In his new state he thinks that the original decision was morally right.

Given my earlier arguments in the addendum to ch. 1, it seems that I cannot say that the agent's having a wrong moral belief makes his state of mind *not* morally reprehensible, for I have argued that the agent who does not know that what he is doing is wrong (because he does not know that certain kinds of act are wrong) does not thereby escape fulfilment of the M-condition.

So it looks as if I must say that this is a case in which the agent knowingly made a morally reprehensible uncaused choice which led to subsequent morally reprehensible choices.

Furthermore, there is nothing about the case which rules out the possibility that the changed agent remembers the original choice and endorses it (because he now, wrongly, thinks that it is right).

Is the agent now blameworthy? I feel that he is not, despite the fact that he seems to fulfil all of the conditions which my arguments suggest to be sufficient.

And this seems to suggest that I either need another condition, in addition to memory and causal connectedness (see n. 15), or that I must revise, or possibly abandon, my original claim that moral beliefs do not escape moral reprehensibility.

One move which might seem tempting would be to make a distinction between mistaken moral beliefs on the basis of their causal origin, claiming that those caused, for instance by insanity, are not morally reprehensible.

But I cannot see any philosophic merit in this manoeuvre. The belief that it is right to torture an innocent man is morally reprehensible however it is caused. (Remember that at this moment we are concerned about what it is for a state of mind to be morally reprehensible, and not about whether the agent should be held responsible for having such a state of mind or acting as the result of it.)

Another apparently tempting, but similarly misguided, move would be to argue that moral beliefs are only morally reprehensible if they are avoidable and to say that since insanity-caused mistaken beliefs are not avoidable, they are not morally reprehensible. But this can be objected to on similar grounds to the first suggestion. A morally objectionable belief does not lose its moral repulsiveness because it is unavoidable. If we are tempted to think that it does, I think this is because we are confusing the issue of moral reprehensibility with the issue of moral responsibility. Furthermore, if we do think that the belief's unavoidability makes the agent not morally responsible, then this might be because we are not yet rid of the illusion that there is an independent C-condition for moral responsibility, cf. n. 11.

11. It might be argued that if the original choice has determined subsequent M-state motivations, then X has no choice but to endorse the original choice, and that if this worries us, then it shows that we are committed to a could-have-chosen-otherwise condition for moral responsibility. But, in keeping with my overall argument, I would suggest that if we are worried, over the fact that X has no choice but to endorse the original choice, this is not a worry that X cannot choose otherwise, but rather that X is being forced to choose against his desires and, since in the case envisaged this is clearly not true, the worry would not be appropriate.

12. Here, I am agreeing with Parfit that 'mere loss of memory seems insufficient'. (*Reasons and Persons*, p. 326).

13. But see n. 10 for an objection to this. To overcome this objection we should have to add to causal connectedness and memory, the condition that the present chooser remains aware that his original choice was morally wrong.

14. The Stoics held this view (see Sorabji, *Necessity, Cause and Blame*, p. 66); Hume can be seen as an advocate of it because of

his insistence that causation consists in constant conjunction, and Davidson because he believes that causal sequences must instantiate exceptionless laws.

15. Cf. Anscombe, 'Causality and Determination' pp. 63–81, van Inwagen, *An Essay on Free Will*, pp. 138–42, and Sorabji, *Necessity, Cause and Blame*, ch. 2.

16. Anscombe, 'Causality and Determination', p. 67.

17. Van Inwagen, *An Essay on Free Will* pp. 139–40.

18. Someone might object to this as follows: 'Our concept of causation involves the idea of necessary and sufficient conditions, and *sufficient* conditions are those which are invariably followed by what they are conditions for: therefore, our concept of causation must involve the idea of necessitation.' I think Anscombe has provided a convincing answer to this. She suggests that the common notion of sufficiency involves the idea of something's being *enough* for something else, and she seems to imply that the idea of something's being enough is the idea of sufficiency which is connected with the common concept of causation. She goes on to suggest that there is no incoherence in the question: 'May there not be enough to have made something happen—and yet it not have happened?' ('Causality and Determination', p. 66.)

But the fact that there is no incoherence does not mean that we would accept the claim with equanimity that there was enough to make something happen although it did not happen. Many of us would feel that this was something which cried out for further explanation. And this suggests that our notion of 'enough' *is* connected, in a way which falls short of entailment, with the idea of invariance. The connection is loose enough for us to be able to entertain the thought that it is logically possible, but we would need to be provided with further argument as to its real possibility. Perhaps this reflects the fact that while the ideas of quantum mechanics are beginning to become a part of our common thought, they are not yet so deeply entrenched as to have replaced the older ideas of classical mechanics.

19. There are analogies between my position and that of Fischer who argues in 'Responsibility and Control', that even if moral responsibility is compatible with the inability to do otherwise it is open to the incompatibilist to argue that it is not reconcilable with determinism because determinism involves 'actual sequence compulsion'. Fischer suggests (p. 38) that the reason why the inability to do otherwise (called by him 'lack of control') 'normally rules out responsibility is that it normally points to actual sequence compulsion'. Thus, I take him to be arguing that the inability to act otherwise might be nothing more than a by-product of what really

worries us about determinism. This is my position too. And while I do not agree that what worries us is "actual sequence compulsion", I do agree that what worries us is something about the determining causal sequence which is independent of its ruling out the possibility of acting otherwise, namely the fact that the sequence consists in states and events for which we are not responsible.

Chapter 4

1. Strawson, 'Freedom and Resentment', pp. 18–20, argues that the incompatibilist's general fear of determinism is not reflected in our everyday practices.
2. Bowlby, *Child Care and the Growth of Love*, pp. 41–42.
3. Tutt, 'Justice or Welfare?', pp. 6–10, compares two models of how juvenile offenders should be dealt with. According to what he calls "the Welfare Model": 'criminal behaviour is clearly linked with social, economic and physical disadvantage. Therefore, any state intervention should be aimed at alleviating these disadvantages as much as, if not more than, punishing the individual offender. . . .' He goes on:

   > in its extreme form the welfare approach would argue that delinquency is a 'pathological' condition and therefore the individual should be exonerated from personal guilt. This underlies a plea of "diminished responsibility" for an adult but is common to much thinking about delinquency which suggests that children from deprived family and social backgrounds are inevitably impelled into delinquency and have little or no control over their own destinies. (p. 7.)

   It is not clear from Tutt's description of what he calls "the Justice Model" whether it relies totally on compatibilist intuitions or includes some incompatibilist ones. He says:

   > Firstly, proponents of justice see offending behaviour as a matter of individual choice affected by opportunity. They stress the notion of free will, that the individual is in control of his own behaviour, that if an opportunity for criminal behaviour arises it is a matter of individual choice whether or not the individual commits an offence . . .

   > Secondly, if offending behaviour is a rational response to certain situations then it is reasonable to hold the individual responsible for his actions and accountable for those actions. (p. 6.)

I think that these contrasting approaches to the treatment of young offenders are misleadingly named by the author. For both seem to involve contrasting claims about what is just based on contrasting ideas about whether or not the offender is morally responsible.

4. Someone might take issue with this example by claiming that any person who is selfish must have had a deprived childhood, but this is not convincing. No doubt any selfish person has been 'deprived' of whatever it is that would have made him less selfish, but one cannot say on this account that he has suffered emotional deprivation. Some research suggests that over-indulgence by mothers (coupled with lack of involvement by fathers) can produce affectionless, psychopathic personalities (see Hilgard, Atkinson and Atkinson, *An Introduction to Psychology*, p. 489). But even if it were true that selfish people were only produced by emotional deprivation, it is justifiable to imagine that selfishness could be the result of a non-deprived childhood in order to test the claim that it is his non-fulfilment of the U-condition which excuses the selfish offender.

5. I owe this suggestion to Derek Parfit.

6. See Bowlby, *Child Care and the Growth of Love*, pp. 66–7: 'But the desire for love, repressed though it is, persists, resulting in behaviour such as promiscuous sex relations and the stealing of other people's possessions.'

7. It should be remembered that according to the arguments in Chapter 2, lack of self-control only excuses if the offender's action can be explained as having been motivated by that lack of self-control in a way which precludes fulfilment of the M-condition. And since we are concerned in this Chapter to find whether there are blameworthiness conditions by reference to which an agent who has fulfilled the M-condition might be excused, we can ignore the reference to lack of control in the passage quoted.

8. I am, of course, assuming that the offender could not be responsible for his own deprivation. It might be logically possible for an agent to be causally (and morally) responsible for his own emotional deprivation, but it would not be empirically possible.

The sort of logical possibility I have in mind is this: a person makes an uncaused M-condition request to a supernatural agent that the agent should transform him into someone who will never take the interests of others into account. The supernatural agent grants his request in an unexpected way, by subjecting him to such severe emotional deprivation that he becomes completely callous.

One reason for the empirical impossibility of such a case is that for emotional deprivation to work, by which I mean for it to succeed in producing people who are completely callous, children need to be subjected to it long before they are old enough to be able to think in moral terms.

Chapter 5

1. 'P. F. Strawson Replies', p. 264.
2. See Watson (ed.) *Free Will*, p. 10; also Ayer's remarks in 'Freedom and Necessity', pp. 17–18.
3. Cf. Chisholm, 'Human Freedom and the Self', p. 28.
4. See Goldman, *A Theory of Human Action*, pp. 63, 112.
5. See Davidson, 'Freedom to Act' and also Goldman, *A Theory of Human Action*, p. 49.
6. Nagel, 'Moral Luck', p. 37.
7. Nagel seems to allude to these anxieties again in *A View From Nowhere*, pp. 111–12.
8. I think that some of this discussion may have been inspired by a lecture by J. A. Foster, at Oxford, in Hilary Term 1983, on 'Induction, Causation, and Freedom', and by Thorp's use of the terms 'activity' and 'passivity' in his discussion on pp. 107–15 of *Free Will*.
9. I think Richard Taylor believes in something like this, although he does not express himself in this way. See his *Action and Purpose*, p. 60.
10. Shaffer discusses, and then dismisses, something like this principle in *The Philosophy of Mind*, p. 109, although his arguments are different from mine. The claim he considers and rejects is this: 'If something A has a property and A causes B, then B must have that property also.'
11. It might be thought that the c.t.p. can be easily refuted by mentioning emergent properties. But, despite appearances, the c.t.p. does not imply that there can be no emergent properties; it merely implies that there can be no emergent properties whose presence would be inconsistent with causing properties. In this respect, the c.t.p. and the more general principle about properties, i.e. whatever is in the cause will be transferred to the effect, are not like the principle which Descartes seems to be relying on in The Third Meditation, namely there must be as much reality in the (efficient total) cause as in the effect.
12. Although I see this argument of Nagel's as one which can be given on behalf of the agent-causationist, those agent-causationists with whom I am familiar do not deny that acts are events. What they

deny is that act events can be further broken down into causing events consisting in the agent's mental states. See the discussion later in this chapter.

13. See Davidson, 'Agency', p. 53.
14. Ibid. 52–3.
15. Davidson, 'Freedom to Act', p. 65.
16. This is Thomas Nagel's claim about the subjectivity of consciousness; see 'What is it like to be a bat?'
17. I originally thought that this second form of the argument was quite powerful, but doubts raised about it by Paul Snowdon persuaded me to rethink.
18. Paul Snowdon has said that he is not persuaded by the implication that we can distinguish between uncaused psychological events for which X is responsible and those for which he is not by reference to the active–passive distinction. He asks what it amounts to to say that something is active (or done)? I acknowledge that I have not explained the distinction, and I do not know whether I could without resorting to phrases like 'making something happen as opposed to having something happen to you' which could themselves only be explained by invoking the terms 'active', 'doing', 'passive' which he finds problematic. However, I hoped (and still hope) that readers would have enough of an idea (however vague and inarticulable) of what the distinction amounts to, to agree with me that deciding and choosing fall on the active rather than the passive side.
19. O'Shaughnessy discusses this in ii. 297–302 of *The Will*.
20. O'Shaughnessy's account seems to share the Davidsonian assumption that intending to do X involves holding that doing X is best, but this is counter-intuitive, for surely one can intend to do something which one does not think is the best thing to do. I owe this point to Paul Snowdon.
21. Here, I agree with Feinberg who says that even when all the facts are in, I still have a certain amount of discretion when it comes to decisions ('Action and Responsibility', p. 111).
22. *The Will*, ii. 300.
23. Ibid. 297.
24. Cf. ibid. 301.
25. Melden argues like this in *Free Action*.
26. Both objections are made by Davidson in 'Actions, Reasons and Causes'.
27. Paul Snowdon has pointed this out.
28. Davidson argues in 'Mental Events' that whenever there is a causal sequence there is a law which governs it and suggests that such laws would always have to be described in the language of physics

(or, perhaps, neurophysiology). Pears implies that generalizable (and hence law-like) descriptions of an agent's desire to do A could be couched in the language of commonsense psychology. (See 'Sketch for a Causal Theory of Wanting and Doing'.)

29. 'Sketch for a Causal Theory of Wanting and Doing', pp. 99–100.
30. 'Actions, Reasons and Causes', pp. 9–10.
31. In 'Predicting and Deciding', Pears suggests that an agent could both predict his decision and engage in a process which comes close to qualifying as a decision making process. Pears then seems to take it that he has shown that an agent could both predict his decision and genuinely decide, but I do not think he has made a case for the latter claim.
32. *Intention*, p. 18.
33. O'Shaughnessy, *The Will*, p. 296.
34. This is reminiscent of the famous claim by Leibniz that 'motives incline without necessitating'. But Leibniz meant that it was not *logically* necessary for a person's motives to issue in action and this would not satisfy the U-condition libertarian who requires a non-causal link between motives and action. (See E. M. Huggard, *Leibniz Theodicy* (London, Routledge, 1952) and C. D. Broad, *Leibniz, An Introduction* (Cambridge University Press, 1975) both mentioned in Cottingham, *Rationalism*. See also 'Lettre a Mr. Coste de la Nécessité et de la Contingence', in J. E. Erdmann (ed.), *Leibniz Opera Philosophica* (Berlin, G. Eichler, 1840), 447–9, quoted in Chisholm's 'Human Freedom and the Self'.
35. Thorp, *Free Will*, p. 132.
36. This objection was suggested to me by some remarks of G. Strawson in an early paper, 'The Impossibility of Self-Determination'. But Strawson has said that he is not committed to this; instead he is concerned to argue that even if there can be reasonless, free, moral-responsibility-entailing choices, it is not such choices which are of central interest when we worry about whether we are free. Rather, we want to know whether we can be free when we act for reasons. Cf. his discussion in *Freedom and Belief*, ch. 2.
37. But a revised conception of praiseworthiness is proposed in ch. 7.
38. 'Are Moral Requirements Hypothetical Imperatives?' p. 15.
39. It might be thought that my use of the term 'reason' is ambiguous: (a) 'reason' *qua* motivating psychological state, and (b) 'reason' *qua* consideration which can serve as a justification for acting in a certain way. Foot is mainly concerned in her paper to argue that the reason-giving force of moral judgements depends on human interests, and this suggests a predominant interest on her part in (b) type reasons. But she begins her paper by discussing whether a man's reasons (*qua* motivating psychological states) for acting as

he does must include a desire. McDowell is concerned exclusively with reasons as psychological states.

40. See Hume, *Enquiry*, p. 293.
41. This term is used by Bond, *Reason and Value*, p. 12.
42. Goldman uses the term 'standing wants' as distinct from 'occurrent wants' in *A Theory of Human Action*, p. 86.
43. McDowell, 'Are Moral Requirements Hypothetical Imperatives?' pp. 16–17, 21, 23, 26, 29.
44. The claim that desires are necessary for motivation, which I am arguing for, is the claim that unless the psychological states of an agent include either an occurrent desire or an affective-inclining disposition, he will not be moved to try to act. But another way of construing the claim that desires are necessary for motivation is to say that unless the psychological states of an agent include a desire of some kind, he will not be moved to *want* to act, i.e. that a desire to act can only be generated by preceding states which include a desire. This *is* false. (See the above argument about enriched cognitive states.) If this is the thesis McDowell was attacking when he denied that the motivating power of reasons derives from their including desires, then I agree with him.
45. See Hilgard, Atkinson and Atkinson, *Introduction to Psychology*, pp. 466, 470–1.

Chapter 6

1. *Freedom and Resentment and Other Essays*, p. 18.
2. Ibid. 18.
3. In 'Accountability', Bennett distinguishes between moral and non-moral reactive attitudes by calling the former 'principled'. But this is not sufficient. Moral reactive attitudes are *morally* principled in the way I have suggested.
4. The psychological theory of cognitive dissonance suggests that the belief about injustice might disappear because it makes things awkward for us. If this happened, it would do so as the result of an unconscious psychological process, and this does not affect my point which is that we could not deliberately drop the belief simply because we did not want to think of ourselves as acting unjustly.
5. Cf. Rawls, *A Theory of Justice*.
6. Lecture 1, from the series *The Varieties of Free Will Worth Wanting*, p. 24. (Not reproduced in the book, *Elbow Room* (Oxford, Clarendon Press, 1984) which was based on this series.)

Chapter 7

1. Below, I suggest that we should revise this conception of praise-worthiness.
2. As noted in ch. 3, Kant argues for this in *Religion Within the Limits of Reason Alone*.
3. Cf. Williams, 'The Idea of Equality', p. 234 and 'Morality and the Emotions', p. 228.
4. Despite appearances, Feinberg is not arguing for incompatibilism in the paper from which this passage comes.
5. Hospers, 'What Means this Freedom?', p. 137.
6. Ibid. 137.
7. Cf. Ake, 'Justice as Equality'.
8. If the conception of praiseworthiness were revised along these lines, it would mean that contrary to the traditional view advocated in ch. 5, someone could deserve praise even if he were simply prepared to do the right thing (e.g. for a selfish reason), so long as his act involved an effort.
9. Of course, talk of desert is only appropriate if we accept that we are committed to a compatibilist *justification*. Those who are not convinced should substitute the words 'would be judged to owe less' for the words 'would be deemed to deserve to pay less'.
10. *Punishment*, p. 28.
11. I wrote this before the latest government proposals on crime, one of which is that some criminals should be punished within the community by being 'placed under curfew and allowed to stay at work and pay 10 or 20 per cent of their income in compensation rather than face a jail sentence.' (*The Times*, 4 April 1988, p. 1) Here, beliefs about what the offender deserves to pay seem to be directly linked with beliefs about the amount of suffering caused to his or her victim. It was also claimed in *The Times* that 'the proposals aim to bring home to criminals, particularly young criminals and first offenders, the consequences of their actions.' It is not entirely clear if the motivating rationale for this aim is deterrence, retribution, or reform. (The reference to young criminals and first offenders could suggest that the motive is either deterrence or reform or both.)

Appendix

1. Kant assumes that because judgements of the form 'X ought to have done such and such' imply that 'X could have done such and such', reproachful ought judgements are inconsistent with the truth of determinism. But it is precisely the assumption that the

could-have-acted-otherwise claim can only be interpreted in a way which is inconsistent with determinism which the compatibilist contests. (See B562, 579 (n. *a*) and B583 in the *Critique of Pure Reason*.)

2. All textual references to the *Critique of Practical Reason* are to T. K. Abbott's translation, 3rd edn. (London, Longmans, Green 1883).

3. One further respect in which Kant's argument in the *Critique of Practical Reason* differs from that in the *Critique of Pure Reason* is that in the latter work Kant believed he was only able to establish the possibility of freedom, whereas in the *Critique of Practical Reason*, he claims to establish the fact of freedom. He claims that in knowing we are bound by the moral law we know that we have free-will. I have mentioned but not emphasized this because it is not relevant to my interest in the argument which lies in its claim to show that freedom from determinism is a necessary condition for morality (via its claim to show that a desire-independent ability to act is a necessary condition of morality). But this neglected aspect of the argument is simply the other side of the coin from that side which I am considering. For the argument that freedom is a necessary condition of the existence of moral requirements is at the same time a demonstration that it follows from the existence of moral requirements.

4. Very near the beginning of Chapter 1, Kant explicitly links his notion of free will with the existence of moral rules, claiming that there cannot be such rules, unless pure reason can be practical, i.e. unless the human will can be moved independently of desires and inclinations, by reason alone. He says: 'Supposing that pure reason contains in itself a practical motive, that is, one adequate to determine the will, then there are practical laws; otherwise all practical principles will be mere maxims' (p. 105). According to my interpretation, much of what follows in the first chapter is a defence of this claim.

5. It might be thought that Kant was proclaiming the existence of a supreme moral principle in the form of a demand that we should work towards the suppressing of our desires and inclinations so that we would be able to fulfil moral requirements when the occasion demanded it. This would run counter to Kant's insistence in the *Critique of Practical Reason* that desires and inclinations can provide some of the content of a moral volition, so long as they are being acted on because to do so is in accordance with the moral law. Leaving aside the question of whether the endorsement of such a principle would have been inconsistent on Kant's part, there is something curious about the suggestion. We could

not say of such a principle that it commanded its own motivation, i.e. that it required that we set aside desires in order to set aside desires. We would have to take it that the act of setting aside desires was a moral act, whatever the motivation. And yet, this way of putting it, the suggestion that one could fulfil such a demand as the result of a desire, seems paradoxical.

6. I suggested in ch. 7 that we should revise this conception of praise-worthiness.

7. But there are difficulties in reconciling the belief that benevolent desires can form the core of a moral motivation with the belief that the agent whose act is motivated by such desires is praise-worthy because his act was motivated by them. For we take it that, for the most part, the desires we have, we have as a matter of luck. And (as I have argued in ch. 7) it seems counter-intuitive to claim that what we have as a matter of luck can be the reason for our deserving praise or blame. (See Nagel's 'Moral Luck' and Williams's perceptive remarks about Kant in 'Morality and the Emotions', p. 228, and 'The Idea of Equality', pp. 234–6.) It is (partly) this difficulty to which I think Kant was reacting when he insisted that action as the result of desires could not be morally praise-worthy. If Kant equated the notion of 'moral action' with the notion of an 'action for which the agent deserves praise', then this could, to some extent, explain what to many philosophers is his counter-intuitive insistence that the act which results from benevolent desires cannot be moral.

8. Atkinson makes this point in 'Categorical Imperatives', p. 14.

9. In ch. 1, I suggested that the absurdity of the claim lies in the fact that it contains an implicit contradiction and not, as might be thought, in its attributing of a desire-dependent ability to act.

10. In this respect too, there are strong analogies between Kant's position and one of the main themes in Nagel, *The Possibility of Altruism*. Nagel holds that rationality is central to ethical motivation and that it allows each individual to stand back from his own desires and inclinations. But he does not suggest that rationality is supersensible, although he sees it as something which enables us to engage in metaphysics.

11. Kant, Groundwork of the Metaphysics of Morals, pp. 66–7 n. 16. in the Paton translation *Moral Law*.

Bibliography

AKE, C., 'Justice as Equality', *Philosophy and Public Affairs*, 5 (1975), 69–89.

ANSCOMBE, G. E. M., 'Causality and Determination' in Sosa, E. (ed.), *Causation and Conditionals* (Oxford University Press, 1980), 63–81.

—— *Intention* (Oxford, Basil Blackwell, 1980).

ATKINSON, R. F., 'Categorical Imperatives', *Proceedings of the Aristotelian Society*, Suppl. Vol. 51 (1977), 1–18.

AYER, A. J., 'Free-Will and Rationality', in van Straaten, Z. (ed.), *Philosophical Subjects* (Oxford, Clarendon Press, 1980), 1–13.

—— 'Freedom and Necessity', in Watson, G. (ed.), *Free Will* (Oxford University Press, 1982), 15–23.

AYERS, M., *The Refutation of Determinism* (London, Methuen, 1968).

BENNETT, J., 'Accountability', in van Straaten, Z. (ed.), *Philosophical Subjects* (Oxford, Clarendon Press, 1980), 14–47.

BOND, E. J., *Reason and Value* (Cambridge University Press, 1983).

BOWLBY, J., *Child Care and the Growth of Love* (Harmondsworth, Penguin Books, 1983).

CHISHOLM, R. M., 'Human Freedom and the Self', in Watson, G. (ed.), *Free Will* (Oxford University Press, 1982), 24–35.

COTTINGHAM, J., *Rationalism* (London, Paladin Books, Granada Publishing, 1984).

DAVIDSON, D., 'Freedom to Act', in *Essays on Actions and Events* (Oxford, Clarendon Press, 1980), 63–81.

—— 'Agency', in *Essays on Actions and Events*, 43–61.

—— 'Actions, Reasons and Causes', in *Essays on Actions and Events*, 3–19.

—— 'Mental Events', in *Essays on Action and Events*, 207–25.

DENNETT, D., *The Varieties of Free Will Worth Wanting*, John Locke Lectures given at Oxford in Trinity Term, 1983, published as *Elbow Room: The Varieties of Free Will Worth Wanting* (Oxford, Clarendon Press, 1984).

DESCARTES, R., *Meditations*, trans. Sutcliffe, F. E. (Harmondsworth, Penguin Books Ltd., 1968).

EDWARDS, P., 'Hard and Soft Determinism', in Hook, S. (ed.), *Determinism and Freedom in the Age of Modern Science* (London, Collier-Macmillan, 1970), 117–25.

FEINBERG, J., *Doing and Deserving* (Princeton University Press, 1970).

—— 'Action and Responsibility', in White, A. R. (ed.), *Philosophy of Action* (Oxford University Press, 1973), 95–119.

FISCHER, J. M., 'Responsibility and Control', *Journal of Philosophy*, 79 (1982), 24–40.

FOLEY, R., 'Compatibilism', *Mind*, 87 (1978), 421–8.

FOOT, P., 'Reasons for Action and Desires', *Proceedings of the Aristotelian Society*, Suppl. Vol. 46 (1972), 203–10.

FRANKFURT, H., 'Alternate Possibilities and Moral Responsibility', *Journal of Philosophy*, 66 (1969), 829–39.

—— 'Freedom of the Will and the Concept of a Person', *Journal of Philosophy*, 68 (1971), 5–20.

—— 'Three Concepts of Free Action', *Proceedings of the Aristotelian Society*, Suppl. Vol. 49 (1975), 113–25.

—— 'Identification and Externality', in Rorty, A. (ed.), *The Identification of Persons* (London, University of California Press, 1976), 239–51.

GLOVER, J., *Responsibility* (London, Routledge and Kegan Paul, 1970).

—— 'Self-Creation', *Proceedings of the British Academy*, 69 (1983), 445–71.

GOLDMAN, A. I., *A Theory of Human Action* (Princeton University Press, 1970).

HILGARD, E. T., Atkinson, R. C., and Atkinson, R. L., *Introduction to Psychology*, 6th edn. (New York, Harcourt Brace Jovanovich, 1975).

HONDERICH, T., *Punishment* (Harmondsworth, Penguin Books (Peregrine), 1976).

HOSPERS, J., 'What Means This Freedom?', in Hook, S. (ed.), *Determinism and Freedom in the Age of Modern Science* (London, Collier-Macmillan, 1970), 126–42.

HUME, D., *Enquiry Concerning Human Understanding*, Selby-Bigge, L. A. and Nidditch, P. H. (eds.) 3rd edn. (Oxford, Clarendon Press, 1975).

KANT, I., *Critique of Pure Reason*, trans. Kemp-Smith, N. (London and Basingstoke, Macmillan, 1973).

—— *Groundwork of the Metaphysics of Morals*, trans. Paton, H. J. as *The Moral Law* (London, Hutchinson University Library, 1972).

—— *Critique of Practical Reason*, trans. Abbott, T. K., 3rd edn. (London, Longmans, Green, 1883).

—— *Religion Within the Limits of Reason Alone*, trans. Greene, T. M. and Hudson, H. H. (New York, Harper and Row, 1960).

KRIPKE, S., *Naming and Necessity* (Oxford, Basil Blackwell, 1980).

MCDOWELL, J., 'Are Moral Requirements Hypothetical Imperatives?',

Proceedings of the Aristotelian Society, Suppl. Vol. 52 (1978), 13–29.

MELDEN, A. I., *Free Action* (London, Routledge and Kegan Paul, 1961).

MILO, R., 'Amorality', *Mind*, 92 (1983), 491–8.

MOORE, G. E., *Ethics* (Oxford University Press, 1972).

NAGEL, T., *The Possibility of Altruism* (Princeton, Princeton University Press, 1978).

—— 'Moral Luck', in *Mortal Questions* (Cambridge University Press, 1979), 24–38.

—— 'What is it like to be a bat?', in *Mortal Questions*, 165–80.

—— *The View From Nowhere* (Oxford University Press, 1986).

NOZICK, R., *Philosophical Explanations* (Cambridge, Harvard University Press, 1981).

O'SHAUGHNESSY, B., *The Will*, ii (Cambridge University Press, 1980).

PARFIT, D., *Reasons and Persons* (Oxford University Press, 1986).

PEARS, D., 'Sketch for a Causal Theory of Wanting and Doing', in *Questions in the Philosophy of Mind* (London, Gerald Duckworth, 1975), 97–141.

—— 'Predicting and Deciding', in *Questions in the Philosophy of Mind*, 13–38.

RAWLS, J., *A Theory of Justice* (Oxford University Press, 1971).

SHAFFER, J. A., *The Philosophy of Mind* (Englewood Cliffs, Prentice-Hall, 1968).

SMART, J. J. C. and Williams, B., *Utilitarianism: For and Against* (Cambridge University Press, 1973).

SORABJI, R., *Necessity, Cause and Blame* (London, Duckworth, 1980).

STRAWSON, G., *Freedom and Belief* (Oxford, Clarendon Press, 1986).

—— 'The Impossibility of Self-Determination', unpublished paper.

STRAWSON, P. F., 'Freedom and Resentment', in *Freedom and Resentment and Other Essays* (London, Methuen, 1974), 1–25.

—— 'P. F. Strawson Replies', in van Straaten, Z. (ed.), *Philosophical Subjects* (Oxford, Clarendon Press, 1980), esp. pp. 260–6.

TAYLOR, R., *Action and Purpose* (Englewood Cliffs, Prentice-Hall, 1966).

THORP, J., *Free Will* (London, Boston and Henley, Routledge and Kegan Paul, 1980).

TUTT, N., 'Justice or Welfare?', *Social Work Today*, 14/7, 19 Oct. (1982), 6–10.

VAN INWAGEN, P., *An Essay on Free Will* (Oxford, Clarendon Press, 1983).

—— 'Ability and Responsibility', *Philosophical Review*, 77 (1978), 201–24.

WATSON, G. (ed.), *Free Will* (Oxford University Press, 1982).

WIGGINS, D., 'Towards a Reasonable Libertarianism', in Honderich, T. (ed.), *Essays on Freedom of Action* (London, Routledge and Kegan Paul, 1973), 33–61.

WILLIAMS, B., *Morality* (Harmondsworth, Penguin Books, 1973).

—— 'Morality and the Emotions', in *Problems of the Self* (Cambridge University Press, 1976), 207–29.

—— 'The Idea of Equality', in *Problems of the Self*, 230–49.

WISDOM, J., *Problems of Mind and Matter* (Cambridge University Press, 1934).

WOLF, S., 'Sanity and the Metaphysics of Responsibility', in Schoeman, F. (ed.), *Responsibility, Character and the Emotions* (Cambridge University Press, 1987), 46–62.

Index